Faith Fuel

for
Individuals and Churches

By James J. Stewart

ISBN No. 978-0-615-50930-3

Other books by James J. Stewart:
The Loving Prophet
Faith and Yosemite
Walking in Faith
Lasting Love

Foreword

Do you struggle with your Christian faith? When pressed, most Christians have to admit that this is the case. Are there times when you want help understanding what the Bible teaches us? Even pastors have such times, and that leads them to research and discussions with colleagues. Have the pressures of life weakened your faith? All of us have "dark nights of the soul." All Christians experience spiritual winters from time to time.

Sometimes the fire of our faith gets down to barely glowing embers. When a campfire gets down to embers, we have to add more fuel in order to get the fire going again. When their spiritual fire gets low, Christians need some kindling or tinder to get the fire blazing again. In these pages, you can ponder the struggles Christians face. Here are more than two hundred fire starters–faith fuel–reflections on what the Bible teaches us. They were written to help church members in congregations located in several regions of the United States.

Several have pointed out that there have been more changes in church life during the past half century than in the previous several centuries. Some Christians like to point out that we are living in a time predicted in 2 Timothy 4:1-5. Whether this is true or not, it is vitally important that Christians live their lives as faithful reflections of the teachings of Jesus Christ. It is also essential that Christians not become discouraged in these difficult times, letting their spiritual fires get low. This book is designed to help Christians keep their spiritual fires burning faithfully.

Table of Contents

Faith Fuel
<u>JANUARY</u>

Personal Faith

Life's longest journeys are often between our head and our heart. As we get older and hopefully wiser, we make the journey more often. Just because we make the journey frequently however does not mean that the journey gets any easier! When a person becomes a Christian, one early lesson is that Christ has commissioned each of us to help others to come into a productive relationship with Him. It is called disciple making. Most Christians know this, at least in their heads. What is in our hearts is often considerably less certain!

A common misconception about being a Christian is that it means obeying the Golden Rule. "Do unto others as you would have others do unto you." There is nothing wrong with the Golden Rule within the limits of its scope. Most people interpret the rule as being loving and nice to all people. Indeed, Jesus was loving and nice to most people, but he was stridently critical of those who were not otherwise living out the imperatives of the "Kingdom of God." Needless to say, one does not have to be a Christian to be loving and nice! To be a fully functional Christian each of us makes the journey from our heads to our hearts. We learn to share the person as well as the teachings of Jesus.

Being the church does not simply mean maintaining the church and nurturing its members. Being a fully functional church means spending time, energy, and money in efforts at introducing other people to the living Christ. A good rule of thumb is to spend more than 10% of the church's time, energy, and budget on making Disciples. Sometimes the church has to delay or sacrifice pet projects in order to fulfill Christ's Great Commission.

Another Year

An open book begins another year,
And Christmas doesn't seem at all too near.
The football games fill ears with bursting cheers,
And quiet thoughts of Christmas bring some tears.

Can gifts be now so quickly lost and spent?
Can joy be quickly lost in paying rent?

Faith Fuel

Does God look down and know how much its meant
To me to know the joy that's heaven sent?

I wonder as I look ahead today–
To one more year of struggle day by day:
Will minds be focused just on making hay,
Or is life more than seeking higher pay?

There's hope in all of this I usually find.
There's more to life than just the daily grind.
One cannot see the future in the mind,
But play and toil release that bitter bind.

Anticipation is the fuel at hand.
We wait expectantly for luck to land
On our front doorstep just as though we planned
To make our mark on this our native land.

Finding the Holy

What is your favorite place to look for God? It is true that one can "find" God, or be found by God, in any time or place. There is no formula. The most consistent place to experience both the intense intimacy and the supreme power of God is in a community of faith at worship. Jesus said, "Wherever two or more are gathered in my name, there I am in the midst of them." The experience of millions of people testifies that what Jesus said is true.

Despite this testimony, public worship for many people is not their favorite place in which to encounter the presence and power of God. There are many who naively insist they do not need Jesus for an intimate relationship with God. Some even try to provide convoluted intellectual reasons why one does not have to know Jesus in order to be a Christian. As Pascal once put it, "The knowledge of God is very far from the love of Him."

I dedicated my life to Christian ministry. As in a marriage, I committed myself to serving the church "for better or worse, in sickness and in health, to love and to cherish" until I go on to the larger life. It was like marrying the impressions of what I read about my bride rather than the real thing however. It was more than ten years before I finally experienced how real and powerful our Savior really is. There is no way I can go back to resting my faith on intellectual understandings of God,

8

Jesus, and the Holy Spirit. Intellectual pursuits still keep my mind sharp. All of that is like an appetizer. The Christ of faith is the main course.

Discovering Our Gifts

"Do you believe that Jesus is the Christ, the Son of the living God, and do you accept Him as your personal Savior and Lord?" Rev. John W. Hanna asked me that question. I said, "I do." After being baptized, I was a 'newbie,' and I did not have a clue as to what God had in store for me. Many people are in the same boat when they are baptized.

It was years before I realized that the Holy Spirit was at work within me, empowering spiritual gifts I had been given as part of being a follower of Jesus Christ. Although the Bible speaks of the Holy Spirit prior to Jesus' coming, Jesus told his followers that He was sending the Holy Spirit to His followers after He ascended to heaven. Even His closest inner circle of friends did not realize how important that was until the first Pentecost after Easter. Pentecost marks the day for Christians when the Holy Spirit was given with power to the church.

There is some debate as to how many spiritual gifts are listed in the New Testament. Lists are found in Romans 12, 1 Corinthians 12, and Ephesians 4. When we read these three passages, we find twenty-four gifts: prophecy, pastoring, teaching, missions, wisdom, knowledge, encourage-ment, evangelism, giving, helping, mercy, hospitality, faith, leadership, administration, miracle working, healing, tongues, the interpretation of tongues, poverty, celibacy, intercession, exorcism, and service. Several people have said I have the gifts of knowledge and teaching. In over three decades of ministry, I have only met one person who actually had more than three gifts. Many have only one.

It is very important to understand some basic facts about spiritual gifts. First, everyone who surrenders to the authority of Jesus in his or her life is given at least one spiritual gift. The Bible does not specifically say this, but it is implied. Second, not everyone has the same gift, but all gifts work for God's glory. (I Corinthians 12-14). This is important to remember so we do not have unrealistic expectations of one another. Finally, everyone has seen instances where one of these twenty-four gifts are manifest, but that does not necessarily mean that the person has that gift.

In his letter to the people of Corinth, Paul encourages all to prophecy, but that does not make everyone a prophet. Conversely,

Faith Fuel

Mother Teresa demonstrated a lifetime use of the gift of mercy, but those of us who do not have the gift of mercy still must be merciful. All of us have occasions where we must give, help, show faith, serve, evangelize, or do other things as the spirit leads us and empowers us. For instance, God expects us to tithe, and God expects us to share the good news of Jesus with others. People who give generously without hesitation, and people who regularly bring people to Christ have the gifts of giving and evangelism.

Whatever we are called to do, the important thing is to respond in faith. We are to act out our faith. We are called to be Christ-like. Whenever we encounter someone who does not know how much God loves them, we have an obligation to tell that person about Jesus and His life, death, and resurrection. This is called witnessing to who we are. Whatever our gift or gifts, God wants to use those gifts through us for His glory. His divine power is readily available to us so that we may serve Him. God is always faithful. God is our hope. In pursuit of the life God has given us, we find our joy.

Epiphany

On the church calendar, the season that is between the end of Christmastide and the beginning of Lent is called Epiphany. Epiphany Day is intended to commemorate the descent of God in the form of a dove down upon Jesus at his baptism. An epiphany is an appearance of God.

During Solomon's lifetime, God appeared to him more than once. When Solomon became king, God had appeared to Solomon, and, among other things, God granted Solomon wisdom that has never been equaled. Using the gifts that God granted him, Solomon amassed great wealth and power, but his wisdom brought him the greatest fame. Wisdom seemed to pour out of him like water out of a fountain. God's gift came ever so easily to him. He became famous, and then his wisdom became legendary. Stories about him became more and more unbelievable. This outpouring of wisdom brought curious people from great distances.

Among those who came great distances was the queen of Sheba. According to the scripture, she came to "test" him—to find out how much of what she had heard was true. She was impressed to say the least. Because of the wisdom God had given Solomon, the queen of Sheba paid Solomon tribute in gold and other precious things. It is an example of how the wealth of Solomon was accumulated.

Faith Fuel

This ancient story also illustrates another important point. Just because we find favor in God's sight does not mean that we are completely insulated from the world in which we live. God had actually appeared to Solomon–more than once–as testimony of God's favor. Personal appearances by the Creator among us is a powerful incentive to do everything we can to please God. Yet, those around him still put Solomon to the test. History shows that in his later years, Solomon failed those tests. Solomon became disobedient and went after other Gods at the urging of his non-believing wives, both being violations of God's instructions. Solomon succumbed to temptation, and he and his children paid the price.

All of us face temptation. Even God's Son, Jesus Christ, faced temptation. We are told in the gospels that after resisting temptation in the wilderness, the Devil departed from Jesus "until an opportune time." This would seem to indicate that even though we are not told of other encounters with temptation, there must have been other occasions when temptation reared its ugly head at Jesus. The stories of temptations faced by God's favored ones give us insight into how we can face our own temptations. We can pass all of these tests because we can do all things through Jesus Christ, who strengthens us.

Beginnings

"Moses wrote down their starting points, stage by stage, by command of the Lord; and these are their stages according to their starting points."(Numbers 33:2 NRSV)

Is a new year a starting place or an ending place? Are we about to end a year or to begin another? Do we think of the season as an embryo to be developed and birthed? Do we think of the season as an infant to be nurtured, or as a child to be disciplined? Is the season a time of maturity, one to bear fruit? Is the season a time of senility, one to be endured and simply tolerated?

God told Moses to make a record of starting places. It was a record of journeys begun and goals reached. What would the record of our lives be like if we simply recorded the things that we began each year? How would our record read if it simply showed the beginnings launched and the goals reached? The record of our lives looks far better if we remove the struggles and the pains. Does this mean that we should try to forget or ignore our pain and struggle? Should we not learn from all of that? By no means!

11

Faith Fuel

One of the most famous, beautiful, and joyful places in the entire world is Disneyland. On a typical day thousands of people forget their troubles and enjoy a different world. The enjoyment of the guests is made possible by the hard work and struggle behind the scenes. Disneyland's very beginning was difficult, with Walt Disney's struggle to convince his brother to build it. The park begins with a beautiful concept. The goal of the park and its employees is the enjoyment of the guests. In between that goal and that concept is toil that cannot be eliminated or ignored.

In the same way, our lives are filled with beginnings and with goals. In between are pain, toil, and struggle. All of it is part of our lives. All of it is part of growing towards fulfillment. If we spend too much time thinking about the pain and struggle, we quickly become miserable. If we spend all of our time looking at the total picture we accomplish a great deal but find limited enjoyment.

December provides opportunities, built into the holiday spirit. There are opportunities to continue our thankfulness for gifts received, lives delivered, and goals achieved. There are opportunities to celebrate beginnings and goals. There are opportunities to celebrate life in terms of its rewards. We can let happy memories be beginnings– and let dreams be goals. Enjoy!

God's Timing

In the book of Ecclesiastes, there is a famous verse that says there is a time to be born and a time to die. As with many verses in our scriptures, there is a variety of interpretations of this verse.

Usually this verse is applied to persons like ourselves. Some argue in a fatalistic sort of way, saying that the verse indicates that life has no meaning except for the current moment. There are those who use this verse to argue in favor of capital punishment. Ironically, there are also those who use this verse to argue against capital punishment.

In the heat of rhetoric, the verse has been applied to justify the cause of the so-called "Pro-Life" cause. Beyond the rhetoric, some of the extremists of this movement have used this verse to justify violence to "save the unborn." Again, in an ironic kind of way the so-called "Pro-Choice" movement has been known to quote this verse in its defense.

When this verse is quoted and applied to other life forms, the use of this verse becomes even more slippery. The extermination industry kills millions (perhaps billions) of insects and other animals

Faith Fuel

each year without giving a second thought to those animal's "right" to life. Most of us do not give a second thought to swatting a fly or putting out roach bait. In other parts of the world and in other religions, however, such "crimes" are almost unthinkable.

In this country, questions are being raised with sometimes-violent rhetoric, with regard to the use of animals in medical research. Now we are raising questions about the right to quality of life as it becomes possible to live longer and longer. This one little phrase written so long ago, "a time to be born, and a time to die," is now taking on new meaning.

It is the task of church people not to count themselves with those who find an ancient verse and twist it to meet their own agenda. Rather, it is our task to be wise enough to keep scriptures in context. To do this means to be knowledgeable with regard to the entire Bible. To do so goes beyond weekly worship, to daily study and prayer. When called to be the people of God, we are called to this as part of our discipline.

It is usually not wise to apply formulas to Christianity, but simple logic dictates that in order to be knowledgeable, we must study our Bibles daily—and not just read them. Thirty minutes daily would seem to be a necessary minimum.

Christmas Aftermath

The Christmas campaigns to reach out to the community were over. While visitors did come as expected, and while the churches had more visitors for Christmas than the previous year, they did not have as many as they had hoped. In a straw vote of leaders, some of the them expressed their discouragement with the process. I pointed out to my congregation's leaders that when I was doing undergraduate work at California State University at Long Beach there was an epigram on the masthead of the student paper that read, "Life is what happens to you while you are making other plans."

In the church however, we actually have a different perspective available to us, if we take the time and trouble to look. It is God's perspective. While we cannot see things through God's eyes, what we *can* do is see how we relate to a God who sees things differently than we do.

Isaiah 40:30-31 reads, "Even youths will faint and be weary, and the young will fall exhausted; but those who wait for the LORD

13

Faith Fuel

shall renew their strength, they shall mount up with wings like eagles, they shall run and not be weary, they shall walk and not faint." [NRSV] This provides useful perspective.

Sometimes God performs very obvious miracles–God helps us to "mount up with wings like eagles"–totally setting aside logic or natural law. We have the eyes to see these miracles because we are people of faith. Those not of the faith use such labels as "amazing" and "luck."

At other times, God magnifies our resources and efforts–God helps us to "run and not grow weary"–giving great results to what we believe is "ordinary." As people of faith, we usually speak of this as God's "blessing our efforts." Those not of faith again use such labels as "amazing" and "lucky."

At still other times God helps us to be the best possible stewards of what we have in our current situation–God helps us to "walk and not faint"–helping us to endure and to persevere. As people of faith, we describe this as God being "with us in our time of trial." Those not of faith call this "toughing it out" or use another euphemism.

The church is an institution of the world as well as the Body of Christ. As people of faith, we can seek the power of God to fly in faith, run without weariness, and to walk with steadfastness. Our temptation is to be people of the world, looking for luck or wanting to survive. The choice is ours. When we get discouraged, it is a good indication that our faith is shaken or at least weakened. At the same time, however we cannot become weary of well doing. We have to try to be almost as patient with God as God is patient with us!

No one on Earth knows everything God has planned for the coming months and years of the church. We must believe however, that as long as we have the strength and the resources, we cannot fail our mission as a church. Our call is to reach out to those in need with the Good News of Jesus Christ, along with his nurture and love. Indeed, that is our mandate! We are not yet part of the church's past history. Our obituary has not been written yet! God has not given up on us, so let us not give up on those who need Jesus Christ!

Responding to Needs

"Find a need and fill it!" That was the slogan I heard over and over again a number of years ago, when I attended the Robert Schuller Institute of Successful Church Leadership. "Find a need and fill it" partly expresses the basic approach of Jesus in his earthly ministry. Many churches today are rediscovering this fundamental concept. Healthy churches that are thriving and growing are willing to shape their ministries in terms of the needs of their communities. They avoid re-launching programs from the past based on past success. In fact, they avoid thinking in terms of past successes altogether when trying to plan for the future. In these churches there is a willingness to sacrifice everything–their sense of history as well as all of their resources–for the sake of those in need.

The crucial reason for the health and success of these churches is their sense of who is in charge. These churches do not fall into the trap of arguing the democracy of lay leadership versus the autocracy of clergy leadership. They do not even think in terms of shared clergy/laity responsibility and authority. Many of these churches, both conservative and liberal, actually ask aloud the question, "What would Jesus do?"

In a cultural exchange program, the Philadelphia Orchestra had a tour of China under the direction of Eugene Ormandy. In one of the cities, the resident orchestra began to play Beethoven's Fifth Symphony, and they played it very poorly. After the first movement, the conductor handed the baton to Eugene Ormandy. The transformation was amazing! It was as though Beethoven were being played by an entirely different orchestra! In that experience, the section leaders developed a new appreciation for the gifts and skills of Eugene Ormandy–gifts and skills they had taken for granted.

In the same way, it is all too easy to take for granted the role of Jesus Christ in our churches. Like the section leaders of the Philadelphia Orchestra, we may even think only in terms of our contributions to our little section of our world. As the Chinese musicians discovered, when a "master" is in charge of the music, wondrous things begin to happen. In the same way, our churches make better "music" when we pay attention to the Master in Charge. From one point of view, evangelism is the music heard by the world as churches do their ministries. Jesus calls all of us to be part of the concert. When we find a need and fill it, we make the music of Holy Joy!

Christian Life Basics

"The general means of perfection" refers to a list of actions or personal attributes that should be a part of a Christian's life in some of

15

the old tracts, some of which are still published. These means of perfection are purported to be as follows:

a. Faithfulness in small things
b. Self-control and self-denial
c. Order and regularity
d. A habit of prayer
e. A frequent recourse to solitude
f. Reading spiritual books and meditation
g. Frequentation of the sacraments

Faithfulness in small things can be a tall order! With a bit of determination, it is easy to be faithful in the big and obvious situations we encounter, but it is more difficult to pay attention to small bad habits.

Self-control and self-denial are not popular with the "me" generation. Such things imply discipline, which is not very popular in society these days even within the church. Order and regularity also imply discipline. We all enjoy staying within our habit patterns, but we do not wish to conform to a standard of values that would mean change.

A habit of prayer is easy to maintain if the prayer is honest. It is even easier if a time of the day is set aside which is not violated like early in the day. Frequent recourse to solitude is a habit that grows upon the individual. When serving churches in California I used to enjoy going to Yosemite by myself periodically for reflection, meditation, and "walks with God." Reading spiritual books and meditation may simply mean reading several chapters of the Bible each day. That is a good foundation to which one may add other spiritual books. "Frequentation of the sacraments" to some Christians simply means having communion on a regular basis, although some branches of Christianity do not speak of "sacraments." Some people also do much more, by attending or participating in baptisms, weddings, funerals, and healings. When was the last time you thought of all of this as "means to perfection?"

Saying No

One of the things that mark maturity as an adult is decision making. Knowing when to say "yes," and knowing when to say "no," is a skill learned from hard experience. Some people who lack this skill have trouble saying "yes" at all. They may have a low opinion of themselves. They might be cynical about the world. As a result, their

Faith Fuel

lives are lacking in vitality and joy, because they are reluctant to say "yes" to opportunities that come their way.

Other people have difficulty saying "no." It may be arrogance that leads them to believe they can do everything. Sometimes it is a desire to please. As a result, their lives are filled with unnecessary stress, robbing them of much of what God offers them.

Christians who have good decision-making skills usually have a good relationship with the Holy Spirit. They do not resist the Holy Spirit is leadership and authority. To be intimate with the Holy Spirit often means being possessed by a beautiful force and having an awareness of a spiritual presence. These people are almost always prompt and well organized. They also have a serenity and peace within themselves that spills over and brings healing to others.

People have always had trouble describing the Holy Spirit. The oldest records in the Hebrew Scriptures equate the Holy Spirit with the "breath" or "wind" of God. In the New Testament, the Spirit is the power that drives John the Baptist, is the power that anoints Jesus at his baptism, and is the power that launches the church on the day of Pentecost. It is human nature for many people to be reluctant to allow this power to be the driving force in their lives because most want to "be their own boss." Our calling however is to be like Jesus, for the Apostle Paul teaches us, "to set our minds on the things of the Spirit."

New Year Happiness

Each January most of us find occasions to shout, "Happy New Year!" Is your new year really happy? Do the peace and joy of the little Christ child still linger with you throughout the year? Alternatively, do you go back to business is usual after Christmas is over? It is amazing how each year people go to such elaborate means to prepare for Christmas, and then the day after Christmas, they return from the mountaintop experience, back to the valley of the shadows at the rate of a dive-bomber. Why do so few people linger at or near the top? Why not come down the mountain at a more leisurely pace? True, some of us leave the decorations up until after New Year's Day, but why does talk of peace and joy and good will all stop on December 26th?

The answer is found in the seventeenth chapter of the gospel according to Matthew. Jesus, along with Peter, James, and John, go up on top of a mountain. There the disciples see Jesus transfigured before them. That particular vision was perhaps the greatest experience those men had in all their lives up until that time. Peter wanted to preserve the event, and he offered to build "booths" there–a kind of monument. Immediately Jesus led them back down the mountain! Jesus went back to work (business as usual) and healed an epileptic. Peter, James, and John had to come down off the mountain and return to the valley of the shadows. Remember however, that Jesus came down the mountain with them. At Christmas, we have an intense awareness of the Christ-child in our midst, much like seeing a transfiguration. Jesus is just as much with us on the day after Christmas. When the decorations come down, we have to have a keener awareness to notice Jesus' presence.

Therefore, it is back to business as usual after Christmas. For those who have the eyes to see, peace, joy, and good will can linger. We may consign our bodies to the valley, but our hearts can linger on the mountaintop!

God's Holy Word

After a church school lesson one Sunday, I was approached by an older member who asked, "How did you get to know the content of the Bible so well?" With a smile I replied, "I read it daily!" I have sometimes pondered our differing attitudes towards the Bible within the church. The more cynical folks among us believe they can learn the Bible by a kind of osmosis–that they can soak it in through worship or through church school lessons. On the opposite extreme are those who study their Bible systematically and daily. Doing systematic Bible reading is not as hard as it may appear to the cynics. It is certainly neither boring nor repetitious. It is easy to find enjoyment in reading through the Bible in one year.

Not long ago I had a very surprising experience. I was reading part of the gospel of Luke, which I have read and studied dozens of times.I came upon a paragraph that I did not remember ever reading before! I actually asked myself, "When did that get in there?" It began to percolate in the back of my mind, and later I preached on the text with a passion that is rare for me. About the same time I discovered that passage in Luke, I discovered the therapy to be found in reading Psalm 119 aloud. Previously, it had intimidated me because it is so long. The beauty and inspiration is wonderful, so it is worth discovering again.

Over twenty years ago, I decided to start reading the Bible systematically. I decided that this systematic reading was to be separate from studying the Bible for teaching or preaching. It also had to be separate from any inspirational reading I wanted to do. I divided

Faith Fuel

the Old Testament into two parts: Genesis through Job and Psalms through Malachi. Then I divided the New Testament between the four gospels and the rest of the books. Since then, I have read one chapter from each of those four sections each day. The gospels repeat once every eighty-nine days, and the rest of the books of the New Testament repeat about every five months. The Old Testament sections take fifteen to sixteen months to repeat. The resulting pattern is nearly random. It takes nearly forty years for the New Testament pattern to repeat, and the Old Testament pattern will not repeat in my lifetime.

I have made at least two significant discoveries by reading the Bible systematically in this way. I have counted seventeen themes that are woven throughout the Bible's text, and on any given day in the schedule, there is always at least one of those themes found in all four of the texts for the day. I have had days with as many as three themes in all four texts. The other thing I discovered is the Bible's power to transform the reader. As a child, I first experienced the Bible's power to inspire. As I grew older, I recognized the Bible's ability to teach those willing to learn. Now I know the Bible can transform lives in amazing ways.

God's Truth

In the eighth chapter of John, Jesus says, ". . . you shall know the truth, and the truth shall make you free." Later, in the fourteenth chapter, Jesus says, "I am the way, the truth and the life . . . ." Truth is a major issue of the New Testament, and in our daily lives. The advertising companies seem to believe that truth is to be bought, sold, and manipulated like any other commodity. It is difficult not to become jaded in our attitude toward truth. To take clarity further away from reality, the media treat opinions as factual until successfully refuted.

The most disturbing passage on the subject of truth is II Timothy 4:3-4. "For the time is coming when people will not endure sound teaching, but having itching ears they will accumulate for themselves teachers to suit their own likings, and will turn away from listening to the truth and wander into myths."

How many people do we know who have wandered into myths? In the 1960s, there were many people who became lost in the myths of hippiedom. These people had their values either distorted or lost entirely, as they sought temporary fun and pleasure. In the 1970s and 1980s, we talked piously of values education. At the same time, teenagers were often confused and lost in the shuffle. Now, confusion

19

dominates young children's lives, where toys, games, cartoons, and comics make a concerted effort to establish values, which at best are rooted in the shallow soil of the present moment.

It is encouraging to see growth in churches where the truths of important issues are cherished more than the day-to-day politics of congregational life. These churches have a healthy spiritual life and a sustained joy. They are growing because they are cherishing the truth, the gospel, and life's enduring values.

Getting Closer to God

It all starts out beautifully: "In the beginning God created the heavens and the earth." . . . "And God said, ..." The Lord has been speaking ever since, but it seems people just do not listen. It would not at all be a surprise if at some time or other the Lord said, "I know that you believe you understand what you think I said, but I am not sure you realize that what you heard is not what I meant!"

The institutional church usually attaches rather exclusive ideas to God, using such words as infinite, eternal, omnipotent, omniscient, and omnipresent. These words acknowledge the truth that God is not such that we can run all the way around Him and take pictures. Such a relationship would be overwhelming if it were not for God's sending His Son. By learning how to relate to Jesus, it becomes possible to relate to God in a more personal and creative way.

It is no small wonder that many people say that they believe in God but do not know what they believe about God. For them, knowing God is low on their list of priorities. It is that same kind of priority keeping that keeps some "Christians" from knowing the Lord of their lives.

When we really get to know our Lord Jesus, it is easier to keep our priorities in proper order. We can relate to God in a positive, creative, and effective way. We can describe God and our relationship to the Lord in terms others will understand. To do that, we have to open our ears and eyes to all the ways God chooses to be revealed to us. It may mean silencing our own voice and those around us long enough to hear what God has to say. After all, the Voice did say to the Psalmist, "Be still, and know that I am God!"

Faith Fuel

Discipline

My life began to be focused upon parish ministry when I was twenty-five. As I first began to preach, I used either a manuscript or an outline. Gradually, I began to rely upon a source of inner wisdom, the Holy Spirit that God provides when I need it. I am certain that seeking that inner wisdom requires a high level of discipline.

One of the most important factors in my background that has shaped my personality was more than a dozen years of piano lessons. The two-fold discipline of daily practice and weekly confrontation with my teachers made discipline imperative. That discipline gave me mixed feelings. I enjoyed the pleasure that came from the results of those lessons and practice. I also detested the time spent on practice, when I wanted to be doing other things. I also hated facing the seemingly relentless criticism of the teachers. My last teacher was the exception. An important result of all of that practice was discipline. Discipline can be added to faith, through both rigorous Bible study and extended prayer. As a result, at least four things happen.

(1) Discipline provides structure, particularly when our faith is little more than a feeling. Sometimes our faith is little more than a thought or idea. The structure provided by discipline helps us to think through and talk about our faith. Faith is a living and growing thing, and our faith needs a framework just as surely as our flesh needs a skeleton to give it shape.

(2) Discipline provides direction to our faith when it is floundering. Having direction in our faith helps us focus on a problem and deal with it creatively.

(3) Discipline provides strength when we are weary of things that will not go away. Discipline toughens the muscles of our faith.

(4) Discipline creates appreciation for the gifts that God has given us. Study and prayer helps us discover gifts and strengths we never knew we had.

Of course, discipline means work, but you will find that the results far exceed our expectations or our input.

A Christian's Software

We live in a computer-dominated age, and most of us have strong opinions about them. Most have been touched by computers, even those not owning one. I see the computer on which I am writing this as a kind of metaphor. There are two primary ingredients to a computer system. The hardware is the computer itself. It includes an electronic processor, which of course is what the computer really is, and it can be likened to our human brain. Attached to that processor are devices for putting things into the computer, including disk drives, a touchpad or mouse, and a keyboard. In human terms, these things are like our ears and eyes.

Also attached are devices to show what the computer is doing or has done. Those devices include a display (monitor), a printer to put things on paper, and a small speaker. There is also a device called a modem, which allows my computer to talk with other computers. In human terms, these things are like our mouths.

All of this hardware would be virtually useless with out the second prime ingredient in a computer system. This second ingredient is called software. The software guides the hardware so that the information is processed in the way in which we want it to be processed. In short, the software helps the hardware make decisions. In human terms, this corresponds to our own personal system of doing things. It can be said that Christianity is a software system or program for our brain (the hardware).

The people who design software are called programmers. In my humble opinion, the greatest programmer who has ever lived is Jesus Christ. If we allow Jesus to "program" our minds, then we can live the fullest and most satisfying life that is possible—the Christian life. Are you willing to let Jesus "program" your own personal software?

Power to Change the World

A few years ago, Arthur F. Corey made this provocative statement about power: "Power is an emotionally charged word. When we possess it, we call it influence, but when it is held by someone else, we are content to use the ugly word. Yet there is nothing wrong with power; it takes power to get things done. Power is the application of intelligence to force. A river may be a terrific force, but it develops useful power only when directed through a turbine."

Today, the word **power** generates differing images of political power, economic power, atomic power, and electrical power. These powers stimulate our minds to think of many other kinds of power. From early childhood, all of us have had dreams of power. These childhood dreams carry forth into our adulthood, but by that time, our dreams of power become far more sophisticated. All of us dreamt at one time or another of having power that is beyond our regular God-given gifts, and such dreams offer a lot of temptation.

The story of Jesus' temptations in the wilderness offers an example. The Tempter offers three different possibilities of power to Jesus. Just as it was totally inappropriate for Jesus to succumb to those temptations, so it is inappropriate for us to step beyond our limitations. This does not change the fact that often we need power that is greater than what our own poor resources can provide.

What most people do not realize is there is power legitimately available to all of us, and which is greater than any power so far mentioned, but we do not fully explore its potential because we just cannot believe that such power is available. Like Peter Marshall, we can discover that "praying is dangerous business," but we can also discover that the rewards are beyond our wildest dreams.

God's Dreams

When I was growing up, one of the songs made popular by Walt Disney had a text that began "A dream is a wish your heart makes. . . ." If anyone in the twentieth century knew about dreams, and about making dreams become real, it was Walt Disney. He was a dreamer. He was a person who knew that a part of him never wanted to grow up. He was willing to dream big and then concentrate on making that dream come true. His ongoing dream throughout his life was to bring happiness to every life he touched.

As we read the Bible, whenever the people of God had a vision of where they were going and were obedient to God's will, the people made tremendous strides of progress. Miracles happened in every quarter when they were obedient. Whenever God's people lost sight of the vision God had planned for them, they wandered aimlessly until they got back on the right track.

In churches, planning is absolutely essential for the future. If we fail to plan, we plan to fail! The most important thing is to dream for God rather than to dream for ourselves. When we plan for the future of the church, we need to ask some very basic questions of each dream. Will it glorify God? If it only glorifies the local church, it will ultimately fail. Will this dream help more of God's people than any other way of using these same resources? We need to make the maximum use of what God gives us. Deliberate mediocrity is debasement, and it is a sin.

23

Faith Fuel

There is an abundance of examples of churches that have been reborn and revitalized when they decided to let God show them a vision of their rebirth, and they decided to follow that dream. There has always been tremendous growth associated with clinging to the vision that God gives. Then the church simply leaves it to God to supply the time, energy, and resources for us to give God the glory.

A Blind Trust

My first message for one church was based upon two verses of Psalm 37, which begins, "Trust in The LORD and do good . . . ." Since then I have stepped out in faith many times. Such exercises in trust yield fantastic results. As one goes on trusting God, it does not get easier because God keeps challenging us with bigger possibilities.

When we do not have previous experience on which to base our decision to trust, we have to find some other source of motivation. When it comes to trusting God with something we have never trusted God with before, the best motivation is love. Sometimes God invites us to try something really risky while seeming to say to us, "If you love me you will trust me with this one."

There is an evangelism workshop entitled, "Fishing on the Asphalt–How to Share Your Faith Without Being Obnoxious." It was created by Herb Miller for the National Evangelistic Association. All of us have heard what scriptures say about sharing our faith. It is another thing altogether to take what we have heard and say, "Okay, God, I will trust you with this one and begin sharing my faith with people who need to hear your good news." The workshop offers a plan of action.

1. Make a list of two or more people who you know to be un-churched.
2. Pray every day for these people and their problems.
3. After a week of this, begin showing an active listening interest in what is going on in their lives, responding in love as best you can.
4. Ask them what they think either of Jesus or of the church, and listen for their complete response.
5. After you have heard them out, share with them what you believe.

If you are ready to step out in faith but are still a bit fearful, ask a couple of your friends to form a "Fishing Club."

Faith Fuel

Discovering God's Will

The will of God can be a hot topic of discussion. In Christian circles, all seem to agree that we should do the will of God. There seems to be quite a bit of argument as to how one goes about determining what the will of God really is. Even more controversy arises between people who honestly believe they have God's will nailed down, but who disagree as to the particulars.

Sometimes it is simply a matter of stepping out in faith. Davy Crockett used to put it in a secular way when he would say, "Be sure you're right, and then go ahead." It is often not that simple. In Bible times, God's will was declared by God directly, or it was declared by prophets, Jesus, the Apostles, and other religious leaders. Religious leaders continued to be recognized as authoritative until recent years. Since World War II, however, different criteria have been recognized by society.

When Moses encountered Yahweh at the burning bush, he told God to choose someone else because he was not leader material and because he was a poor speaker. When Jesus called one young man to follow him, he told Jesus that there was something more important for him to do–to bury his father. Today we continue to follow this human inclination. When God's will becomes manifest to us, we often respond by saying, "That cannot be God's will because I have got a better idea!"

"Tithe? I think I owe it to God to pay my other bills first."

"Do evangelism? I think God would rather the professionals do it."

"Forgive my enemies? They do not deserve it."

"Love my enemies? I have not got the energy."

God's will is ever before us. If we have the eyes to see and the ears to hear, then hearing simply becomes a matter of stepping out in faith.

The Adventure of Growing Up

"There he made his home in a town called Nazareth, so that what had been spoken through the prophets might be fulfilled, "He will be called a Nazorean." (Matthew 2:23 NRSV)

Jesus grew up in the small town of Nazareth. We can be very sure that the childhood experiences of Jesus were typical of small town life. He would have had far different experiences if he had grown up in a big city like Jerusalem. In a small town, there is usually a powerful sense of community. Small town community life is like that of an extended family. If nothing else, people watch out for one another as self-protection. As with a large family, each worker has his or her role. In the case of Jesus' earthly father, people went to Joseph when there was carpenter's work to be done. As Jesus grew in wisdom and stature, He learned the importance of the personal touch. If Joseph built a chair for someone, it was designed for that person individually. Jesus learned when a carpenter needed to carve a yoke for oxen, the yoke had to be carved precisely to fit the muscular structure of the animal, making the yoke "easy."

Moving away from Christmas into another year, the best growth happens through personal interaction with other people. The gift-giving season may be over except for special occasions, but there are other kinds of giving. When we do our work, we can make it impersonal and ordinary, or we can work with our minds focused on the person or persons who will benefit from what we are doing. A job that we do can be an uncomfortable burden or it can be an easy one. We can accomplish our tasks with the mechanical precision that comes from repetition, or we can approach each task with an awareness of the skills that we have from experience, and the gifts that we have from God.

As the babe in the manger began to take his first steps, He no doubt stumbled. As He learned to walk, practice made it easier. It took time however, to learn to walk with the dignity and poise that belonged to the King of Kings. We celebrate the New Year precisely seven days after our celebration of Christmas. As our celebration of Christmas begins to fade into history, we have little time to think about the Christ Child's days of infancy or toddlerhood. Our minds focus on the big celebration of the New Year, rather than focusing on a flight to Egypt or a journey home to Nazareth. What if you and I had grown up in Nazareth? Would we notice a Christ child in our midst?

Moving Forward on Faith

I began one particular day by doing something different. I always try to begin each day with prayer, but that day I got on my knees and reviewed with God what we had been through together since I had made the decision to go into the ministry. I found myself being grateful. I did not think I had say "thank you," because God knew

I was. Since beginning the Christian ministry, not all of it has been easy or painless.

I decided years ago that I was not working for the "visible" church. If I had not made that decision, I probably would have quit. God is not an employer from whom I can walk away. I understand those who have considered it a few times. In the course of the stupidity that comes from anger, frustration, disappointment, fatigue, and. burnout, the temptation to give up is there. Every congregation I have served has had a majority of people who made me glad I am in all this. Even when I was working for Disneyland and later as a music teacher, deep down somewhere I knew who really was My Employer.

Many years ago, I was called to be the pastor of a small congregation in southeast Texas. It was a beautiful, delightful, warm, friendly church. There were plenty of young, dedicated, energetic members. They practiced excellent stewardship. They had a vital interest in evangelism. They were growing in church school attendance as well as worship attendance. Since I had served there previously as a student, I already knew and loved many of them. It was hard to say "no." Somehow, I knew that I was not supposed to be there.

A few weeks later, another pulpit committee obviously felt their church's problems were thorny. Nevertheless, they had a guarded optimism. I knew that it was congregation where I was supposed to be. I felt like I was in a state of "limbo." I knew where we had come from, and we had charted a good course, but the most able-bodied of the crew were just learning to sail. The Holy Spirit, the "wind" of God, empowered us to go forward together. We kept our ears open to the voice of our Pilot and Captain, Jesus Christ. We were led by His faithfulness.

Approaching Faith with Song

The vast majority of Protestants learn their theology from the texts of the hymns they sing. An interesting and rather accurate way of learning about what a person believes is simply asking them to give you a list of their favorite hymns.

Music has always been a vital part of religion, and our Bible is full of references to both instrumental and vocal music. During the last century, however, music has been used most of the time to entertain, to escape, or to mask background noise. Controversies have arisen regarding both the types of music used in worship, and the appropriateness of applause. If the music glorifies God, and it is performed with the intention of pleasing God, it is appropriate for worship. If the music does not glorify and please God, it has no place in worship. Applause is an expression of thanksgiving. If we are expressing thanksgiving to God for what God has done and is doing, then clapping our hands for God is appropriate for worship. If our applause and thanksgiving is for the performance and performer, then our worship is no longer focused completely on God. It is inappropriate for worship.

Music is one of our greatest vehicles for approaching God. It is possible however, when making a journey, we can get entranced with the vehicle or the driver instead of watching the road and remembering the destination. In our case, worship is the road and our destination is The Eternal.

The Power of Hope

One of the comments I frequently have heard after church is that people need to hear messages of hope. It is a wonder why Christians sometimes act as though there is no hope left. Hope is one of the three great ingredients in the foundation of Christianity. Along with love and faith, Christianity focuses on hope.

A Christian is on a journey to life. Death is a doorway in the sky. We journey on a path centered on trusting in God, the source of our hope. Faith helps us conquer our greatest challenges.

The Christian is not just someone who desires eternal life, but also expects it with hope. The true Christian is someone who believes that Jesus is the Christ, accepts Him as Lord and Savior, and centers their hope on Christ.

It is very important for us to know that we can do all things through Christ who strengthens us. It is also important to us that we are "In Christ" and "new creations." The deeper those facts seep into our hearts, the more we are filled with hope. When we get discouraged, we can find great comfort and renewed hope when we remind ourselves that we can do all things through Christ who strengthens us.

Faith Fuel

Sight Beyond Sight

Many are familiar with the song from *Man of La Mancha* entitled "The Quest." Those who do not recognize that title might know the song as "The Impossible Dream." Christians are often ridiculed when we talk about how all things are possible with God. We often feel foolish when we see things through God's eyes - when we see the possibilities of God's grace and power.

There is a natural human tendency to perceive our world only in terms of what we can actually see and hear. As Arthur Schopenhauer put it, "Every man takes the limits of his own field of vision for the limits of the world." Our public educational system often makes it worse by discouraging imagination while encouraging memorization and acceptance. The result can be knowing facts without understanding them, or seeing how those facts are useful. Unintentionally, the sciences can sometimes discourage creative thinking while overly emphasizing hard data.

Within the church, we are people in the same world as everyone else. Even when leaders begin to see things through God's eyes, it is extremely hard to convince everyone else that the vision is according to God's will. At a district meeting some years ago, we were supposedly trying to catch a glimpse of the future of the region. Instead, we wasted precious time bemoaning the past and belaboring the present. Vision gave way to pious pragmatism. Unable to set our spirits free from the past, young and old ended up stumbling just past the present and falling short of the future. William Blake once said, "What is now proved was once only imagined." The future of the church depends upon our tapping into the imagination of Christ. After all, it is His church! Our eternity is in His hands.

Gifts and Limitations

On my prayer list are a number of people with extraordinary gifts. I am thinking in particular of Susan (a lawyer), John (a preacher), Vanessa (an artist), Richard (a composer), and Debra (an entertainer). These people have amazing gifts. All identify themselves as Christians, though some practice their faith more than others do. Two are divorced, three are married, two bear fruit from abundant spiritual gifts, and one is estranged from God. All are in reasonably good health, all

29

have a favorite passion, and all have friends who believe their gifts are truly phenomenal. Only two have given serious thought to the divine source of their gifts.

Also on my prayer list is a banker wrapped up in her problems. She seldom recognizes her gifts except when she periodically goes to church. There is a model who limits her vision to her physical assets, and she sees most churches as the camp of the enemy. There is a legal assistant who has finally begun to awaken to God's constant presence and power, but does not recognize their significance.

Each of us has both gifts and limitations. At times, our gifts are obvious, like great intellectual or artistic talents. Sometimes our limitations are obvious, as with those who are physically or mentally challenged. We are the only ones who give much thought to our gifts and limitations outside of employers. Good stewardship means making the most of our gifts. Good sense means knowing when not to challenge our limitations.

Congregations have gifts and limitations too. Sometimes congregations perceive limitations where there are not any. Quite often, their gifts are not fully realized. With God's help, however, we can be all that God has created us to be.

Listening to What We Read

In *Christianity Today*, Richard Foster said, "The Bible is not a textbook. Nor is a manual to be studied, mastered, and mechanically applied." This statement is the preamble to an interview with Eugene Peterson, the Bible scholar who published a translation of the Bible entitled *The Message*. In his latest publication entitled *Eat This Book*, Peterson introduces his readers to the ancient Christian practice of spiritual reading. Mr. Peterson believes that we should reflectively "listen" to the Word of God until it fills the soul.

I was raised in a Christian home, and my family went to church nearly every Sunday. My brother and I went to Sunday school nearly every Sunday as well. In my undergraduate days, I never took a course in religion, nor did I take any courses in philosophy. Then I attended seminary, where I was taught how to read and study the Bible accurately and effectively. About six years later, I attended my first evangelism workshop, and I began to recognize a hunger for something more in my life.

Faith Fuel

A few years later, I began systematically reading the Bible. I came up with the reading schedule that many in the congregation are following. By doing this for the last twenty years or so, I have engaged in the ancient Christian practice of *lectio divina*. I did not know about *lectio divina* at the time. I simply started practicing it, evidently at the prompting of the Holy Spirit. The term *lectio divina* means "holy reading." The saints of the Dark Ages and middle Ages devised this mode of reading the Bible for transformation. It does **not** mean reading large portions of the Bible, such as reading an entire book. Although there is a place for Bible study, *lectio divina* is not "study" actually. It is a way for the mind to be immersed into the heart, in order to find the loving goodness of God. It is very much like the experience of reading poetry repeatedly until the text becomes part of who you are and how you see the world.

Those who do *lectio divina* in retreat settings divide it into four parts, either (1) reading, reflecting, praying, and contemplating; or (2) listening, reflecting, praying, and obeying. It is important to understand that these parts should not be seen as sequential. The four overlap and mingle, and the result is a connection with the Holy Spirit. *Lectio divina* could be an approach used by spiritual growth groups. Those who have been following a daily Bible reading schedule can form groups that meet in homes.

Being Read by the Bible

A person need not be a musician to make sounds on a musical instrument. Given time, one can learn to have fun beating a drum or making a simple melody on an instrument of choice. In a similar way, people do not have to be Christians to read the Bible. Given time, one can find enjoyment learning Bible stories and sharing them. On the other hand, to play an instrument so that it makes a difference in one's own life and in the lives of others, a person has to have talent and has to practice. To know the Bible well enough to make a difference in one's own life and in the lives of others, it does not require talent, but like playing an instrument, it does require practice.

When I was four years old, my Mom introduced me to Harriet Nelson, who began teaching me to play the piano. She taught me to read music, how to hold my hands and arms while playing, and some simple fingering techniques. After three months, I was doing all those things. After nine months, she was still teaching me the same things, and my Mom could tell I was getting bored. Just like playing an

31

Faith Fuel

instrument, if we can read to start with, we can learn where the books of the Bible are and where to find our favorite stories quickly. If that is all our teacher teaches us, however, we soon get bored.

When I was five, Mom introduced me to Francis Frothingham. I learned how to become emotionally inspired by what the composers put into the music. When I did not feel music exactly as she did however, she insisted I was not playing correctly. I started complaining again. In a similar way, we can learn how to find inspiration from the Bible. Some psychologists use the Bible for therapy even when they do not consider themselves particularly religious. The Bible is more than nice stories and inspiration however.

When I was eight, I began to take lessons from Ethel Willard Putnam. She taught me to use good technique, find the composer's original intentions, and squeeze the most pleasing results out of performing. I liked the results, but she did not know how to balance praise with criticism. I gave up on piano lessons for a while. As a parallel, we can sometimes engage in excellent Bible study, but if the student and teacher do not communicate well, the results might not be what they could be.

As a junior in high school, I was asked by the school's orchestra director to play George Gershwin's *Rhapsody in Blue* with the orchestra. I engaged the services of a professional jazz pianist to help me. Throughout my career, I have occasionally sought instruction to improve my abilities as a Bible teacher and pastor. It is common for Christians to do specialized study of the Bible under special circumstances.

When I decided to major in piano and voice, in order to get my Bachelor's degree, it was required that I take additional piano lessons. If I had taken lessons from my new teacher, Dorothy Judy Klein at the beginning, I might have become a concert pianist instead of a pastor. She taught me the importance of knowing the music apart from the techniques necessary to perform. I learned the importance of living with the music before performing for others. Ideally, she would like to get her students to memorize the music before they sat down to try to play it! In seminary, I learned how to analyze and communicate various texts of the Bible for the purposes of teaching and preaching. I did not realize at the time how important it is to read and live with the Bible as a whole. I spent years discovering what the Bible had to say about my life's agenda. During that time, I also focused on teaching congregations what the Bible had to say about their agendas. Then I began to apply my lesson from Dorothy Judy Klein to the Bible. I had catching up to do, so I began reading four chapters of the Bible each day. I studied the Bible less, and I read it more. It was a difficult discipline at first, but I was determined to spend more time getting to know the Lord of my life.

I am glad it was not too late for me to discover that the Bible as a whole has its own agenda. It is an agenda that transforms the life of the one reading it. I still study the Bible, but I do not simply want to know what information it may provide as I read it. The more I read the Bible and surrender to its text, the more *it reads me*. That may not make sense to you, but it is absolutely true.

Literate Faith

There are countless people who notice that, when they read the Bible aloud, they *experience* the scriptures differently. The truth is, words on a page are lifeless, but words spoken and heard have a life of their own. Long before Bibles were printed and available for everyone to read, they were spoken and heard. Ask three good readers to read a scripture as though they are the ones telling the story. You will get three very different versions!

When you are reading the Bible, does the Bible read you? Is there a passage in the Bible that you can recite without reading it? If not, turn to the 23rd Psalm in the middle of the Bible, and read through it several times. The more you read it, the more you will feel part of the text. That is when the Bible begins reading *you*. When you begin to experience the Bible reading you, go to God in prayer, and talk with Our Heavenly Father aloud about the conversation that seems to have begun as you were reading. As your mind begins to wander onto other subjects (and it will!), talk with God honestly about what is on your mind.

Have these scripture-begun conversations with God on a regular basis. You will find that a transformation begins to take place. Gradually, the Holy Spirit begins to heal the hurts that trouble our minds and spirits. These conversations begin to strengthen and refresh who we are. Our spiritual gifts begin to flourish and bear fruit. Our training and talents are improved. The result is a life more filled with what the New Testament identifies as the fruits of the spirit. James 3:17 says, "But the wisdom that is from above is first pure, then peaceable, gentle, willing to yield, full of mercy and good fruits, without partiality and without hypocrisy." (NKJV)

Many years ago, a man named Roger Carstensen founded The Mission for Biblical Literacy. For about fifteen years, he was the President of the Christian College of Georgia. He and Fred Craddock sometimes traveled together, providing teaching seminars to churches. In 1976, he set out on his own, founded the Institute for Biblical Literacy, and began offering weekend or weeklong experiences called "The Feast of the Scriptures." Today, the Mission for Biblical literacy continues out of the offices of Peachtree Christian Church in Atlanta, Georgia. Roger was not particularly interested in getting people to memorize passages of the Bible. What he passionately did want people like you and me to do is immerse ourselves in the scriptures. When we thus engage ourselves with the scriptures, the scriptures begin to speak to us and with us. To someone who has never done it, none of this seems to make sense. When I first heard about it, it made little sense to me even to try it.

I met Roger at a preaching seminar, where he taught about a dozen of us how to preach story sermons. In hindsight, I think it was meeting Roger that eventually led me to have such a passion for Biblical literacy. I learned it is not a matter of knowing all the information contained in the Bible. It is a matter of experiencing the scriptures, and thus connecting with God. There is no doubt in my mind that Roger was immersed in the Bible, and that the Bible would read him as he read the Bible. Praise God, this kind of experience is not limited to the clergy. Reading the scriptures enough for the scriptures to begin reading us takes time, but is amazingly worth it. All that God does, God does well.

Of Winter Storms

The stormy winds, they blow so cold, our eyes can't see the sky.
We walk about with bodies numb — sometimes we think we'll die.
We concentrate on simple tasks, survival is our mode:
We want to do the basic things, not take on heavy loads.

We know from life's experience that storms do pass on by,
And when they've passed we might enjoy a clear and cheery sky.
We seldom think of dangers past, our lives are filled with *now*.
Deliverance is just accepted, no "I wonder how . . . ?"

And then there's times when danger's huge, and slaps us in the face!
We're simply overwhelmed with pow'r, — —our ego's been displaced!
We're stunned and humbled, weak and scared, we lift our voice on high,
The Power's holy presence brings a peace, and then a sigh.

Faith Fuel

So You and I are not alone, we look to God above.
Our God is watching over us, so constantly with love!
So in God's love we have no fear, for we can know God's Son;
And we can know redeeming grace, — our stormy battles' won!

Faith Fuel

Time Enough

"For you yourselves know very well that the day of the Lord will come like a thief in the night." (I Thessalonians 5:2 NRSV)

A few years ago, Robert Heinlein wrote a book entitled *Time Enough for Love*. It is a story of a very unusual man and his descendents. This peculiar man had learned as a young adult that a distortion in his genetic make-up made him immortal. Quite literally, he had all the time in the world to do what he wanted to do. There was time enough to love to the fullest. Time enough...?

Since the very essence of God is love, then love cannot be a momentary surge of emotion or something that easily diminishes with time. In a letter written to a Christian community in Ancient Greece, the Apostle Paul told his readers that love never ends. [I Corinthians 13:8] Made in God's image, reaching our potential for love takes time. Is there time enough...?

Love is not something we feel but something we do. Love is not something that we create within ourselves. Rather, love is part of who we are that we can share with others. Love does not flow in gushing rivers that diminish in dry seasons. Rather, love flows from artesian springs that are steady and dependable. Time does not diminish love....

Great reservoirs are not filled in a day or even in a few months. Ponds are drained and filled in a day; lakes and seas are not. Supplying a relationship with a reservoir of love takes time. If in the time of Abraham or Moses God had sent The Christ, the necessary foundation would not have been laid. After many generations, the relationship between God and God's children was ready for the incarnation of love in Jesus Christ. There had been time enough....

The shores of a reservoir of love are secured by liking, loving, and trusting. The larger the boundaries are of friendship, the larger the reservoir is of love. The actions of love deepen a relationship–patience, kindness, tenderness, and the restraint of jealousy and arrogance. Trust is made of mountains and hills that are not easily moved, giving security to a relationship. Mountain lakes are slowly shaped by time....

The earth–and all that is in it and surrounding it–was created by God. All is sustained by God, sustained by God's love. In the image of God, we are filled with love given to us to share. God so loves us that we are given to one another. God so loved the world that God gave God's self as a person in Jesus. There had been, and is, time enough.

Faith Fuel

For the Love of God

It has been said that one of the most important phrases in the English language is "I love you!" In a healthy marriage, both parties need to hear it and say it on a regular basis. Human love often has conditions attached. Human love is easily put to the test by tough times and the unexpected. Human love is strongly tied to trust and comfort. We find it easy to love someone we trust or like.

Trained marriage and family counselors find that relationships are built with three primary ingredients–liking, loving, and trusting. If one of those ingredients is missing or in short supply for either party in a relationship, that relationship begins to weaken and falter. Those who have been through the trauma of divorce have often found that they go on loving their former spouse even if they no longer like or trust that special person.

All of these traits of human love contribute to our amazement when we speak of divine love. Countless people have been amazed when they have found God continuing to love them, even after they know they have failed or betrayed the Holy One. Sometimes that amazement turns to awe when a penitent sinner seeks forgiveness. That awe comes from the overwhelming quantity of love poured out upon those who humble themselves.

In most discussions of human love and divine love, there is a strong tendency to limit the discussion to these two lines of thought. We find it easy to compare human love for humans with Divine Love for humans. There is a third facet to these loving relationships that often gets little or no attention.

Most of us are familiar with the popular exclamation, "For the love of God!" Often of course, this expression is simply an expletive, and the person saying it does not think much about what the expression means. In some cases, the person saying "For the love of God!" is suggesting that someone do something in response to God's love for us. In a few cases, the person saying "For the love of God!" is affirming God's love as their motivation to action. How often does this expression "For the love of God!" refer to our love for God?

How often in our prayer lives do we pray something like this: "I know that you love me O God, and I love you too!" Just as surely as it helps a marriage for each partner to say aloud that they love the other person, the same is true of our relationship with God. How often do we make a conscious decision to do something not for ourselves but simply because we love God? So often, we have sung of Jesus being our friend. How often do we make a conscious decision to do something because we want to be Jesus' friend?

Yes, this is a different way of looking at things. Approaching life in this way may seem like a silly exercise to some. Try comparing how these different expressions sound:

"For the love of God!" or "For my love for God!"
"For the love of Christ!" or "For my love for Jesus!"
"Jesus loves me, this I know." or "I love Jesus, this I know."
"Jesus gave his all for me." or "I'll give Jesus my all for Him."

How do you worship for the love of God? How do you pray for the love of God? Are you doing the ministry to which you have been called, for love of God?

Unconditional Love

It seems to be human nature to love that which we decide is beautiful. In our personal relationships, we respond lovingly to those people we deem to be attractive. We also respond lovingly to those who express themselves well and to those who have physical or intellectual prowess. As our relationships begin to develop, we build our love for people based upon what we find appealing, and upon the things people say or do.

A natural consequence is our love for others tends to be conditional. Our continuing to love someone tends to be on the condition that we continue to respond to that person with the same positive feelings. Some psychologists say either it is impossible to love unconditionally, or it is foolhardy and illogical to do so. Some people admit that their love for someone is conditional, but they insist that it has to be that way.

Jesus teaches us by word and example that unconditional love is both possible and rewarding. The Apostle Paul makes it clear when we examine I Corinthians 13: 4-7. Examination of this passage reveals that Christian love is not so much a response to the person we love, but rather a response to the call of Christ. We can say because of Christ's call to love, we *decide to love* rather than *respond with love*.

To love unconditionally involves risks. Conditional love helps feed our own egos, which may be bruised if we are rejected. Unconditional love nurtures our relationship with Jesus Christ, so we grow towards loving more fully each time we decide to love.

Faith Fuel

Doing Love

Lauryn met Joe's gaze the first time at a business convention. As they began to be acquainted, Joe was taken more and more with Lauryn. Joe was impressed that she was attractive, intelligent, poised, and articulate. He made the decision to love her. No! He did not "fall" in love! He was not overcome with lust. He was simply fascinated, and that led to his decision to love her. Having made his conscious decision to love Lauryn, Joe also realized that if Lauryn were to make a similar decision and commitment to love him in return, he would be perfectly content to spend the rest of his life with her. Does this sound preposterous? Is it unbelievable? Does it sound like a soap opera or maybe a romantic comedy, with Joe making a complete fool of himself? Would he stop loving Lauryn if she did not love him in return?

Most of our world thinks of love in terms of an emotional response to someone or something. The expressions "fall in love" and "learning to love" are common phrases in our everyday speech, but we never hear about someone deciding to love. Jesus' sacrifice on the cross was a direct result of His deciding to love us. He decided to love all humankind so much that it required his life. It was a decision to love when He made the conscious decision to set his face to go to Jerusalem to die on the cross. Christians are truly Christians when they have decided to love Jesus. Most of us hardly knew Jesus when we made that crucial decision. The decision might arguably have been an emotional one. Nonetheless, it was a decision to love.

Living the Christian life so that we love our neighbors as ourselves means we regularly decide to love. We decide to be patient and kind. We decide not to be jealous or boastful. We decide not to be arrogant or rude. The challenge is to continue deciding to love even when that love is not returned, or is thrown back in our faces. The challenge is to decide to love, even if it means making complete fools of ourselves. Unlike the case of Joe and Lauryn, the even greater challenge is to decide to love even when you are not so positively impressed.

The Power of (Non-Sexual) Hugs

An old story tells of a man who checked a book out of the public library, because on the spine of the book it said, "How to Hug."

Faith Fuel

When he got the book home, he was disappointed to learn that he had checked out the sixth volume from a set of encyclopedias!

Who have you hugged today? That may seem like a frivolous question. Actually, it is a question that applies to our physical, emotional, and spiritual health. Hugging is good therapy. It is nearly always non-threatening. It is good for us, even if the hug is not returned! The reason is quite simple: all of us need to touch and be touched. Hugging is the most "massive touch" you can give someone! Give a child in an orphanage a hug, and they all will plead for a hug. If you visit a convalescent hospital and touch someone, he or she will remember your visit. If you give that person a hug, he or she will cherish the memory.

Jesus said to love our neighbors. Many people think they are being good Christians if they simply tolerate everyone. Some go further, and speak kindly or even lovingly to their neighbors. Still fewer give truly warm handshakes while looking the person in the eye and smiling. Still fewer give pats on the back or a squeeze of the shoulders. Have you given any hugs today?

In Christian singles groups, I have encountered a remarkably consistent phenomenon, and that has been overt hugging programs. I have seen hugging demonstrations, and heard hugging "code words" spoken at every time imaginable. Once a group begins to hug, it is rather infectious.

Groups that hug have warmer fellowship, closer friendships, and deeper caring. People that hug are generally happier and more at peace than people who do not hug. Have I made my point? Can my readers take a hint? We can do a better job of loving our neighbors. Who have you hugged today?

Relating to God

Since becoming a pastor, the most common problems brought to me have involved relationships. I obtained my clinical certification in counseling in anticipation of this.. Most of the time, the relationships in question were between people, rather than between individuals and God. These problems between family and friends can often be dealt with fairly easily. The counseling was often in informal settings–even over the telephone. Sometimes though, the problems were more serious.

Faith Fuel

One of the tools I am certified to use is the *Taylor-Johnson Temperament Analysis*. Most often, it is used to survey how well two people know each other. I have administered this survey to people who have lived together for years who really did not know each other at all. I have also given it to people who have known each other for less than two months who knew each other like a book! It is simply a matter of effective communication.

Our relationship to God often suffers from the same malady. Some of us blunder through life for years, fully aware of how well God knows us, but refusing to acknowledge how little effort we have put into getting to know God through Jesus. Let us face it: Jesus is not a beautiful balloon drifting in and out of our lives. Jesus is a person of substance who, as our constant companion, is our ultimate friend. We can always depend upon Him. We cannot see Him in the flesh, but we can see the results of His efforts on our behalf. It is not just a matter of talking to Him. We need to let Him communicate with us.

Loving with Trust

Nothing perplexes people more than trouble with relationships. I have counseled relationships between parents and teens, husbands and wives, and just about every other kind of relationship. The biggest challenge is helping people with their relationship to God.

The three essential ingredients to a full-blown successful relationship are trusting, liking, and loving. If any one of these ingredients is missing for either party in a relationship, there is the potential for trouble.

While in seminary, I learned to love a very special woman. She turned down my proposal of marriage and married someone else. That first marriage dissolved after a relatively short time, and it was devastating to her as a devout Southern Baptist. She sought counseling, and she discovered that she suffered from "beautiful woman syndrome." In her many years in beauty contests, she learned to distrust men at the most basic level. If for no other reason, lack of trust between her and her former husband did them in.

In the Broadway musical *Oliver*, a bar maid is madly in love with a notorious criminal. She trusts and loves him, but she admits she does not like him. He liked her and loved her but did not trust her. During the drama, he kills her, but to her dying breath, she still loves him.

41

Faith Fuel

A number of years ago, I was analyzing my relationship to God on these terms. I realized that I liked God because of all the great things that I could see and attribute to God. I also loved God because of the ways in which I had experienced God at work in my life. John 3:16 was inspirational to me, but it meant little more. I had trouble - as many people do - in the trust department. Trusting God to achieve His dreams for our lives is difficult indeed. It is a matter of giving more than lip service to the Christian faith.

As the son of a science teacher, I try to be pragmatic and spontaneous. I know the facts of the Christian faith. Logical conclusions are based on both facts and assumptions, however. In light of the facts, and assuming that God wants what is best for me, my conclusion must be to trust. I came to that conclusion easily once I invited Jesus into my heart. He became my best friend and constant companion as well as my Savior.

Preparing to Love

Resolve to be patient! God is not finished with us yet. Jesus experienced at least as much suffering as we have, so his responses to our prayers are tempered by personal human experiences here on earth.

Resolve to be kind. Everyone we meet has his or her own cross to bear. It is arrogant for any of us to assume that we are the only ones who experience our particular kind of pain, and God is here to help us.

Resolve not to be jealous! God blesses each of us with our own personal compliment of gifts. God has already given us far more than we deserve, so being jealous of someone else is selfish at best.

Resolve not to brag. We do not really accomplish anything worthwhile without God's help. If we simply have to brag, let us brag about the help we are getting from our Best Friend and Companion, Jesus Christ, from whom we have received all "our" gifts.

Resolve to be humble. We do not have to be a doormat in order to keep our pride under control. It is better - and more honest - to acknowledge God's efforts through us.

Resolve to be courteous. In a society increasingly noted for its bad manners, it is all the more important for Christians to be gracious.

Faith Fuel

Resolve to be flexible wherever possible, without sacrificing good morals and ethics. Having our own way is not nearly as important as doing things God's way.

Resolve to keep tempers under control. Mud thrown is ground lost! Let us trust God to forgive, redeem, and teach us to do the same.

Resolve to find your joy in what is done right. Praise God for flubs redeemed and injustice vindicated.

Resolve to carry burdens graciously. Complaining about our burdens does not help others carry theirs any more than it forces them to carry ours. It is better to work together for mutual support.

Resolve to let God be God, to let Christ be King, and to let the Holy Spirit carry on when we cannot.

Resolve to center hopes vertically rather than horizontally. Seen from God's eyes, our daily walk is a path towards eternal life with God.

Resolve to find triumph! Since Jesus Christ endured the cross and triumphed over death at Easter, we too can triumph over any present crisis.

Love never ends! Real love flows from God and passes on through us to others. We may choose to interrupt the flow of that love. We may choose to divert it temporarily. Love itself, however, never ends.

Have It God's Way

Over nineteen centuries ago, the Apostle Paul wrote a letter to the Christians in the picturesque community of Corinth. Corinth was (and is) situated on a little isthmus of the Greek peninsula with the Adriatic Sea on the West and the Aegean Sea on the East. This beautiful spot was the setting for a church divided into many factions, divided both from within and from without. The city's culture was both strongly intellectual and strongly hedonistic. The biggest problems came from within.

The divisions were not entirely along theological lines. No, the divisions of the church happened when groups within the church took one important aspect of the life of the church and made it the central issue: To put it another way, they took an important thing and tried to make it the main thing. The Corinthian church became a problem church. If ever there was an expert who knew how to help problem

43

churches it was the Apostle Paul. Nineteen hundred years have come and gone and Paul's advice to churches is still relevant.

As we search Paul's letters looking for a common theme, we find a gem in the so-called 'love chapter,' I Corinthians 13. One statement there would apply to almost every church problem as well as every problem that would plague a relationship. Paul said, "Love does not insist on its own way."

Years ago, there was an advertising campaign with the slogan, "Have it your way!" Church problems usually seem to unravel when we lovingly say that to each other–and to God. It is a matter of resisting the temptation to demand our rights, instead serving one another in the name of Jesus.

The Call to Care

At the core of the Christian faith is the injunction that we should love one another. Until Jesus came, no one fully and clearly understood the importance of love. No one knew really how God wanted us to love one another. One of the Greek words for love, *agape*, was rarely used until the Christian era.

Many of us in the Christian community believe when we lead our lives so as not to hate anyone, we are obeying Jesus' commandment to love. We assume this because we believe that the opposite of love is hate. That assumption is a tragic trap. The opposite of love is not hate: Hate is merely a distortion of love. The opposite of love is apathy.

When we do not actively demonstrate our love and concern for someone, we do not love them at all. It is easy to justify our not showing Christian love by saying, "I just do not have loving feelings for that person." This also is a tragic trap! Christian love is not a response of the heart but a decision of the mind. To love someone with Christian love means being willing to love them. In I Corinthians 13:4-7, Paul drives this point home by saying that love is patient, kind, and not jealous. One must decide to do these things!

Whenever we say, "I do not care," we are denying Jesus' call to love. Whenever we say, "It does not matter to me," when our help is really needed, we are betraying our faith. We are called to care, to be involved, to be concerned, to love, and to shun apathy. Yes, we are each called, and our response to that call is crucial to our faith.

Faith Fuel

Tough Love

One of the ongoing struggles in the Christian life is with trying to love those with whom we do not see eye to eye, those who constantly irritate us, and those who are sinning against us or against God. Another struggle is determining when to exercise "tough" love when all of our loving efforts seem to fail.

The first step is always forgiveness. Forgiving someone may not mean excusing them. Forgiving someone does not mean we have changed our mind, and that the offense was acceptable after all. Forgiving means letting go of our anger as soon as we can. Such anger is destructive to us internally, and it distorts our ability to deal logically with the problem. Someone once approached Jesus and asked if he should forgive his enemies seven times - a large number by Jewish standards. Jesus' response was an exaggeration that pointed to not placing a limit on the number.

The next step is to determine what we believe about the offense and the offender. When we are angry or hurt, it is hard to separate the facts from our assumptions. This can be dangerous to our emotional health, and sometimes to our physical health as well. Assuming the best intentions in a person can be just as destructive as assuming the worst. We cannot always base our analysis of the present situation on past experience!

Finally, we have to live with the actions we take. Writing off a relationship or cutting off communication is usually just as destructive to us as revenge is. In most cases, the loving response is the best one, unless the loving response consistently does not produce the desired results. In such cases, tough love is mandatory.

Unexpected Love

With all of the advances we have made in recent years, we have retreated in our understanding of such things as love, beauty, and honor. Science would have us limit our understanding of love to the sexual or social chemistry between people. Some scientists would have us believe that all behavior is chemically induced. Media editors would limit our understanding of beauty to its outward appearance, even though appearance may be enhanced by makeup or plastic surgery. Pundits would limit our understanding of honor to paying our dues, only when we get caught doing something inappropriate or unlawful, rather than as a record of overall behavior.

Faith Fuel

It has become difficult to express a genuine interest in friendship with a new acquaintance without motives being questioned. Unexpected love makes many uncomfortable. Because of news stories about predators, our motives are also often questioned if we pay high compliments on someone's appearance if that person is not related or a close friend.

Love is truly love only when it is unconditional. Genuine love is not something we feel, but something we do. True beauty can be experienced in the heart or in the mind without the input of our eyes or our ears. Beauty's impression lingers beyond appearance. Honor is measured by the character of each man or woman and not by the events that shape them. All of this is "made flesh" in the Christ who died for us, who invisibly embraces us, and who never lets us down. Christ is love, beauty, and honor made flesh.

The Power of Patience

"Love is patient" seems like an easy statement to make. Before we can really work with that statement, we have to understand what it means. Loving means enduring things simply because we care. It also means tolerating a lot from people simply because we love them. The patient person is a persistent person. We need to see that love is patient from these three different angles.

We seldom think about God being patient with us, but there are biblical examples. After God had chosen His people, the Jews would stray away from where they were supposed to be going. They would forget what they were supposed to be doing. They would forget how they were supposed to be living. God would patiently call them back, admonish them, and start them back in the right direction again. The mother of James and John asked for priority placement of her sons in heaven, and Jesus patiently reminded everyone of the importance of humility. The greatest of all is the servant of all, a lesson that Jesus repeatedly taught.

Then there is the direction of humanity's lack of patience with God. We go to the Lord in prayer, we spend time telling God what we want, and we tell God we want it right now. Patient prayer is different. It says, "If it is Your will!" It says, "Lord, you know my needs better than I do!" It says, "Lord, you know what I want, but do You want it for me?"

God often wants the same things that we want, but since God sees history from an entirely different perspective, we just cannot see why God times things the way He does. It is a matter of comparing

Faith Fuel

God's timing with our timing.

Love means having the patience to endure until God brings us our great blessings. Love means having tolerance of God's ideas for our lives. It means having the tolerance to love God enough to believe what He says is right, instead of believing what we think is logical. Love also has the persistence with God to pray unceasingly for that which we know is right, for the benefit of others as well as for ourselves.

We can easily see how patience is manifested in love when God asks us to love our neighbors. If we really love our neighbors, we have patience with those who disagree with us. If we really love our neighbors, we have patience with those who make mistakes at our expense. Love means having patience with those who do not see what we see or hear what we hear. Jesus tells us to love our enemies, because in loving them, we learn the patience we need to love those who are close to us.

Loving people have the endurance to handle those who disagree with them. Love has the endurance to handle those mistakes that are made at our expense. Love has the endurance to look as well as see, and to listen as well as to hear. It has endurance and strength for those who cannot cope. "Love is patient" means having the tolerance to handle the opinions of others, even though they are in disagreement with our own. Love means having the tolerance to forgive mistakes made at our expense. Love means having the tolerance to listen more carefully, to try to hear what others hear, and to try to look yet again. Love looks through other people's eyes, to see what they see. Love is patient; love does endure, does tolerate, and has persistence. When we reach that point where we are ready to give up on someone, to say we cannot handle that person any longer, it is then we need to remember the words of the Apostle Paul: Love is patient!

Kindness Caresses the Heart

The Apostle Paul says a lot about love in I Corinthians 13:4-8a. He begins by saying that love is patient and kind. Paul uses a particular word for *kind* that appears nowhere else in the Bible. Even in the Greek translation of the Old Testament, the word is not used.

Used outside of the Bible, writers of that era did not mean simple kindness. It meant divine overwhelming compassion. It also meant grace–unearned, unasked for, undeserved love. That is what the Apostle Paul means, saying that love is kind. That implies a lot!

47

Faith Fuel

Jesus tells two parables illustrating this kindness. In the parable of the loving father, the prodigal son comes to his father and asks for his inheritance prematurely. The father decides to give his son what he wants, and the son takes his inheritance, goes, and squanders it in loose living. After having "come to himself", the son returns. As the loving father sees him coming in the distance, he runs out to meet him, embraces him, welcomes him, and overwhelms him with kindness. Love is kind!

In the parable of the Good Samaritan, a man in desperate need cannot even ask for help. Two people who should have the love of God in their hearts pass by without helping, but a Samaritan gives him the compassion and grace that Paul refers to when he says that love is kind.

God's kindness for us communicates His grace and His compassion. Repeatedly the Hebrew people messed up their lives, turning away from God. They were in spiritual darkness. God granted them compassion and grace, and He restored and redeemed them. In the New Testament, humanity was still in bad shape. God's people had turned from God, becoming legalistic. God sent Jesus out of His compassion and grace—divine kindness. We are called to reflect that kindness back towards God by being kind to others.

Kindness must come from us, yet often when we pray there is no kindness in our prayers. We say to God, "Why did You do this to me? How dare You! How could You hurt me so?" We say to God, "I want, I want, I want NOW!" There is no kindness in our prayers. Prayer is to be the loving person's response to the Creator, responding with adoration, contrition, confession, thanksgiving, intercession, humble supplication, and submission. That is our kindness that we are to send back to our God.

Kindness caresses the heart. The love of God that we share with our neighbors is a reflection of God's kindness. We are to share kindness with everyone we meet. This is the compassion and grace God shares with us. When we meet someone, we are to pass this on, saying that we understand his or her suffering, and by remembering that everyone suffers. We are not the only ones in the world that have problems! We let our neighbors know that we suffer with them. This is our kindness. We let the grace of God flow, supplying out of our own resources, because these resources are ours by the grace of God.

Paul says love is kind. Such love means compassion and grace, reflected back to our God. In doing so, we find fulfillment and the abundant life that is promised by our Lord Jesus.

Faith Fuel

Zealous But Not Jealous

"Love is not jealous," says the Apostle Paul in his first letter to the people of Corinth. It seems to be a simple statement to make. Since God is love, a logical conclusion from the statement "love is not jealous" would be that God is not jealous. We read in the Old Testament however, that the Lord God is a jealous God. It is assumed that jealousy is a natural reaction for a loving person, yet the Apostle Paul says, "Love is not jealous."

When we look at the original Greek of the New Testament, we find that the word used for jealous is the same word used for zeal. Jealousy and zeal both come from the same root meaning, "to boil over." Many of us have seen someone who was so jealous they were boiling over with it. Others have known people who were so zealous they were boiling over with enthusiasm! The difference is in focus. The difference is between being *zealous for* someone and being *jealous of* someone. The Bible makes a distinction between being zealous and being jealous.

Love knows no envy. Still, some think it natural for people to be envious at times. It is seen as part of the human condition to be envious. There is an old joke that says, "There are only two kinds of people in the world–those who are rich, and those who wish they were!" The tenth commandment says, "You shall not covet." Coveting translates as envy.

God is a zealous God, but He is not an envious God. How could God be envious? He gives us everything we have, so there cannot be any envy. Envy is almost the antithesis of love. Where there is envy, love is shoved aside, and awful things can happen. Love knows no envy. God is not envious of us, but He is zealous for us. Zealous, in that He wants the very best for us. God wants our undivided attention. Jesus said, "I came that you might have life and have it abundantly." That is God's zeal in our behalf.

All of us may have dreams of being king of the world or President of the United States. We are sometimes envious of God's power. We have this desire to be in control. In essence, we say, "Lord, I do not want you to be in control. I want to be in control. I want to be autonomous. I want to pull my own strings." This is not the kind of love we are called to share. It is envy. It is the very antithesis of love. God does give us the freedom to make our own decisions. That is the beauty of it! When we put God in control, we have more control over what happens in our lives than when we think we have control. It is a

49

paradox.

We are called to love our neighbors as ourselves. We are to do it unto the least of our neighbors. We are supposed to be channels for God's love, letting out the love that God places in us. When we do that, there is no room for envy. Instead of being envious of our neighbor, we are zealous for them. Zeal has the same root as jealousy, but it is on the other side of the coin. We are zealous on their behalf, so we want what is best for them. No matter what they have, we want them to have it. We want them to have joy. We want them to have abundance, even if we do not have it ourselves. It is "zealousy" rather than jealousy. That is the heart of loving others–having zeal on their behalf instead of ours. That is loving them the way God loves us! Love is not jealous!

Loving Is Not About Us

"Love is not boastful," says the Apostle Paul. It would seem better to turn it around by saying, "Love is humble." Humility is an umbrella word covering several areas, but Paul is very specific. The Greek word translated as 'boastful' is only used that one time in the entire New Testament. Paul is using a special word for this particular quality of love. It is crucial to understand what has become known as "Christian love" or agapé love. We are saying three things about it.

First, we are saying there should be no selfish ambition when we love–we should not love for our own benefit to climb up on our own ladder. We are not to love in order to gain something. There are people who say, "I love you" to get something. Politicians do it, lonely people do it, and people who hunger for something will do it. Sometimes the words are expressed in order to feel good inside. Sometimes we express the words of love so that others will express those words back at us. This is not love–it is boasting. Imagine someone saying, "Hey, I love you, isn't that terrific? Aren't you glad I love you? Do not you feel good knowing that I am giving you some warm fuzzies by saying I love you! Does not my loving you make you feel like you've got to do something for me in return?"

Second, when we truly love, we do not love with a desire for our personal prestige. We think very little of those who like going into a hospital with the idea that if they do enough volunteer work, the nurses will notice them as a good person, and the doctors might even notice them as somebody who cares. It is a counterfeit of love, for the purpose of selfish ambition and for status. A variation is loving someone because we feel that particular person needs our particular love. It means loving someone because we think God will look favorably upon us if we do. We are taught to love our neighbors as ourselves, and to love as fully and completely as possible. We are supposed to love for loving's sake, not so that we can move up the ladder to heaven.

Finally, love does not boast because it does not focus on ourselves, saying, "I have got this capacity to love, I am supposed to love. I have all this love to share. Aren't I terrific for loving these people?" This is not love! We are to focus on the one we love, realizing that the person needs love, and doing whatever is necessary to demonstrate, for their sake, that God's love is available and ready. We are then showering them with godly love.

Sometimes, all someone needs to do is talk with somebody who will listen. True humility does not mean thinking less of ourselves, but rather thinking of ourselves less. Each of us has a tremendous resource available–a capacity to love that is greater than anyone's capacity outside the church. Love does not boast, but love does love for love's sake. God does not love us out of selfish ambition or desire for personal prestige. God has what He needs. God does not concentrate on God, but rather concentrates His love on His children. If we are to reflect back the love that God has for us, then we have to have a love that has no selfish ambition or desire for prestige. It is a love that concentrates on God instead of on ourselves. When we love others, we are called to love them without concentrating on ourselves. We then truly love because of God's love for us! Love does not need to boast.

There Is No Pride in Love

When the Apostle Paul says, "Love is not arrogant," he covers a lot of territory. The Bible tells us that pride is the source of most of our mistakes and our bad living. All arrogance comes from pride. Paul himself talks about a pride that fills him, but it is not unwarranted pride, so it is not arrogance. Paul takes pride in what Jesus is accomplishing through him. His pride gives credit where credit is due. Paul is also proud on behalf of others. So long as our pride is focused in the right direction, placed in its proper perspective, pride is legitimate. When pride turns in upon itself, and we become preoccupied with who we are and what we do, the result is arrogance that the Bible condemns.

William Barclay tells a story of a man who lived in Europe and started as a cobbler, mending shoes for a living. Then he received

God's call to become a missionary. He went to India, and he had talents he never knew he had. The man's name was Carrie. Before his career was even half over, he had translated the New Testament into twelve dialects in India. One night he was at a dinner with some wealthy people. There was a snob there, and he looked at Mr. Carrie and said, "I understand that you started off life as a shoemaker." Mr. Carrie's response was, "No sir, not even a shoemaker. Only a cobbler." He did not make shoes, he merely repaired them! Here was a man who saw himself for who he was, but had the confidence to accomplish great things for his God.

A Christian's identity might center on who he is and what he has accomplished. A Christian can also consider what he could accomplish, but never has. As we answer these questions, praise God! Praise God for who we are and what we have, no matter what! That is the essence of "love is not arrogant." Love is not inflated with its own importance. Love is not preoccupied with who he or she is. Let us humble ourselves, and say, "Lord, I am sorry, and I am going to try to be better." There is an old nineteenth century slave's prayer that says, "Oh Lord, I ain't what I want to be; oh, Lord, I ain't what I could be; but praise God I ain't what I used to be!" The Lord keeps redeeming us so long as we keep ourselves in perspective. That redemption process keeps on happening repeatedly. That is when real love and growth happens.

When we are not growing, we are stagnant. Stagnation is what happens when we do not grow. It is part of disintegration. Stagnation is ugly and it stinks. That is an excellent reason to keep on growing. All growth comes from God. To keep on growing, we have to keep ourselves in perspective and make our focus on others so that as we grow we can reach farther and farther. Love is not arrogant Love that is seemingly arrogant is stagnant, but love that is not arrogant grows—grows with a zest. Therefore, the Apostle Paul is truly on target when he says that the loving person is not arrogant.

Grace Filled Love

"Love is not rude." It is a shame that the Apostle Paul had to say it negatively. William Barclay's translation of I Corinthians 13:5a says, "Love does not behave gracelessly." When we love, we are graceful. That has a sweet sound to it. If we really are not to be rude, our love must make a conscious effort to be gracious.

Our world is often short on compassion. Americans treat our

world rudely. We have roughly six percent of the world's resources and population. We are using thirty percent of the world's resources, and we are also putting out over thirty percent of the world's output. We have all of this money going out, and all of this stuff coming in, and we are hurting ourselves in the process. The Lord gave us all of these talents to do all of these good things, while He gave others the resources that we want most! God is not saying to us, "All right, you've got to produce, but I will not give you the resources!" No!

If we are going to use our abilities, our talents, and our gifts, we cannot be rude about the use of our gifts. God has given us sufficient resources for us to keep on going, so long as we make compassionate use of our gifts. We know that:

- if the population of the world continues to grow at its present rate,
- if medicine continues to improve the quality of life at its present rate,
- if we continue to use our resources without more recycling,
- if we continue to be bad stewards of our gifts at our present rate,
- and if we continue to be rude with one another by treating each other as objects instead of as persons,

there will be more widespread starvation and suffering.

It is not a question of God giving us sufficient resources to feed the people of the world. God has given us all that we need. Our stewardship of those resources makes the difference. It is not merely a matter of the United States sharing its wealth. It is the way we treat others in the international community.

This is truly the "me generation." We are becoming more and more egocentric: preoccupied with what we as individuals want and need. If the world is going to survive without more widespread suffering, we need to make a compassionate transition from the rude "Me Generation" to the compassionate "We Generation." The problem is widespread, even within the church. A basic disease in politically active Christian groups is in their attitude toward their fellow human beings. They are busy pointing their fingers, saying others have a problem, instead of humbly admitting that we are all in this ship together. We have a problem! Whenever someone points their finger and says, "They have a problem, but I do not," that is precisely the arrogance, the lack of love, and the rudeness of which the Apostle Paul speaks in I Corinthians 13.

Faith Fuel

We are our brothers keeper. "Their" problem is our problem too. That is what compassion is about. We are to be compassionate towards our fellow human beings. When we look at southeast Asia, east Africa, or anywhere else where there is rampant hunger, disease, and other problems, we cannot say, "Those people have a problem." It is our problem too! It is a problem for all humanity. If our love is not going to be rude, then we are to be compassionate.

Love Is Easy Going

Love is not pushy! Several years ago, I spent some time in the mountains with some youth. As we were sitting around the fire, I gave the youth the opportunity to help me write about this particular quality of love. We read the first part of I Corinthians 13 up to the place where Paul says, "Love does not insist on its own way." Their responses were interesting, as we sat there around the fire 3500 feet up in the mountains.

They started by saying that God does not insist on the way God wants. God gives us free will, God guides us, and God reveals to us what is best for us. God constantly redeems us, and God keeps giving us opportunities to head in the right direction. God does everything in His power to light the way, so that we can know what direction we should be going in, what we should do, and what we should say. God does not, however, manipulate us like puppets and insist that we do exactly as God says. We have our free will to choose whether to do things God's way or our way. God loves us enough that there is no insistence, no absolute power saying we must do something a certain way. God loves us enough to release us to make our own choices and to live with them.

As the discussion continued, we talked about how when our Creator sent us Jesus Christ, there could have been power overwhelming the whole world, so that the world would have no choice but to accept the Son of God. God has that power, but love does not insist on its own way. God offered us His Son and sent His Son into the world, hoping against hope that we would accept Him, love Him, and follow Him. Still, God let us have our free will. There was no love in that crowd that cried, "Crucify Him! Crucify Him!" They were insisting on their own way. They wanted what they wanted from God.

Love is not pushy! The context in which something happens determines a loving response. A parent might say to a child, "You must not do that under any circumstances—you cannot, I will not allow you!" If

54

a parent says that to a child who is very young, that is not pushiness, but simply good training! It is the teaching process. In that context, the most loving thing we can do is to show them what is really needed so that they can learn. We are more responsible for their actions than they are. That is parental love. If a parent says the same thing to someone who has graduated from high school, that is being pushy! When a child grows up, one cannot insist on one's own way.

During the Exodus, the most crucial event in Jewish history, Moses goes to Pharaoh and says, "Let my people go!" He is speaking for God. God could have stepped into history, released His chosen people, taken them out of bondage, set them on the road to the Promised Land, and killed Pharaoh. Instead, God showed His power. God was insistent, and God was persistent. Each time, Pharaoh had the option of letting the people go or not letting the people go. Pharaoh had a choice. God out of love did not insist on His own way. Instead, God taught, led, and inspired until finally, Pharaoh saw that he must let the people go.

When we see someone doing something incredibly wrong, we could step in, take that person by the shoulder and say, "I am going to restrain you. I am going to prevent you from ever doing that again. I am not going to let you make that choice ever again! You're going to do what God says or else." I hope that none of us has that kind of audacity. That would not be the loving way. Instead, we speak aloud and clear! We do everything in our power to guide, to educate, and to help them. We keep on witnessing of God's will and God's love. There are fanatics who believe that they know what God wants, determined to force the world into being the world that they want. That is not God's way. Love is not pushy. Love inspires, love persists, love teaches, and love does all kinds of things short of being pushy.

It is a hard lesson for us to learn. "Love is not pushy."

Love Is Serene

Love never flies into a temper! On the surface, that would seem a logical thing to say. Some Christians wonder what Paul really was talking about in I Corinthians 13, when he said, "love is not irritable." Ecclesiastes 7:9 (NRSV) says, "Do not be quick to anger, for anger lodges in the bosom of fools." We could conclude from that passage that all anger is foolish, but most of us know better. Proverbs 19:11 (NRSV) says, "Those with good sense are slow to anger, and it is their glory to overlook an offense." Then Proverbs 16:32 (NRSV) says, "One who is slow to anger is better than the mighty, and one whose temper is controlled than one who captures a city."

In a synagogue, Jesus asks the leaders of the synagogue if it is right to do good or to do evil on the Sabbath. Then He asks a more direct question: would healing a man mean doing good, or doing evil? He healed the man with the withered hand. The righteous anger of the synagogue leaders angered Jesus! It is a beautiful picture of the magnificent anger of Jesus toward the leaders of the synagogue. This stands in stark contrast to the messages in Proverbs and Ecclesiastes. In the Temple courtyards, Jesus found that the people who had the least to spend, and were hurting the most, were being cheated by the moneychangers and merchants. Jesus took a whip in furious anger and drove the moneychangers out of the Temple. It is magnificent and appropriate anger!

There is an approach of psychological counseling called Rational Emotive Therapy. It says our behavior is determined by our beliefs. For example, many think that for every action, people have an equal and opposite reaction. That is not true! If someone slaps us on the face, and we believe there is a good reason, we will not be angry. On the other hand, if we believe that they are wrong in slapping us, we get angry. The belief about the slap in the face determines the reaction. When we have anger on behalf of ourselves, it is usually based on selfish reasons.

Another kind of anger is on behalf of God. Most people do not experience it very often. When we witness an injustice, our resulting anger is based upon God's design for the world, so our anger is on behalf of God. There can also be anger on behalf of others. When we see other people hurting, we can be angry on their behalf, because there is something wrong in their lives.

There are three basic types of anger—on behalf of ourselves, on behalf of God, and on behalf of others. Where the Bible talks about anger on our own behalf, it is described as foolish. Where there is anger on behalf of God, we are reminded, "Vengeance is mine says the Lord. I will repay." God objects to our taking God's role of taking vengeance. The type of anger that is acceptable or praiseworthy is on behalf of others, and it makes the world a better place in which to live. In those two instances of Jesus' anger, His anger was on behalf of others.

It is a matter of selfish anger or selfless anger. The wise person, as Proverbs puts it, is the person whose anger is selfless. The unloving person, the person who aims that anger at himself or on behalf of himself, is the foolish person. Love knows how to put anger in its place. Love knows how to deal with passion. Love knows how to

56

Faith Fuel

deal with the natural peevishness that sometimes boils up within us. Love knows how to focus anger, so we do not have this petulance and vexation that we sometimes experience. Love can turn anger from something that destroys into something that redeems. Love never flies into a temper. Love is not irritable.

Love Is Not Touchy

Love is not resentful, says Paul in the Revised Standard Version. There are some other translations. It translates literally, "Love does not reckon the evil." The Phillips Translation says, "Love is not touchy." The Cottonpatch Version says, "Love keeps no books on insults and injuries." We have some clues as to what the Apostle Paul is saying to us in the 21st century. The first clue is in the twelfth chapter of Romans beginning with the seventeenth verse, where Paul says, "Repay no one evil for evil, but take thought for what is noble in the sight of all." Jesus teaches us not only to forgive, but also to forget. As Lloyd Ogilvie has pointed out, our cross to bear is not what other people do to us, but it is to bear the memories. That cross is our inability to forget. In his delightful little devotional book called *$3.00 Worth of God*, Wilbur Rees says we should thank God for erasing the records of our past behavior. He says, "That is what hell is, is not it? Having the tape played back?"

Resentment is not in our best interests, and it does not do the other person any good either. It completely ruins an otherwise beautiful relationship. Resentment is like a mold. It has a way of spoiling, stagnating, or souring the best of relationships. When I first began my previous career in music, I became very fond of one of my professors. One day he did something I did not expect that hurt me very deeply. It made me so angry that when I walked in the back door of my home afterwards, I was literally shaking all over. I bottled it up. It literally ate me alive, and it was the main reason I got acute gastritis. I prayed to God to help me forgive. That was only part of it. I did forgive that person. In prayer, I went through a lot of my past, and I consciously decided to forgive every single person who ever tried to hurt me.

If we are to be forgiving persons, we cannot be resentful. As the Cottonpatch Version puts it, we cannot keep books on our insults and injuries. In Tahiti, if you go into a grass hut that has been there for a long time, and you look up towards the ceiling, you will see odd little things hanging from the ceiling. They are reminders. Every time a Tahitian is hurt very badly, he makes for himself a little reminder and

57

hangs it up in his house so that he can never forget what that person did to him. That is the very opposite of what Jesus teaches.

One of Jesus' disciples went up to Him and asked how many times he should forgive a person who had wronged him. In rabbinical law, it was said the good Jew forgave a person three times, and after that, it was not necessary. This disciple asked if he should perhaps forgive him seven times, saying, "I'll do more than the law requires–I'll do more than the scripture demands of me." Jesus responds, "You must forgive him even seventy times seven," or have unlimited forgiveness for your neighbor.

Forgiving is only the beginning. Sometimes the forgetting occurs naturally with time. A child might do something terrible, get a spanking, and then be sent to his or her room, deprived of dinner. Years later, the child may still remember the event. Blessings upon blessings, the parent has forgotten the whole thing. That is what forgiving love is all about. It is not just about forgiving, it is forgetting. Love does not keep a record of wrongs. Love is not touchy. Love is not resentful.

The Blessing of Truth

The NRSV translation of I Corinthians 13:6 would seem to make no sense: "(Love) does not rejoice in evildoing, but rather rejoices in the truth." The Greek word for truth, *alêtheia,* is variously translated as *certainly, most, rightly, truly,* or *truth.* Some people wonder, however, that it is a basis for joy. One predominant Biblical theme says we should rejoice whenever God overcomes evil.

Many are reluctant to talk about evil, and pretend that evil does not exist. Evangelicals tend to be more conscious of it, but there is a danger. Some see everyone caught in a tug-of-war, with the devil pulling us one way, and God pulling us the other direction. From that viewpoint, if we do something right, give God the credit, and if we do something wrong, give the Devil credit. Then we do not have to take any real responsibility for what we do. I prefer to believe that God created us to make choices for ourselves. We are not puppets on strings.

What do we do when we do not know what to do next? "Therefore take up the whole armor of God, so that you may be able to withstand on that evil day, and having done everything, to stand firm," says Ephesians 6:13 (NRSV). Having done everything, and not knowing what to do next, we stand fast in our faith in God. There is evil

58

in our world, and we have to admit that. If things can go wrong, they will–evil will see to it. We may not be thinking of evil when we talk about Murphy's Law, but evil is what we are talking about.

The Bible says we should rejoice anytime evil is overcome. That is why "Love does not rejoice in evil doing." Love takes no joy in seeing evil happen. That is material only appropriate for horror movies! Love rejoices in the right. Love rejoices in the truth. Love rejoices when evil is overcome.

"Love rejoices in right," but what does the Bible mean by "right?" The essence of righteousness is to love as fully as God would have us love. We try to be the fully loving person that Jesus is. When we are the channels for divine unlimited love, then everything that we do through that love is righteous. It confirms and strengthens the relationship with our God and with others.

I have discussed various descriptions of love. Love is patient, kind, not jealous, not boastful, not arrogant, not rude, and not insisting on its own way. All of those qualities of love aim at this conclusion: "Love does not rejoice at wrong but rejoices in the right." The right or the righteous confirm a loving covenantal relationship with our God and with our fellow human beings. It means rejoicing when evil is overcome. It means rejoicing when love is substituted for evil. It means rejoicing because evil is put in its place. Psalms 97:10-11 (NRSV) says, "The LORD loves those who hate evil; he guards the lives of his faithful; he rescues them from the hand of the wicked. Light dawns for the righteous, and joy for the upright in heart." The psalmist speaks of rejoicing, gladness, and pure unadulterated joy. There is joy because the Lord is with us, and because the Lord supplies us with the love that we need. Evil is overcome. We put on the whole armor of God and stand fast. That is the loving response. That is the way to do the loving that God calls us to do. Love rejoices not at wrong, but rejoices in the right.

Love Overlooks the Pain

"Love bears all things," says Paul in I Corinthians 13:7. The literal Greek translation is, "Love covers all things." It seems this particular Greek word can be translated "to bear," "to endure," and "to cover." I Peter 4:8 says, "Love covers a multitude of sins." This does not mean that love must be blind to all faults. There is no indication anywhere in the New Testament to say that love itself is blind. Proverbs 10:12 says, "Hatred stirs up strife, but love covers all offenses." That does not mean love is blind to those faults. Instead, it means although we see them, we overlook them. As with the raising of a child, the child makes all kinds of mistakes as he or she grows up, but the parents love that child anyway. The parents overlook, but they are not blind, and they know the child makes mistakes. They know the child is naughty at times, and as far as teenagers are concerned, they know that love becomes almost unbearable at times because one has to overlook some of these faults.

When we go to visit at homes, some people notice everything. A television commercial years ago advertised for a spray wax. The mother-in-law came with white gloves and noticed everything–even the finest speck of dust that might show up somewhere. Most do not go that far. We cannot allow those things to affect our love for these people. If there is a violent argument going on in another room, we overhear it, and we wonder about the love that this family shares. We still are to love them. If something is dreadfully wrong that we do not expect, we do not allow that to affect our love for those people in that household.

Two men are walking down the street toward you. One is wearing a tuxedo and the other one is wearing torn jeans and a torn, dirty T-shirt. They are spaced apart from each other, not walking together. As you pass both of them, each asks you for your cell phone so they can make a phone call. To which one will you more likely give your phone to make a phone call? Unfortunately, our love is affected by what we see. Love is not so much a response of the heart as it is a decision of the mind. Divine love, *agapé* love, is a decision of the will. Either you decide or you do not to love someone you see. The Apostle Paul points out that we should love all of our neighbors the way Jesus taught us to do. When we read in I Peter, "Love covers a multitude of sins," it really does mean that love atones for others' sins.

Love not only covers sins of the other person, it covers our sins as well. Love atones for the manifold faults of the lover, the loving person. In Luke 7, towards the end of the chapter Jesus is invited into the home of a Pharisee, who takes him in, they sit down, and they begin discussing things. A crowd gathers. A woman described as a sinner kneels at His feet, and she lets her tears fall on His feet as she wipes His feet with her hair. She takes a vial of ointment and anoints His feet. The Pharisee is indignant and says to himself, "If this man really is a prophet, then he would know this woman is a sinner and he would not allow this to take place." Jesus knew otherwise.

The more we love, the more we are forgiven, not only by other people, but by our Lord and Savior. His Love does atone for us. That is the crux of the matter. "Greater love has no one than this, that one lay down his life for his friends." By Jesus doing this, the sins of the world were forgiven! The sins of the world were atoned for! Love is the qualification for divine forgiveness.

We must love. That is our obligation, and not merely a response of embracing. One embraces everyone equally, forgetting the sins. Love never gives up, and we never give up on the people we love. There is nothing love cannot face, because love knows no limit of its endurance. Love covers all things. Love bears all things.

Love Intertwined with Faith

"Love believes all things!" says I Corinthians 13:7b. That does not mean that we are to be naive. Rather, there is a linkage between faith and love. In the New Testament, we find faith and love intertwined. Few people have a faith strong enough that we can go to a mountain and say, "Be moved," and believe in our hearts that it will move simply because God will do what we ask. From God's perspective, all things are responsive to God's will. We know God created the heavens and the earth, and we can see the meaning of this statement "love believes all things" in that perspective. If God says to a mountain, "Be moved," it happens!

If we wholly love God, we believe everything that God has to say to us. There are three things intertwined here–faith, belief, and trust. If we honestly do not believe that a mountain is going to be moved when we say so, we do not believe God by His power will respond to what we want. Perhaps we are afraid of that power. Prayer is a scary thing if one really believes in the power of prayer. "Whatever you ask in prayer, believe that you receive it and you will...." That is more than most of us can handle.

In the Old Testament, we find men casting lots to determine the will of God. If we have our choice between praying for what we want and casting lots for it, most people would rather pray. When engaging in truly sincere prayer, we feel closer to God. Our loving relationship with God becomes more complete because we sense God responding and answering. Our belief becomes so strong that we do not allow doubt to interfere. When doubts arise, we must acknowledge them and resist them, because all things are possible through prayer. Love does believe all things. If we believe all things are possible through prayer, then that is when our love for God is more complete. The loving person truly believes the door is open. The loving person truly believes that when they ask they shall receive. The loving person truly believes that

Faith Fuel

when they seek, they will find. Then, when they knock, the door is opened.

Jesus says in Mark 11:24, "So I tell you, whatever you ask for in prayer, believe that you have received it, and it will be yours." (NRSV) Jesus does not make it something that happens a long time in the future. He tells us, "Whatever you ask in prayer, believe that you receive it and you will." We can have trust and confidence in the Lord because love believes all things.

I heard a clergyman argue that this is the most impossible verse in the New Testament because we all doubt at least a little. Doubts can be dealt with so they become unnecessary and inconsequential.

If you believe your prayer is being answered ...
If you believe that your God loves you and you love God ...
If you believe out of that loving relationship anything is possible –

... that is believing all things, and there is no point in doubting.

I began to grasp this concept years ago when I prayed a prayer that I honestly believed would happen. It was one of those impossible dreams, but I believed it would happen. Then I began to feel uncomfortable with my prayer. I simply prayed, "Lord take this little seed of faith and nurture it and help it grow." I had this little bit of absolute faith. I said, "Help me hang onto this little seed of faith, Lord!"

That is the challenge. Grasp just a little bit of absolute faith in some little spot in your life. Ask God to nurture that seed of faith. As that seed grows, you will all discover that through God's love, love believes all things.

Hope Filled Love

We may struggle with the Apostle Paul's statement, "Love hopes all things" in I Corinthians 13. When Paul says to his people in Philippi, "How I long to see you," is it just simple desire? Hope actually means desire combined with expectation.

In the Old Testament, God is seen as the source and the object of hope. If ever a group of people were in utter despair, it was the Hebrew slaves in Egypt. Moses came to these people and lifted them out of that despair to hope. Suddenly, they had a God who was on their side who loved them. Sometimes the Bible speaks of God as a rock

62

Faith Fuel

that cannot be moved. Other times it looks at God as a refuge and a fortress. If we think of God as a refuge, the bosom of God is a fortress against which nothing else can stand. In our response, there must be trust. When the Hebrews were trapped against the Red Sea, they did not trust God at all. They actually wondered why they did not remain slaves in Egypt! When there is utter despair, the only possible antidote is trust. Gradually, the people of God developed an eagerness to take refuge in Him. Eventually they developed confident expectation; confidence that they can expect the very best from our God. Linked to it is waiting with patience and courage.

In the New Testament, hope involves a relationship with God in Jesus Christ. Our hope is actually focused not on Jesus, but *through* Jesus. Jesus is a window unto the Almighty. When you point through a window, speaking about a beautiful tree, you are pointing to the tree on the other side of the window, not at the window itself. When we point to Jesus and say, "There is God," we are looking through Jesus and seeing the perfect will of God manifested through Jesus. It is through Jesus that we have our hope.

Again, hope is expectation as well as desire. Hope is the watershed of the Christian faith. If we look at all the other major religions of this earth, the one distinguishing characteristic of the Christian faith is its hope. The human response for all of this hope is unshakeable confidence. There is also rejoicing. Whatever we sing, it should be sung with joy. Hope is being able to endure our day-to-day existence because our hope is in the Lord.

There is another aspect of having the Christian hope, and it is boldness. It is a thrill to listen to teens boldly talk about their faith, saying, "Jesus is my Lord!" and to freely admit it in front of their peers sitting beside them. We do not see that kind of boldness, excitement and rejoicing among adults often enough. Another response is the glorious freedom we have in Jesus. We are free to live out life, because we have the hope, the desire, and the expectation of eternal life. When we are baptized, it is our Calvary. Death is just a transition–nothing to be afraid of anymore for those who have hope. Faith is defined by the Christian hope and Christian love. Our hope is defined by our faith and by our love. Our love is made manifest in our faith and in the hope we express.

Hope without love is grim. Can you imagine hoping for something and not loving the prospect of what you hope for? Love without hope is fruitless. Love without a future is static, and it goes nowhere: It cannot grow. Hope and love are bound together. When we say that love hopes all things, we are expressing the very foundation of the Christian faith. We can say with assurance, confidence,

63

Faith Fuel

expectation, and desire, "I want to spend the rest of my life with Jesus Christ."

Love That Thrives

"Love endures all things" is a statement that can be easily misinterpreted. Does it imply stoic acceptance, which is unfeeling and uncaring? Near the top of the list of the "Seven Deadly Sins" of Pope Gregory the Great was *acedia*, which literally translated can mean, "I do not care." That is not what the Apostle Paul means when he says, "love endures all things." William Barclay translates it, "Love bears all things with triumphant fortitude."

In Biblical times, slavery was common. A slave was seen merely as an animate tool. In a Christian household, both the master and the slave might be Christians. Though both had a common relationship with God, they did not alter their roles. We live in a time where slavery is abhorred, and we often fail to understand the fullest meaning of this word translated "endure." The suffering of the slaves led to the betterment of the household. The suffering and endurance of that person meant greater things for someone else. The problem with the institution of slavery was that it was involuntary. Christ's teachings transcend cultures. Jesus said that the greatest of all is the servant (slave) of all.

We can see this in the example of Jesus. Jesus was without flaw, lived the perfect life, and endured all the way to the cross. The cross was transmuted from being an instrument of torture and death, into being an instrument of victory and eternal life. Death was transmuted from being an end in itself and a source of hopelessness, into a source of being a transition from this life to the next. The law itself was transmuted by the cross, and by Jesus' suffering and endurance. Because of Jesus' endurance of the cross, the law was transformed from an instrument of control to an instrument of love.

A profoundly influential thing in my life was enduring thirteen years of piano lessons. A major part of who I am is rooted in the discipline of those lessons. There are unpleasant things I endure, which I do purely for the sake of the ministry of Jesus Christ. That endurance comes out of my joy, and out of my love for the people with whom I am working. This can find its roots in those thirteen years of piano lessons once a week, coupled with six to seven days a week of practice.

64

Faith Fuel

We are called to love God without limit and without reservation, no matter what. At times when love is thwarted, when evil seems to be prevailing, we are still called to endure with the hope that such endurance will transmute us. All of this is summarized by this very important phrase of the Apostle Paul in I Corinthians 13: "Love endures all things."

Real Love Is Eternal

"Love never ends," says I Corinthians 13:8a (NRSV). To put it another way, "Love is eternal." Scientists talk about infinite things. Mathematicians use infinity as a device in doing a number of critical calculations. When scientists and mathematicians talk about infinity however, it is an incalculable distance or amount within our created universe. The human mind hardly comprehends the infinite in any useful way outside of science and mathematics. This is not a new challenge.

An eon is a stretch of time so long that no one can fathom it. Plato, a few years before the birth of Christ, coined a new word: *aionios*. What he literally meant was eternity. Eternity means having no beginning, no end, no change, and no decay. Whereas an eon means indefinite time that cannot be measured, eternity has nothing to do with time or anything measured. There is nothing created or destroyed in eternity. There is no past, present, or future. Eternity can only be applied to God.

The Greek word which we translate eternal literally means without time, growth, past, present, or future. There are two ways 'eternal" is used in the New Testament. First, it is used in terms of covenant. When God makes a covenant with us, it has a beginning but has no end: Time is literally meaningless as far as God's covenant is concerned, and that covenant cannot be destroyed.

The other way 'eternal' is applied is hope. Our hope is eternal. The idea of eternal life is crucial to Christian faith. It is fundamental to our understanding of who Jesus Christ is, who God is, and how God works. 'Eternal' is coupled with life forty-four times. Eternal life was central to the teachings of the early church. It is predominant the writings of John, Paul, and all the other writers of the New Testament. In the Psalms, "His steadfast love endures forever" is repeated many times. Steadfast is coupled with love dozens of times in the Bible. Love is constant. That brings us right back to the statement, "Love never ends." Love is steadfast. Love endures forever. We can celebrate the ultimate source of the love we receive from our mothers and fathers, for all love comes from God.

Once we acknowledge that idea, we begin to get a feel for how much our God loves us. Moreover, we get a feel for how important it is to let God's love flow through us, so that others might see God's love in us. Love is patient and kind. Love is not jealous or boastful, nor is it arrogant or rude. It does not insist on its own way. Love is not irritable or resentful. Love does not rejoice at wrong, but love does rejoice in the right. Love does bear all things. Love does believe all things. Love does hope all things. Love does transform all things with triumphant fortitude. Love never ends. Indeed!

The Essence of God

Christians live out a journey into a widely misunderstood subject–love. We make the assertion that God is love. There are several words which translate "love" from the Greek. *Phileo* is translated as 'love' over thirty times in the New Testament. *Agapao* is a verb used about the same number of times. Used most often is the noun *agapé* used more than 130 times. Before the Christian era, *agapé* was part of the Greek language but seldom used. Christians noticed this word and began to use it during the first century. Since the time of the Christian era, *agapé* has become known as Christian love. It is understood to be the highest form of love. There are two other Greek words for love, but *storge* and *eros* are not used in the Bible.

There are three areas in which *agapé* functions. We see agapé in terms of God's love for humanity. I John makes the assertion that God is love. William Barclay says, "Just as we never see electricity but see its effects, we never see God, but we do see the effects of God." As I have said, Christ is like a living window. We are on one side of the window, and God is on the other side. The closer we get to a window, the more we see what is on the other side. The closer we get to Jesus Christ, the more we see of God. The light that shines through that window from God is love! Jesus was the ultimate loving person. The cross is the focus of God's love in human history. God was willing to sacrifice his own son so you and I can be redeemed.

God redeemed us on the cross by allowing His Son to die there. God's love is fulfilled by overcoming death through the resurrection on that first Easter. God's love for us is seen in the character of Jesus, and that character is brought to focus on the cross.

Faith Fuel

When God creates, God creates in love. When God redeems, God redeems in love. When God judges, God judges in love.

Agapé is prominent and manifest in our response to God. All genuine love comes from God. Our love for God is simply a reflection of God's love for us. Christian love is expressed in endurance that triumphs. It is also reflected in obedience, a willingness to do God's will. We are willing not simply because it is law, but because we love God. We then express love for God through following faithfully in the footsteps of Jesus. Perhaps most of all, our love for God is expressed in faith and absolute trust in God. Faith shows love for God when that faith is genuine.

The other area in which agapé functions is in our love for others. Jesus' summary of the law of the Bible was to love God with all our heart, mind and spirit, and to love our neighbors as ourselves. Agapé-love expressed for our neighbor is not love generated within ourselves. Christians can think of themselves as "love valves." In order for God's love to flow from us to others, we open ourselves to let the love flow from within, because God dwells within us. When we love our neighbor, it is a matter of letting that love flow out of us. The loving person is then complete, whole, and a fulfilled person.

Unlimited Love

When reading the sixth chapter of John we often focus on the 35th verse, where He says, "I am the bread of life." In that section of John's gospel, there is a verse we often pass over too quickly. Freely translated, verse 38 says, "I have come not to do my own will but the will of him who sent me." What kind of person can say that it is not their own will that they want to do, but someone else's?

It might be someone who simply will not take responsibility for their own actions and would rather do what somebody else tells them to do. They can always blame somebody else if something goes wrong. The other possibility is that this is someone who truly is a great lover. This kind of love is overwhelming!

Love is more a decision of the will than it is a response of the heart. You can love a person the moment you meet them. You do not know them, you do not know what their strengths and weaknesses are, and you do not know what he or she is up to. You love someone with no strings attached, taking a chance on being hurt! That is unconditional love.

Faith Fuel

This brings us to the subject of will. God's very nature is love. God's will is to love, and God's will for us is to love. God sent Jesus into the world that we might be redeemed. It was God's intentional will that Jesus live a normal life to a ripe old age. It was God's circumstantial will that Jesus be allowed to be crucified as man intended, but God's ultimate will cannot be thwarted. It was God's ultimate will that humanity be redeemed. God's ultimate will was made manifest in the resurrection of Jesus the Christ. God's ultimate will is revealed in the eternal life of Jesus and in the gift of eternal life to all of us who will accept him as Savior and Lord.

God's intentional will revealed God's love. He really did want Jesus to be a terrific gift to humanity, and the gift was given with no strings attached. God's intentional will reveals God's love. By following God's example and Jesus' example, our intentional will has to be to give of ourselves, to give of our very life to others without strings attached. God wants our intentional will to be to love others without reservation. We are to be selfless and focus ourselves on giving to others.

It was God's will under the circumstances to allow God's creatures to have their own way. Therefore, we cannot by any means try to force our will or the will of our God on anyone else. This is a classic mistake that too many Christians make. We must love people without strings attached. We cannot make our love conditional in terms of loving only those who agree with us, and who follow our moral precepts. That is not what the Bible teaches. We are to love everyone without strings attached.

If we look at God's ultimate will not being thwarted, then we see we are redeemed through the resurrection of His son. Our love for others, our conduct, and our way of doing the will of God cannot be conditioned by what others do, even if we do not like them. Our ultimate will must be the will of God. God's will cannot not be thwarted. We are called to love our God with all our heart, body, mind, and spirit, and to love our neighbors as ourselves. We have the power to do that. We have the resources for love unlimited. It is a matter of having the will to love with no strings attached.

Love Is More Than a Feeling

Recently I read an article by Scot McKnight in *Christianity Today* entitled "Spiritual Eroticism." Hundreds of years ago the phenomenon of "courtly love" developed, where people fell in love in a purely emotional and non-physical way. These people were often otherwise happily married, but were intoxicated with the feelings of fantasy and avoided the harshness of reality. These people only wanted the experience of loving and did not want the real presence of the one they loved. This "courtly love" eventually evolved into our ideals of romance and romantic love.

There are people in the church today who love singing of their love for Jesus, but some give very little thought to loving Jesus when they are not singing about it. In the same way, some people love the idea of learning about Jesus and love learning what He teaches. Some of these same people give little thought to what Jesus wants to teach them when they are not listening to a sermon or attending Bible study. Some people love the feelings associated with learning about Jesus more than they love Jesus Himself.

When I was in seminary, I provided the music for revivals on several occasions. The preacher, Gilbert Davis, was excellent. He gave the people the Bible-based fiery sermons that they wanted, and people ate it up. I discovered in those experiences that some people love the feelings associated with being confronted with their sins and surrendering their lives again. Some people would go to as many revivals as they could so as to experience those feelings of repentance and revival.

There are also countless people who say they believe in God but do not trust God. There are those who enjoy reading about Jesus, but they want Him to be historical—not as intimately close as their next breath. There are those who just "know" that if they are good people they do not need a community of faith to help keep them on track with their Savior. Yes, there are many people who talk the talk, but who do not walk the walk. There are also people who go to church for who and what they see. This has been true for 2000 years. Sadly, in this post-Christian era, there are increasing numbers of people who see church as an unreal and alien world.

No matter how great the feelings we may have when worshiping, it is crucially important that we not simply enjoy the feelings, but worship God in awe of His presence and power. Good feelings are not enough! Yes, we can enjoy getting those great feelings, and it is great to get a small measure of God's presence into our hearts. We must also focus, however, on what we joyfully give with our voices and out of the core of who we are, to the One who supplies everything.

Working in a gift shop in Yosemite Valley, I could often spot people who walk the walk with Jesus. They had joy in their voices and on their faces. If they had children with them, those children seldom whined or misbehaved, but rather shared their parents' joy. I sincerely hope that when I meet people in the marketplace, that they know I am a Christian, even if I am not wearing my cross necklace.

The Seduction of the End

For some people, a special loved one is their whole life. For others it may be a particular thing or a job. Within the Christian community, there are some for whom Jesus Christ's personal companionship is their whole life. For some it is the study of the Bible. For some it is the church as a whole, and for some, the whole world is wrapped up in a particular church on a particular corner.

Many people are concerned with the Book of Revelation and believe that the end is near. Jesus teaches that such "signs" make no difference. Jesus says that we are to be all that we are created to be and living "His" life regardless. The issues raised in Robert Frost's poem are of great interest to those who worry about "the end," and the end of what is important to us.

We cannot afford the "luxury" of worrying about the end of our own lives. Neither can we afford the luxury of worrying about the future of any organization, group, or structure. When a local church makes the preservation of its building its first priority, it is the beginning of the end of that congregation. Even when just a few within the fellowship have this distorted priority, they place the future of the church in grave danger. The tyranny of that few can rob the soul of the congregation of its life.

The future of any church rests upon the prayers of its people on behalf of others who need the church, and not on behalf of a church that needs others. According to the Book of Daniel, three men walked into a fiery furnace, and they were not consumed because they were focused upon God and not upon the furnace. Let us focus upon spreading the Good News of Jesus Christ.

Faith Fuel
MARCH

Getting Ready

Some churches light a succession of candles in preparation for Easter. With one congregation, as we lit the sixth of seven candles on our Lenten candelabra, we began our celebration of Christ's Passion. Traditionally called Palm Sunday, it was the day we remembered Christ's triumphal entry into Jerusalem. To those outside the Christian community, the phrase "Palm Sunday" had no meaning, and that is still true.

Each December we talk about keeping Christmas in perspective because of the commercialization of the season. At Easter, there is a tendency to have precisely the opposite problem. Most of the church recognizes the resurrection of Jesus Christ as the center of the Christian faith. The problem is a tendency to focus only on the comfortable good news and great joy of Easter. The challenge is to maintain that sense of joy while seeing the larger picture of the Atonement. Easter is the climax of the Atonement, and our joy is even greater when Easter is seen in the context of the entire passion of Jesus.

To offer a comparatively mundane parallel, consider any one of the great dramas of the greatest playwrights. The final act in one of those plays is what grabs the audience with its intensity. Yet, if that final act is seen without the first part of the play, as good as it is, that final act is far less impressive. Christ's Passion, the Atonement of Jesus Christ, is the greatest drama of human history. We need to witness the entire drama to give proper credit to The Playwright! This drama was put on for the benefit of all humankind! Palm Sunday is the first scene in the First Act of "The Atonement." There were no intermissions for Jesus–it was the ultimate marathon event. For us, there can be no "fast-forwarding" the video tape. It is inappropriate to put Jesus on "pause" while we go get more popcorn or a soft drink.

Sharing Our Faith

Although flexibility is essential to effective witnessing, by nature it makes training more difficult. There is no witnessing formula that works in every situation. Our witnessing must respond to the needs of the individual. A frequent problem with relating our faith in an effective

71

way is our language. Words like "grace," "sin," "redemption," "salvation," and "atonement" may have either no meaning or a different meaning to someone outside the Christian community. We need to use words that have the right meaning and definite impact on the person with whom we are conversing.

Another problem hindering effective witnessing is labeling. We have a tendency to label our own lifestyle as "Christian," "good," "creative," and "positive," while we label those who do not live our lifestyle as "bad," or "un-Christian." Although our imperative to witness does not mean that we have to adopt the lifestyles of others, we must be fully accepting and loving of all persons regardless of how they choose to live, so long as they are not being destructive physically, emotionally, or spiritually.

Good witnessing usually does not involve rigid doctrine beyond the basic beliefs in one all-powerful God and in Jesus as the Christ. The details can be absorbed gradually over time. While the Bible should be seen as legitimate authority for beliefs, we need to recognize diversity in interpretation, and we need to use our minds as well as our emotions when responding to the Bible out of faith.

Just as surely as we know the good news of the Christian faith, we also need to live and spread this news that is too good to keep to ourselves. Are you doing your part?

No Worries

Care can be defined in several interesting ways in the dictionary. We see the implications of what it means to care when we look at some of the synonyms of the word. Care means the mind is weighed down by responsibility. Care can also mean being agitated by apprehension. Being concerned implies being troubled in our mind because we are personally interested, because we are related, or simply because we love. An old word, solicitude, implies great concern and also means thoughtful or hovering attentiveness to someone who is in pain, who is ill, or who is otherwise distressed. The word *anxiety* means an anguished uncertainty or fear of failure or misfortune. Worry suggests fretting over matters that may or may not be real cause for anxiety. This is not merely an exercise over definitions!

Jesus' teachings tell us to love one another, but Jesus also says not to be anxious or worry because God will take care of us. This is not a contradiction! Jesus asks us to care for one another, taking responsibility for one another. Jesus asks us to have concern for one

Faith Fuel

another–taking a personal interest, affirming our relationships, and expressing our love. Jesus asks us to have solicitude for one another in that we are called to be attentive to one another.

Jesus does not want us to have anxiety. We are not to fear either failure or success. We are not to fear the consequences of the past or have anxiety over the future. Likewise, we are not to worry about things that are not in our control or worry about things for which we are not responsible.

We can practice the art of doing these things by taking our belief in the priesthood of all believers and really ministering to one another. Even the telephone is an instrument of ministry. Encouragement is a ministry. Prayer is a ministry. It is all a matter of caring.

As we look to the future, let us remember to always look beyond ourselves and onto the needs of others. This is not our church– it is Christ's church. He risked everything for our sakes. To be the church often means caring enough to risk it all for His sake. It may merely mean sacrificing the status quo. It may also mean risking the loss of everything for the sake of those in need.

Prayer with Patience

Lauren Buck Medieros coined a word I have found very useful: "*Praytience*." It reminds the user of the word that there is a close relationship that should be maintained between prayer and patience. Just as surely as prayer is rare among un-churched people, when an un-churched person does resort to prayer, it is usually during some kind of emergency. Such prayers are seldom patient. Active members of churches often do not approach prayer with any more patience than un-churched folks do! The Apostle Paul says that love is patient. It is incredible just how patient God is with us. As we nurture a healthy relationship with God, it seems logical to work at being just as patient with God as God is patient with us!

Coming at *praytience* another angle, it is a word that is both horizontal and vertical. When we find it difficult to deal with a person, prayer is often the ingredient that makes it possible to be patient. When we find situations difficult and frustrating, prayer is the key ingredient that gives us the patience to deal with those situations positively and creatively.

Those in leadership positions in the church often find church work frustrating and discouraging because one-fourth of the people usually carry three-fourths of the responsibilities. The result is burnout unless prayer is a primary ingredient in their work. Let us be patient when we pray, and let us pray when we need patience. Praytience! Praytience! Praytience!

Symbols Can Be Useful

I have a sterling silver cross which was given to me many years ago. I do not wear it all the time. One of my nieces, when she was much younger, asked me why I was wearing a necklace, and I found it difficult to explain to her why I did not think of it as a necklace. It seemed as though her mother was more embarrassed by the question than I was. I told my niece it was a symbol of my faith, and I also told her that it served in difficult times to remind me of who I am. She asked, "What's a symbol?"

A desk dictionary of mine gives one definition of symbol as ". . . something that stands for or suggests something else by reason of relationship, association, convention, or accidental resemblance; especially: a visible sign of something invisible . . . ."

The cross I wear stands for my faith, and suggests a relationship between it and Christ's death, burial, and resurrection. It is a visible sign of an invisible fact: those who accept Jesus as the Christ and as their risen Lord have the promise of salvation through a loving relationship of faith confirmed by actions.

The cross that I wear is a proclamation of my faith. Some may argue that I should wear a cross all the time, and perhaps they are right. Proclaiming my faith and proclaiming Christ is risen by simply wearing a cross is not enough. I must communicate that awareness to others in every legitimate way possible. Symbols are useful so long as they are used not just as decoration. It is possible for a person to become a living symbol of their faith. Why not?

Believing Jesus

A few years ago, I heard someone say at a luncheon, "Everyone wants to go to heaven, but nobody wants to die!" Everyone laughed. It was both funny and true! There are some similar statements that can be made that are equally true:

74

Faith Fuel

"Everyone wants to know what God's will is, but nobody wants to take the risk of doing it."

"Everyone wants to please God, but nobody has the courage to ask God what will be pleasing to Him."

"Everyone is willing to ask God questions, but nobody is willing to wait for the answers."

Looking toward Palm Sunday, Maundy Thursday, Good Friday, and Easter, we also consider seriously the mission of the church. Whom are we trying to reach? What are our goals? What do we want to communicate to our neighbors? What are their needs? It is significant when Christians risk part of their assets to reach the community with the Good News of Jesus Christ. It is significant when church leaders look beyond current congregational needs to look at the needs of the un-churched. It is significant when church leaders are willing to take risks for the cause of Jesus Christ. Will the congregation invest time and energy? Will it follow through, visiting those who visit? Will they go a second mile—or a third? Jesus said, "I came that you might have life and have it abundantly." Do we believe him?

Self-Idolatry

Violating the Sabbath is surprisingly easy and common. Over and over again the Bible reminds us that one day out of every seven we are to take a day completely off and rest. Why is it that we find this so hard? In a few occupations it is harder to accomplish, but the biggest factor in our violating the Sabbath is a subtle form of idolatry. We act as though the world cannot get along without us. It did for a long time! According to the creation story in Genesis, God rested after spending six days creating the heavens and the earth. If we do not need to take one day of rest each week, we are subtly saying that we have more stamina than God does!

Jesus clearly emphasized that it was acceptable to do good on behalf of others on the Sabbath. On the other hand, Jesus never said that the Sabbath was to be a day when we simply worked for ourselves instead of for our employer! One Sunday I did not have as much energy and enthusiasm as usual for worship. I had been busy all day Saturday, officiating for a wedding. I had tried to take a different day as my day of rest, but it was not the same.

It seems as though my prayer life is also more satisfying and effective when I get enough rest. It is tempting to use my Sabbath day

75

to do personal work that is not related to the church. If I take a full day of actual rest however, I get more church work done, and I get more of my personal work done as well. A day of actual rest may include reading, going to a movie, watching television, or a walk in a park. It does not include cleaning the apartment, mowing the lawn, doing laundry, or doing anything else that actually involves real labor.

Keeping the Sabbath holy enriches our relationship with God, and can contribute to greater intimacy with Our Savior. Try it!

Performers and Saints

In the 10th chapter of Mark, Peter is recorded as saying to Jesus, "We have left all, and have followed you." Peter seems to be saying this with some pride. It is very human to be confident in our faith. Wilbur Rees, one of my favorite contemporary writers, wrote this: "If I am doomed to be a saint, then I want to be a gold cup saint." One of the challenges of being a Christian is that we can become overconfident. Quoting scripture off the top of our heads does not make us Christians. Neither does going to church or church school. Being able to recite, "I am saved by the blood of the Lamb," does not mean you are saved. Claiming to be a loving Christian does not make us loving. There is a difference between being a saint and being a good performer. Everyone may desire to be a gold cup saint, but God simply asks us to be faithful.

The key is submission or willingness to surrender. It is a lot easier to tell God what we want, than to act on what God wants us to do. Jesus says, "Not everyone who says to me 'Lord, Lord,' shall enter the kingdom of heaven." That verse pricks our consciences and makes us think twice about where we are in our faith journey. Are we spending all our time dreaming the impossible dreams of the future? Are we spending all our time living in the rosy past? God wants us to be doing the faithful work of the present, being committed to the God of present action.

Days of Preparation

When Mardi Gras is over, Christ's church begins a forty day season called Lent. Traditionally, a person will give up something important to them for that forty day period as an act of discipline and devotion. By focusing on such a minor difficulty during these forty days,

Faith Fuel

our joy at Easter is enhanced. Many people give up an extra measure of their time or of their resources to the cause of Jesus Christ during this very special time.

When Easter rolls around, will you look back at the previous forty days as Lent or lint? Do we give as much thought to the celebration of Ash Wednesday - the day after Mardi Gras - as we do to the first shopping day of the Christmas season? Do we spend as much of ourselves preparing our homes and churches for Easter as we do when we decorate for Christmas? Do we work as hard spreading Easter joy as we do Christmas joy? The good news that Christ is alive and at work in our lives is at least as important as the news that Christ is born in Bethlehem!

There are people we love very much, who consider themselves quite religious or spiritual, who worship God only when it suits their mood and their schedule. They worship God on Christmas and Easter because they believe they should or because they believe they have to go. Their spiritual life consists of thanking God for the things which they believe God is responsible, and then they ask God for more. How inadequate that is! They are missing out on so much! Easter is a good time to begin another approach.

Lent is a reminder that worship of God involves far more than thanking and asking. Worship also includes expressing our fervent love for God, acknowledging our shortcomings, interceding for others, and surrendering all that we are and all that we have to God. For some, their love for God is greatest before they express it in worship. For others, it is after they experience God's presence and power!

There are two ways we can get complete rest and relaxation. Getting a full night of sleep without interruption is quite satisfying and the most common. On the other hand, spending a seemingly sleepless night praying for everyone we know provides surprisingly complete rest! Spending extra time in prayer is a great way to experience Lent.

A Manger and a Tomb

It is easy to celebrate birthdays. We all love a joyous celebration. When we celebrate Christmas, all of the celebrating seems very natural. Christians celebrating Christmas seldom stop to think just how close the empty tomb stands next to the manger. Christmas just would not be Christmas if it were not for Easter.

77

Faith Fuel

Lent is the time of preparation for Easter. A few Christians go to Wednesday services, but little else is done. We put so little effort into preparing for Easter when it is so important! The birth of Jesus was not–and is not–as important as His life, death, and resurrection.

HE WALKED IN BEAUTY

He walked in beauty in the days
Of healing sick and binding wounds;
And all his loving, healing ways
Were put to death and dark and gloom.
Then all the joys that loving pays
Came at the dawn — an empty tomb.

One day the more, one nail the less
Would not impair the gauge-less grace
Which came from God that day to bless:
For through that window we do face
Our God. So hear our voice confess
That Jesus Christ fills us with grace.

And on that hill, and in that tomb
So still, so stark, so eloquent:
The sounds of silent victory loom
That tell of God's great power spent
Dispelling death and darkness' gloom,
That tells of life that never ends!

Every Christian can worship every Sunday during Lent. Try giving up something important for Lent! Give up something you like, otherwise it is not a sacrifice. Whatever you do, do it for God's glory and your devotion to God's risen Son, Jesus.

Combating Bad Press

When I was at Long Beach City College in California, I came across a poem by Daniel Whitehead Hicky entitled "How Silently April Takes a Battlefield." It says in part, "How silently April takes a battlefield! There is no flare of trumpets, and no drum, to mark the sudden way that she will come. ..." Years later, this poem illustrated what I saw in the path of Hurricane Andrew. The storm came through Homestead, Florida in August of 1992. I arrived eight months later to

Faith Fuel

assist with continuing relief work. I heard many people speak of the area as looking like a battlefield. Andrew came with the heralding of the media's trumpets, coming suddenly with merciless ferocity. There were cries of anguish as Andrew blew and shook South Florida. Then April began taking the battlefield. We began to notice it with the relatively gentle rains that came with the new hurricane season. Like a softly and slowly opening flower in a battlefield, we began to see the signs of definite recovery. God was among us, victorious and redemptive in our midst.

I heard a Jewish woman say, "After Andrew, a lot of people stopped believing in God. Why would God do this to us?" So many of us are still in the habit of speaking of blessings as great luck, while speaking of disasters as acts of God. God got a lot of "bad press" in the aftermath of Andrew. Part of our job as the church is witnessing to our faith, declaring God's continuing creative and redemptive activity. Andrew was part of the evil of our world. Jesus said, "Be of good cheer–I have overcome the world!"

Faith Fuel
APRIL

Holy Week

As the end of Lent approaches, Shrove Tuesday (Mardi Gras) seems like ancient history. These Lenten days are full of rich and sacred traditions. Tradition at its worst can be a mechanical thing of little or no value. At its best, a tradition can add a spiritual boost to faith.

Palm Sunday takes its name from an old traditional processional that originated in Jerusalem as a celebration of Christ's triumphal entry. The whole Christian community in Jerusalem went out in the evening to the Mount of Olives where after a worship service people returned home in procession carrying leafy branches and singing "Blessed is He that comes in the name of the Lord." Sometime later, the ceremony was introduced to the West.

The day before Good Friday, Maundy Thursday, we recognize the evening Jesus had His last meal and instituted the Eucharist (or Lord's Supper). *"Maundy"* refers to the ceremony of foot washing that is depicted in the Gospel of John's account of that evening. Good Friday marks the anniversary of Jesus' death on the cross. It is the only day of the year where tradition says we should not celebrate the Lord's Supper. It is also a time when some churches drape their altars and crosses in black.

Easter Sunday is the chief festival of the Christian year, which was instituted for celebrating the resurrection of our Lord and Savior. It is more important than Christmas because if Jesus had not risen from the dead, we probably would not remember His birthday. The term Easter comes from an old English word, *Eostre*, who was an old Anglo-Saxon goddess, and as a result, the term has no theological significance for Christians.

Easter Monday is sometimes known as The Day of Holy Laughter. It is a day for having good clean fun and telling jokes because we are celebrating how God had the last laugh on the Devil when Christ rose from the grave. The church gave up celebrating the day centuries ago because it was so hard to get people to come to church the day after Easter. In recent years, churches have been celebrating the Sunday after Easter as "Holy Humor Sunday." The focus in these celebrations is the joy of Christ and His sense of humor. The Sunday after Easter sometimes has good attendance because of this day of joy.

Faith Fuel

What Now?

After Easter, some may well ask, "What now?" The chief event of the Christian year is over. Many Christians breathe a heavy sigh and think, "It is a long time until next Christmas!" Some will point out other special days between Easter and Christmas, such as Holy Humor Sunday, Pentecost, World Communion Sunday, or Thanksgiving Sunday. Some may even wish to stretch the point and mention semi-special days, such as Mother's Day, Father's Day, Achievement Day, Freedom Sunday, Labor Sunday, or Reformation Sunday. Those who want to emphasize outreach would also include Reconciliation Sunday. Even so, these dates do not make a complete list. Those who are so oriented to special days sometimes fail to see the beauty of Sunday-by-Sunday church life, and they miss the glory of each God-created day. Some churches give every Sunday a special Sunday name so that more will get this point!

God gives us all kinds of possibilities for our lives, even when we think our possibilities are limited or our choices poor. It is up to us to make the most of what God gives us. It is up to us to make the most of the life we have. It is up to us to make the most of the relationships God helps us to establish. It is up to us to make the most of the faith we have. It is up to us to make the most out of our whole church. It is up to us!

Seeing Miracles

Do you believe in miracles? Have you seen any miracles? How do you respond to those people who say that no miracles have happened since biblical times? The answers to these questions largely are dependent upon how you define the word miracle. If you say a miracle only happens when natural laws are set aside, that limits the discussion. Some people insist miracles are impossible because even God has to obey the laws of nature. Atheists and agnostics often argue against the idea of miracles because one needs a god to perform a miracle.

The most workable definition for Christian purposes is this: a miracle is any event, either natural or supernatural, in which God is revealed to one or more persons. God being revealed means that such an event causes a person to be aware of the active presence or power of God.

There are some interesting ramifications to this definition of a miracle. It means that those who believe in miracles must have some kind of faith. While people may define their idea of God or the transcendent in different ways, one must have the eyes of faith to see in order to see a miracle. Without the eyes of faith, most people will reduce everything to scientific evidence. Those without the eyes of faith see life as a cut and dried sequence of events that have no purpose or lasting significance.

On the other hand, life can be an adventure in faith, and a time of excitement and celebration. It can be a time of taking delight in all that God has provided and is providing. With this perspective, life itself is a miracle, and our relationship to God opens our eyes to miracles all around us. Christians' eyes are open to the greatest miracle of all: Christ's empty tomb! That is why worship is intended to be a celebration!

Transforming History

They decided to eat in the loft. Up there, through the windows, one could see the stars twinkling overhead. It would be good to gather with one's friends for a big meal up there. By candlelight, their shadows would dance upon the walls, and the light's soft glow would add distinctively to the warm and happy mood of their annual celebration.

It was to be a very special party, and everything had to be just right. Although they were used to the rather detailed logistics, a multi-course meal required planning and a lot of preparation. Who would prepare the fresh horseradish this year? Who would bake the eggs in their shells? Who would prepare the lamb according to the usual recipe? How much wine would be enough? Who would see to the social amenities as they arrived?

Many years have passed now since that particular meal was planned and eaten. Today, only a small minority of God's children still continue the annual celebration of Passover with all of its detail. We usually begin by remembering that same meal, but the details and the logistics are radically different. Ours is a two-course "meal," in which the two courses all too often blur into one. Instead of breaking bread, we taste small morsels of bread already broken for us. We do not wait for the fruit of the vine to become wine, but rather we drink the juice that has been pasteurized to protect us. To a pragmatist our ritual may

Faith Fuel

seem mechanical and sterile, but with the eyes of faith–and even with the heart, ears, taste buds, and smell of faith, we meet our Lord Christ face to face in the loaf and in the cup.

Parades Then and Now

People like parades. There is something about seeing a procession of any kind that makes people stop and look. If so, they sometimes applaud and shout encouragement. In the days before television, radio, full color magazines, newspapers, or bound books of any kind, entertainment priorities were much different. Public speaking and plays were the main forms of entertainment, and a parade was a major event–even more so than now.

I am thinking about a rather different kind of parade. There were no floats, no marching bands, no pompom girls, no politicians, and no show business personalities. There was just one equestrian entry, and the rider was not even riding a horse in order to look important. He was not standing tall in the saddle. He did no tricks with a lasso, and the animal on which He was riding did no fancy gaits or steps. Instead of a mighty steed, there was a colt, the foal of a jackass. The rider had no uniform or costume. The rider wore no finery of any kind. He wore a simple tunic, a seamless robe, and common sandals.

The crowd cheered Him on as if He were a fabulously wealthy media czar. They treated Him as a king, yet He wore no crown. An outside observer might have thought He was known throughout the world, but a hundred miles away the masses hardly knew His name. They shouted, "Blessed is He who comes in the name of the Lord!" Everyone who was coming into the city was coming because of the Lord! He sought no trouble, and the people loved Him. Those in power, however, saw Him as a troublemaker.

On Palm Sunday, we gather to remember this parade, and we consider anew the priorities of our modern world. If it were rumored that Jesus was going to ride a motor scooter into our community, how many would come to look? Once the parade was over, would someone plot to betray Him? If He were arrested, would His followers flee? How many would deny knowing Him? The police would probably see that a lynch mob did not prevail, but that is not the style in our century. The trial and appeals would go on for years. . . .

Faith Fuel

The Equalizer

One of the oldest games is King of the Mountain. Jesus' disciples were playing that game in a theological way on Maundy Thursday afternoon. Jesus brought the game to a rather interesting conclusion when he proceeded to wash their feet that evening. A more subtle version of that game is one-upmanship, the version that calls on us to have the competitive edge always. Why are we not willing to approach our neighbors as equals?

If we feel that we are inferior rather than the salt of the earth, we cannot approach others as equals. If we often feel out of place in the midst of groups, we can hardly take a stance of equality. If we feel overburdened with our own problems, our underdog status feeling will keep us from approaching our neighbors with equality. Pain is the most personal thing we experience in our lives. That hurt can put us in a "one-down" feeling. When we approach our neighbors with an attitude of suspicion, chances are we are approaching them from a "one-up" position.

Most of us hold up equality as an ideal, quoting the Declaration of Independence or the U.S. Constitution. Very few of us truly believe that we are the equals of all of our neighbors. God's children engage in war of all types, from global conflicts to family squabbles. If all of us believed we had grounds of equality with every other human being, God's peace would be a reality bringing order to our chaotic world. Jesus tries to teach us to love one another equally. Are we willing to believe that we are fully equal? Wasn't the empty tomb the greatest equalizer of all?

The Big Dinner

When I was growing up, my parents really enjoyed entertaining guests in our home. During the Christmas season, in particular, we would have at least two, sometimes three, large dinner parties. We considered it a large dinner party when ten or more people sat down at the dining room table.

What was the biggest dinner party you ever attended? Those chronicling Jesus' life might argue that for Him, it was the time he served 5000 men plus women and children along the Sea of Galilee. I

84

would argue that the biggest dinner party He ever attended had thirteen men, plus women, slaves, and children.

Actually, that was just one room full of people. There were thousands of rooms in Jerusalem, full of people celebrating the same dinner party - no one room could hold them all. If the records of the Roman Empire are accurate, there were millions of people at that dinner. The numbers are not really the issue however.

Those dinners in my parents' home were not huge dinners because there were many people around the table. Those dinners were gigantic because they celebrated the birth of Jesus Christ. That dinner in the upper room was not huge because others were celebrating throughout Jerusalem. The dinner was huge because it celebrated the deliverance of God's people from slavery in Egypt.

Currently there are millions of Jews in our world, most of whom celebrate the Passover every year. Jesus transformed that Passover meal into something more significant, however. He said, "This is my body . . . This is my blood." His followers have been joining Him in that celebration ever since. I like to do it every time I worship. Some do it less often. For decades, most of the churches around the world have coordinated their celebration of Eucharist or The Lord's Supper to happen on the first Sunday of October. When we worship around the Lord's Table, we are joining millions of Christians around the world in this holy act because He said, "Do this in remembrance of me."

Directed Prayer

A woman called out from the crowd, saying that Mary was truly blessed because she bore Jesus and nursed Him. Jesus, instead of affirming the blessing of His mother, said that the person who is truly blessed is the one who seeks the will of God and does it. Either we want to serve God in whatever capacity we are called, or we prefer to serve God in an advisory capacity instead, telling God what is going on when we feel like praying! God is the initiator of all prayer, and that prayer is to be a two-way communication. We cannot assume, however, that God is not speaking to us unless we actually hear a voice. We cannot believe God is giving us a vision of His holy will if we only see pictures!

When we pray, our minds often seem to wander. The more we try to concentrate on God, the more we find ourselves straying from the subject we are trying to discuss with Him. As we picture in our minds the people and situations for which we are praying, images of other people and other situations seem to intrude. That is good! In truly effective prayer, one goes with the flow, lifting up these intrusions to God along with everything else! By examining these intrusive images alongside of the ones we intended to examine, God is helping us clarify our vision of His holy will.

One June evening, I was praying while driving home. I was lifting up each member of my congregation one by one, picturing each one of them as I prayed. Before I was half-way through my mental list, I heard myself praying for someone I had never met. She was and still is world-famous. In discussing with God why this had happened, I began a new pattern of prayer that continues to this day. Ever since, I have been praying for people in the public eye. I have seen some of those prayers answered. A seeming distraction has led to a ministry of prayer.

It is sometimes a lengthy process to discover God's call upon our lives. We need to discuss things with God from every possible angle, even illogical and undesirable angles. Then we are ready to serve God in whatever capacity we are called.

Prayer Is Like a Steering Wheel
Prayer is like a steering wheel—it guides the roving mind.
Prayers can't be just sent-up flares to God for crises' sake.
To read of saints in scriptures feels like fuel so good to find.
We move through life and care to dare when evil's on the make.
So prayer and power grows our faith as evil's left behind.

Risen Indeed!

He is risen! When Christians hear that in a worship service, many traditionally respond, "He is risen indeed!" Easter celebrates the day that the disciples of Jesus Christ discovered that his tomb was—and still is—empty. The foundation of the Christian faith is built on Easter: on the death, burial, and resurrection of Jesus. Celebrating someone's birthday is a common occurrence because everyone who has ever lived has been born. If the foundation of the Christian faith were based upon Christmas, our faith simply would be built upon the greatest man who ever lived and his teachings. Other religions would argue that the greatest man who ever lived was Mohammed, Confucius, Buddha, Zarathustra, or someone else. Jesus is not who He is to us simply

Faith Fuel

because He was a great man. Even with all the trappings of angels, wise men, shepherds, and the family of Jesus, our faith is not built upon His being born–even of a virgin. That event was admittedly remarkable, but Jesus' birth alone did not change the course of history.

Everything before the first Easter was a prelude to the fulfillment of God's plan for humankind. All Christian interpretations of history and religion are seen through the "filter" of Easter. Jesus is the window through whom we are able to get our clearest view of God. Easter is the historical window through which we see Jesus most clearly. At Christmas, many of us make up wish lists of things we would like to have as gifts during the holiday season. Since Easter is far more important than Christmas, I suggest a wish list for the church as a part of our celebration of Easter.

My first wish is that the church will always be willing to take risks. Everyone in her community should be reached as often as possible with the Good News of Jesus Christ. As part of that wish, it is my hope that everyone within reach of the church will know that it is a place of good news, of healing, of solace, of forgiveness, and of love. As the church reaches people with the Good News of Jesus Christ, it is my second wish that as the church discovers needs, it will meet them. It is my hope that the church will always have both the power and the willingness to minister to the needs of its community in the name of Jesus.

Each one of us can make it our own special project of the year to help one person get to know the risen Christ! Not one of us is responsible for converting people. The Holy Spirit does that. Our job is simply to open people's eyes to opportunities. The most prevalent form of church growth today is friendship evangelism. If you make new friends and bring them to church, the next step is friendship with Jesus.

New Traditions

When I was growing up, it was no big challenge to get palm branches for Palm Sunday. Many people have palm trees in their yards in southern California. It was always a big deal for the children in Sunday school to carry palm branches down the center aisle ahead of the choir, as the choir proceeded down the aisle during the opening hymn. It was really a lot of fun. We looked forward to it each year. Following the Palm Sunday worship service at the church I served in Louisiana, the organist would gather up the palm branches and burn them that afternoon. He would then store the ashes. The following year on Ash Wednesday, we used those ashes as part of the service. An elder and I would dip a finger in the ashes mixed with a little water, and draw a cross on people's foreheads as they came forward at the conclusion of the service. It was an interesting tradition and meaningful to those who participated.

A lot changes as years go by. If a tradition has meaning, and if that tradition does not violate Biblical principles, Christians should be quite willing to participate. Conversely, if a tradition violates Biblical principles or it has lost its meaning and purpose, there is no reason to maintain it. We should not maintain a tradition simply because it is a tradition–it must have reasonable value. I enjoy starting new traditions.

On the Sunday after Easter, many Christians observe Holy Humor Sunday. Centuries ago, church leaders wanted people to come to church on the day after Easter to celebrate God's last laugh on the Devil–the resurrection of Jesus. A couple of decades ago, some churches in the mid-west of the United States discovered this old idea and decided to resurrect it. Since Monday is out of the question for most, the Sunday following Easter is the logical alternative. Palm Sunday through Easter is so very full of activities. It would be a shame for people to miss out by thinking that nothing special will happen right after Easter. Wrong! God wants us to have joyful and constant faith in Him!

Joy and Health

The Christian faith should always be joyful. Religion having no sense of humor tends to be sick. When talking to other Christians, we can describe our Christian selves with joy. In 1964, Elton Trueblood wrote, "We do not know with certainty how much humor there is in Christ's teaching, but we can be sure that there is far more than is normally recognized." I was privileged to meet Reverend Trueblood many years ago at a clergy luncheon. Although he was a Quaker all of his life, at that luncheon he said he liked to think of himself as a C-A-R-E Christian. He explained that C-A-R-E stood for Charismatic Apostolic Reformed Evangelical.

He went on to explain each of the letters in turn. Spiritually healthy Christians, he explained, should all be charismatic in the sense of being filled with the Holy Spirit to share the good news of Jesus Christ. In the same way, our faith should be apostolic in the sense of being authentic first-century faith. We all need reforming periodically because our faith has a tendency to get off track. Finally, the Christian faith should be evangelical in the sense of being consistent with the Bible's teachings.

Very few of us outside of Pentecostal churches tend to think of ourselves as charismatic. Unless we are avowed apostolics or fundamentalists, we are not prone to call ourselves apostolic. We seldom describe ourselves as reformed unless we are part of the Reformed movement. Elton Trueblood made his address to a mainline denominational audience that does not usually identify itself as evangelical. Trueblood made valid points about who Christians are as people of faith, and the humor of it all brought a number of chuckles as he cited examples.

Humor is a great teaching tool, and Jesus knew that. Jesus also knew that life itself has numerous twists and turns that provide opportunities for humor. Everyone who was listening could laugh when Jesus described the Pharisees as people who try not to swallow a gnat while swallowing a camel. The teachings of Christ are full of exaggerations, parodies, and satire. It is appropriate that we follow up on the joy of Easter with a celebration of God's last laugh on the Devil. Why should the joy cease simply because Easter is behind us?

Another Viewpoint

A small church group had been working and traveling together for many months. They had an excellent leader who loved them, and they loved him. He warned them on a number of occasions that their great times together would not last, but none of them wanted to think about the end of such a good thing. After many exciting months together, they had their farewell dinner. Their conversations were typical of an anniversary party, which it was.

Just before the end of the party, the leader got serious. "When I sent you out on extended errands without supplying you with a lot of resources, you did very well, did not you?" They acknowledged that everything had always gone smoothly, and they had all that they needed. "Wherever you go from now on," he said, "you'll need to have money as well as fully loaded luggage. In addition, you must be prepared to defend yourself, because there are battles ahead. My enemies may come after you." They responded that they would be prepared.

It seems very unlikely that any of us would ever find ourselves in that kind of situation. We live in a democratic republic where religion is supposedly a protected right under our constitution. Few if any of us

Faith Fuel

who worship on Sundays give any thought about having to stand up in a hostile environment to defend what we believe. We know that this happens in other countries, but we do not expect it to happen in the United States. It seems somewhat easy to say that we would die for what we believe when there is no real threat of having to do so. It is noble to think that we would die for Jesus if necessary. It seems impossible that our faith will ever be tested in that way however.

The inner circle of Jesus' followers, known as The Twelve, along with their families, probably never imagined they would face martyrdom. Those people were normal, down-to-earth folks who worked hard 5-6 days and then rested and worshipped. We have to doubt that they ever gave serious thought to dying for what they believe in or for their relationship with Jesus. That is precisely what many of them did. The first two paragraphs of this meditation are based upon Luke 22:35-38.

> [35] And He said to them, "When I sent you without money bag, knapsack, and sandals, did you lack anything?" So they said, "Nothing." [36] Then He said to them, "But now, he who has a money bag, let him take it, and likewise a knapsack; and he who has no sword, let him sell his garment and buy one. [37] For I say to you that this which is written must still be accomplished in Me: 'And He was numbered with the transgressors.' For the things concerning Me have an end." [38] So they said, "Lord, look, here are two swords." And He said to them, "It is enough." (NKJV)

Most of those to whom He was speaking died for their faith. It is food for thought.

90

Faith Fuel
MAY

Help with Bad News

Each of us has our own way of handling bad news. Some of us are stoic, covering our emotions completely so that no one can tell how deeply we are hurting or feeling the impact of the bad news. We may be completely silent, saying nothing. We also may express ourselves by detaching our emotions, speaking only about the facts of the situation.

When we cover our emotions or detach ourselves from them, we may be deceiving others, deceiving ourselves, or both. If we simply delay the expression of our feelings until later, it is a simple deception that is perhaps justified. In any case, we eventually have to deal with our feelings. If we do not make the effort to deal with our feelings, we will eventually be forced to do so anyway, with the results surfacing in terms of anger, depression, or physical illness.

The ancient Hebrews were usually wise in the ways that they handled their strong emotions. They often made a public display of their emotions, particularly with regard to grief and anger. King Hezekiah had heard a prophecy spoken against him. He reacted to the prophecy by tearing his clothing and covering himself with the most humble cloth, and then he went into the temple to worship. The wisdom of all of this was that he knew that right or wrong, he needed to humble himself before God.

This would seem to go against much of the popular psychology being published today. Those writers tell us to pull our own strings and take charge of our own destiny. To put it in more pragmatic terms, we are told to fight for our rights. Hezekiah's level of stress went way up when he heard the prophecy against him. If he had chosen to stand up to the prophet, it would have caused his body to put even more adrenalin into his system.

What did he do instead? He chose to let go and let God. He humbled himself before God and turned the situation over to the One in charge of life. He sent for a prophet who he knew he could trust in order to get an authentic word from God, but that was not the most important thing that he did. Far more important was the rending of his regal clothes into shreds and the seeking of sanctuary under the wings of The Almighty.

Unlike Hezekiah, we cannot go running to a prophet like Elijah or Elisha. What we can do is go running to our Savior, Jesus Christ. We know that Jesus will understand because he was as fully human as we are. We know that whether we are right or wrong, Jesus understands us. God loves a humble and penitent heart. God is most wondrous in His power to redeem us when we let go, letting God by God's grace extend His power and love to us.

Love for Our Neighbors

When asked by a lawyer about the greatest commandment Jesus responded that we should love God totally and completely. When Jesus went on to say that we should love our neighbors as we do ourselves, the Gospel of Luke tells us that the lawyer asked a follow-up question regarding what constitutes Jesus' definition of 'neighbor.'

According to Luke, that question led to the parable of the Good Samaritan. That question leads to a different kind of answer for the members and friends of growing churches. In congregations that are growing, members recognize the fact that everyone with whom they come in contact is a neighbor. Growing churches need not worry about proselyting. There is a far more important issue.

There is good reason to share our faith with everyone we meet. When we share our faith with someone who already has a personal relationship with Jesus Christ, sharing the faith encourages them and strengthens their faith. Sharing the faith with someone who already knows Jesus also reinforces our own faith and gives us the courage to go on sharing with others. Sharing our faith with people who already have a healthy relationship with a church encourages them to work harder in their church. It encourages them to be faithful in their calling to that place.

When we invite someone to church who is already churched, their telling us of their relationship to their church should bring us joy instead of shame. Let us rejoice with them! Let us share our successes and failures with one another, learning from one another! There should be no shame in our finding out that they already have a church. Let us be glad that they do and move on!

The fact is that a large percentage of our population has never been inside a church, except for weddings. A surprisingly large percentage has never even attended a Christian wedding. These people are counted as "lost" by Christians.

It is probably just as well that many of our churches have stopped referring to those outside the church as "lost." The biggest misconception about "the lost" is that they are all out there somewhere, in other countries, in other lands, in worlds not our own. At the beginning of the twentieth century, eighty percent of all Christians were to be found in the United States and Europe. Sadly, as we closed out the century, the opposite was true. Eighty percent of all Christians are now living outside the United States and Europe! Churches in Africa, South America, and Asia are sending missionaries to the United States and Europe, as well as to other parts of the world!

We can also remind ourselves that "the lost" are often inside our churches. These are the ones who go to church out of habit or out of hunger for friendship, rather than a hunger to worship God in a community of supportive faith.

All of these people are our neighbors. All are in need of our personal ministry. All are in need of patience and kindness. All are in need of forgiveness and an encouraging word. All of us need the saving grace of God in the friendship and the Lordship of Jesus Christ. We have invited many of our neighbors to dinner this Wednesday. I hope that all of us will remember other neighbors that we will invite next time.

Beyond Survival

When I was in high school, my family went to Yosemite Valley almost every summer. One year, we decided to climb to the top of Half Dome. Since it was sixteen miles of strenuous and steep hiking, we set out early in the morning with sack lunches. It was about two o'clock in the afternoon when we reached the top of the dome. It is an outcropping of granite, so large that a game of football or baseball could be played on its flat top. At the same time, however, its sides drop three to four thousand feet. The shiny face of the sheered off half of the dome drops thirty-eight hundred feet straight down! As we were making the final ascent between two cables provided by the National Park Service, the skies were cloudy, and we began to feel a light mist. There were faint rumbles of thunder in the distance. If we did not get off the dome fast, there was eminent danger to everyone on the dome of being struck by lightning.

When challenges seem to overwhelm us there is a strong temptation to think in terms of survival. We did not look around and enjoy the view as we went down. We did not stop to consider the beauty of God's creation. We did not stop to thank God for the opportunity, strength, and courage to climb this great peak. We concentrated upon survival. We scrambled down between that final set of cables as quickly as we could. Thinking in terms of survival only, we proceeded to get lost. As we focused upon survival, we took a wrong turn and failed to use another set of cables that were part of the safe route down. Thinking in terms of survival, we compounded our errors, going on to by-pass some nine hundred steps that had been carved out of the rock for safety.

When we reached the base of the bare granite at soft soil, we realized that we were a long way from the trail. Except for knowing the general direction in which to proceed, along with knowing we should continue to go forward, we were lost. We followed bear and dear trails, worked our way around a high altitude swamp, and got back to the trail more than three hours later at sunset. We did not reach our car at the trailhead until ten that evening.

At the beginning of Holy Week, we see how Jesus did not think in terms of survival. Knowing what would face him if he went to the temple area, he nonetheless "set his face to go to Jerusalem." He entered the Holy City on Palm Sunday, not as a convicted man but as a king. He courageously moved about in Jerusalem, speaking God's word and healing those who sought his touch. Jesus was never known to function in survival mode. As he faced his accusers and faced the cross there was no hint of his seeking to do anything other than God's will.

Jesus was able to keep himself from thinking in terms of survival because he completely trusted our God. Those who give up possibilities of lucrative income in order to serve the church know just a taste of all of this. The same can be said of those who "cannot afford" to tithe but do anyway. It can also be said of those affluent folks who double tithe, triple tithe, or more.

There is more to it all than this, however. Church congregations cannot afford ever to think in terms of survival. It is the very nature of the church to risk itself for the sake of others.

Prophets and Miracles

Moses said, "Show me your glory, I pray." (Exodus 33:18 NRSV)

Moses had been to the top of Mount Sinai more than once. He knew the way to the top, and he was not afraid of encountering God there. He knew the rewards of being obedient and the alternative

94

Faith Fuel

consequences. He had learned that fully loving God also means fearing God. He had also learned that experiencing God's love casts out fear.

Moses had the confidence of a son with a loving father. While the wrath of God was something to be feared, he knew how to avoid the wrath. He knew how to make his concerns known to God with total humility and profound respect. Moses had learned a lot. He had learned much of it the hard way, like most of us.

In the 33rd chapter of Exodus, Moses is again on that mountain. In a burst of enthusiasm and joy, Moses asks to see God's glory–physically to see God face to face. For Moses' safety God declines, but allows Moses to see the Holy backside after passing by.

Like Moses, most of us see God at work in 20-20 hindsight. We look back on something that has occurred, and, with the eyes of faith, we see divine handiwork. It is an exceedingly rare event in which we see God actually performing a miracle. Just like Moses, we people of faith long to experience a miracle actually happening.

A miracle is an event in which people of faith see God at work. When a miracle is shared with other people of faith, it is received with joy. When a miracle is shared with people without the same faith, it is received with skepticism. When a miracle is proclaimed to be occurring in the midst of a gathering of believers, people may hear that declaration with skepticism unless they themselves have the same perspective. When such a momentary miracle is proclaimed to people of little or no faith, the reaction is far worse. The person may will be judged as a religious fanatic or seen as out of touch with reality.

If one regularly proclaims miracles as happening recently, that behavior is frequently seen as odd or eccentric. If the same were done as miracles are happening, that person might get committed to a mental institution. Society is inherently secular in the legal sense. There is little room for prophets in the twentieth century. Part of our problem is that we do not make room for real prophets.

Keep It Brief!

..."Today this scripture has been fulfilled in your hearing." Luke 4:21 NRSV)

At the beginning of His ministry, Jesus made this statement at the synagogue where he had been raised. It was a crucially important statement in world history, and if enough people had been listening, perhaps history would have been very different. Prophecy is truly

95

prophecy only when it is fulfilled. Too often we realize that a prophecy has been fulfilled through twenty-twenty hindsight. Our **hearing** is the key.

When Christians hear the prophet Isaiah quoted as saying, "For unto us a child is born, unto us a son is given," we see the birth of Jesus as the fulfillment of a prophecy. Jews do not see it that way. They do not "hear" it as Christians do.

Christians see Jesus' being born in Bethlehem as a fulfillment of prophecy, but Jews do not see it that way. Christians see Jesus' being raised in Nazareth as a fulfillment of prophecy, but others do not "hear" the prophecy in the same way.

On the other hand, there are those who see current developments in our world as fulfillment of the prophecies in the Revelation of John. Countless others in the previous nineteen centuries have made the same kind of pronouncements, but so far, they have always been wrong. One of these days, someone will be right, but time will not permit that self-righteousness to give that person any satisfaction. Jesus himself admitted that God had not revealed that timetable to him. It will be amazing to see if God reveals to someone else what God would not reveal to Jesus. Will there be someone there to see and to hear?

Most do not realize is that the prayer used by Alcoholics Anonymous is an abbreviated version of a longer prayer by Reinhold Niebuhr. Every church has an abundance of people who believe they are happy and peaceful, but they probably have never experienced the serenity-filled life. Most of us are serene some of the time and a few are serene most of the time. I want to learn from those people that are "always" serene. I can remember certain people who were so filled with the spirit of Jesus Christ that their serenity filled and radiated from them. A few people come to mind. These people make ideal prayer warriors. They begin by hearing with faith filled ears.

I first discovered Salada tea during the summer of 1961. My Dad had secured a Fellowship Grant for continuing education, and my parents and I traveled across the country to New Jersey. At the local A & P Market, the produce manager tried so hard to sell us his California vegetables until he found out that we had just arrived from California. The national brands were in the store, of course, but Salada was a national brand we had not encountered before. The tea was a little better than average, but what really impressed us was the variety of epigrams printed on the tea tags. As a high school student, I began to collect epigrams because of those tea tags, and later I found good use for them on my church signs. Epigrams are like condensed wisdom, easy to hear.

Faith Fuel

I like epigrams because they say a great deal in a short space–they do not waste words or time. One of my biggest frustrations with church life is with those people who waste so much time in church meetings. It is not just that they make haste slowly–that is good! To paraphrase another tea tag, those meetings can be "...a waterfall of words without a drop of common sense." For the good stewardship of time, we need to insist that our church leaders stay on the subject at hand. Sometimes people can hear something short and to the point, when they will not listen to a more detailed presentation.

Why is this so important? Too often, when we get off subject, we get on subjects that are best left alone. A committee chair should have an agenda, with a set amount of time for each subject if necessary. If the discussion has gone on too long, everyone should stand up and not sit down until the subject changes or the meeting is over. If we are standing and impatient to leave, we often listen more attentively.

The same guidelines apply to individual conversations as well. If you have a question, do not make it an essay, or they will not hear it as well. If you have an answer, make your answer a memorable tune and not a symphony–they just may listen! The important things of life need to be both heard and remembered.

Pursuing the Dream

One of the best blessings ever spoken was delivered by Lloyd Ogilvie a few years ago on his television program when he said, "May God grant you the vision to perceive, the power to believe, and the trust in God's ability to achieve God's dreams for your life."

One is struck by the ideas of vision, power, and trust. We know to move into the future with confidence means having a sense of vision. We know that having a positive outlook requires the power to believe. We also know the greatest things happen to those who trust in God. The striking thing is this blessing's emphasis upon God's dreams rather than ours. How indeed does one determine what those dreams are?

Great athletes and artists become experts by training and practice. Great scientists become experts in their fields by research and experimentation. Albert Einstein said developing the Theory of Relativity was five percent inspiration and ninety-five percent perspiration. One cannot become a Bible scholar without reading the Bible repeatedly and studying what it contains. One does not discover the effectiveness of prayer without praying. The more we read our

Faith Fuel

Bibles the easier the Bible is understood. The more we pray the easier it becomes.

If one of the workers in an organization wants to have an audience with the boss to get something, that worker had best do the required homework. Do you want to know God's dreams for your life? Do you want clear answers to your prayers? Do you want a clear path to follow? Do your homework!

In order to discover God's dreams for our lives we must spend much time in conversation with God's Son, Jesus Christ. That conversation involves at least as much listening and meditation as it does talking on our part. God gave us two ears and one mouth. . . . If we have a solid relationship with Jesus Christ, it is likely that we will get a clear answer when we ask about those dreams.

Everyone's Primary Relationship

When I was doing clinical practice as training for counseling, at least half of my work was helping people work through painful relationships. In marital counseling, for instance, we would always ask three basic questions of both the husband and the wife: Do you like this person? Do you love this person? Do you trust this person?

In the first pastorate I served after obtaining my doctorate, I quickly made the uncomfortable observation that there were people in my congregation that had a richer and fuller faith than I did. I had a desire to say, "Let me catch up so that I can lead you!"

Being the son of a science teacher, I approached the problem in a scientific way. I began to analyze my relationships to the church, to God, to Jesus, and to the Holy Spirit in terms of relationships. I asked those same three basic questions of myself with regard to each of those relationships. I quickly saw that my relationships to the Trinity were sorely lacking in trust, and I began the long process of building up my trust level. I knew that faith was a matter of trust, but I had to make that difficult journey from my head to my heart.

When a church is in crisis and begins to express anxiety about its congregational future, it is usually a matter of faith. Christians, like everyone else, often have a hard time putting their heart where their head is. Christians talk about the church belonging to Jesus. We talk about Jesus being in charge, and about trusting Jesus with what happens in and to the church. We talk about trusting God to provide for what we need and to help us do the ministry that needs to be done. We

98

talk about "letting go and letting God." With all of the talk, we nonetheless are reluctant to risk everything for the cause of Christ. We are reluctant to lay our church's life on the line for the cause of Christ. We are most unwilling to risk dying that others might be saved.

I have been called to take risks for the sake of the ministry of Jesus Christ. That is not easy. I do so in order to lead by example. I have to set aside my fears and love my Lord enough to trust Him. In the days ahead, we need to support one another and encourage one another as we step out in faith together.

A Parody

- I have suffered a thousand deaths, but I have walked with God.
- I have built many great houses for Him, but I have destroyed many of His sanctuaries while warring with my brothers.
- I have proclaimed His Holy Name on national television, but I have refused to acknowledge him among my friends.
- I have littered His lands with bodies murdered by my hands, but I have saved millions of children.
- I have shunned some of my brothers in the streets, but I have openly welcomed them in His house.
- I have orphaned children by warring with their parents, but I have built orphanages to ensure their living.
- I have a power that can cure all of the world's problems, but I pray mostly for just myself, and where no one can see me.
- I have outraged my brothers with theological bickering, but we all heal through the grace of the same God.
- I have written stories that are both inane and profane, but I have made the Bible the greatest best-seller.
- I have offered food and clothing to those in need, but I have refused to offer The Lord's Supper to those of another denomination.
- I was born without sin, but I hunger for it like a food.
- I live in God's country, but I generally use His name as an obscenity.
- I am ashamed, but I am proud.
- I am a Christian.

Faith Fuel

Music in Our Souls

Many of us were quite young the first time we said something negative about our musical ability. "I cannot carry a tune in a bucket!" "I am not the least bit musical!" "I am tone deaf!" "I cannot sing worth a hoot!" Not too long ago a call went out at a major university from their music department. Someone wanted to do research on tone deafness. Ads were placed in local newspapers saying that anyone who considered themselves tone deaf was invited to participate in an experiment. Out of the hundreds of people who showed up claiming to be truly tone deaf, only a very small percentage actually had the affliction. A few years ago, an 87 year-old woman who was usually shy and quiet left church smiling, laughing, and loudly telling jokes to her friends. What had come over her? She had made a "joyful noise" that day for the first time in years, because the organ was finally loud enough so that others could not hear her!

Those of us blessed with good teachers early in life often learn that music is the universal language–the language of God. Even those with no musical talent, those who cannot sing, or even those who are actually tone deaf have music in their souls. Some of us have discovered the happy fact that music is an excellent response to heartburn, to anxiety, to grief, to pain, and to other kinds of suffering. It is truly amazing how God speaks to us through music–even when the music does not have words. Many people cannot settle for an electronic organ in church, no matter how expensive or loud. There is something within some of us that loves worshiping the King of Kings with the King of Instruments–a pipe organ. The Holy Spirit makes itself known to us with the music in our souls. Sometimes finding the power of the Holy Spirit is simply a matter of letting out the music within us.

Faith Fuel

Opinions and Gossip

During a heated debate in the U. S. Senate, one senator told another to "go to hell." The senator under attack, naturally not wanting to go to the theological place of eternal punishment, appealed to the presiding vice president, Calvin Coolidge, concerning the propriety of the remark. The future President of the United States was evidently idly leafing through a book when the question was asked. Coolidge said, "I have been going through the rule book. You do not have to go."

Just because a particular person says something, even if we respect them and believe it to be true, does not make it true!

"The Pope is afraid of sex because he is not married."
"Jill lives on the street because she does not want to work."
"The Russians want nuclear war."
"John continues to be a homosexual, therefore he does not care if he gets AIDS."
"All blacks are inferior."
"All Jews are cut-throat businessmen."
"So-and-so knows what is best for the church."
"If something great happens it is good luck, but if something tragic happens it is an act of God."
"Most gossip is harmless."
"Obese people do not want to be healthy."
"Jesus did not find women attractive."
"A child having a mother is more important than a child having a father."
"It is sacrilegious to think of God as 'Daddy.'"

All of these statements are bigoted, lies, or both, but John 8:31-32 (NRSV) remains true: "Then Jesus said to the Jews who had believed in him, 'If you continue in my word, you are truly my disciples; and you will know the truth, and the truth will make you free.'" It is very important that we talk *with* one another but not *about* one another! The former is honest, but the latter is gossip.

Edifying Others

Encouragement. Have you ever considered some of the words that go along with this word? In terms of assistance, encouragement

101

may mean aid, help, faith, comfort, support, or sustainment. In terms of helpfulness, encouragement may mean support, reassurance, motivation, enlightenment, comfort, or urging.

Early in the book of Deuteronomy, God tells Moses on two different occasions to encourage Joshua because he will be the one to secure the Promised Land for God's people. In Acts 15, it was important for Judas and Silas to encourage the believers. The name Barnabus means "Son of Encouragement," and we can have little doubt as to his importance to the ministry of the Apostle Paul. Paul sent Tychicus to the church at Ephesus, so that he might encourage the believers there. Paul sent him to Collosae for the same reason. In the same way, Paul sent Timothy to Thessalonica to encourage the church there. Paul wrote to the Thessalonians, telling them to encourage one another by following the example of Timothy. The letters of Titus and Peter also speak of the importance of encouragement in the life of the church.

I am encouraging–urging–all of my readers to enter into the ministry of encouragement by using the telephone to reach out to one another. Start the first week by calling everyone on the page where your name appears in your church directory. Each successive week go to another page, and when you get to the end of the directory start over!

This is not a gimmick! All of us need positive words and hugs as we face the difficulties of our lives. When we are helping one another, we find that our own lives go easier. When we offer support and encouragement to those with whom we experience friction, very often that friction is eased. Let us encourage one another–that is power that all of us possess!

Good Risks to Take

Virtually all of our decisions in life involve risk. When we laugh, we risk appearing to be fools. When we weep, we risk appearing to be sentimental. We risk personal involvement when we reach out to another. Not getting involved risks our relationship with God. We risk exposing our real selves when we show our feelings. When we fail to show our feelings, our bodies feel the rebellion in the form of illness. To love someone means to risk not being loved in return, except when we love God. Not loving leads to living that is truly sterile.

To live life to its fullest often means risking death sooner than we would like. Not living life to its fullest may mean that we are dead inside anyway. When we allow ourselves to hope, we risk being in despair later. To live without hope means risking despair immediately. When we try, we risk failure. If we do not try, we have already failed. So long as we are alive, we have opportunities to take risks–physical, mental, or spiritual. We can avoid suffering and perhaps even avoid sorrow for a while, but we must take risks in order to learn, feel, change, grow, and love. In other words, we must take risks in order to truly live.

When we insist that everything remain the same, and when we do not trust new ideas, new friends, and new possibilities, we have given up our freedom. We have chained ourselves to ourselves. When we allow ourselves to have alternatives, we are free. To remain free, we have be willing to take risks. As Christians, we need to risk being a fool for Christ. We have to get involved, to get real, and to love unconditionally. Taking these risks leads to the abundant life that Jesus promises.

What We Are For....

Most of our lives we use words without analyzing their meaning. Take the word "react" for instance. This word is particularly interesting because in one sense, most of us define who we are by how we have reacted and are reacting to our world. To put this another way, most of us define who we are by what we are against!

Christians can define themselves as people who are against evil, sin, hate, indifference, violence, injustice, and so forth. Some Christians might define themselves as being against hunger, poverty, prostitution, and all kinds of "isms" in addition to the first list. Other Christians might define themselves (in addition to the first list) in terms of being against abortion, smoking, drinking, dancing, going to the movies, or reading certain books.

Americans may define themselves in terms of being against Communism, terrorism, pollution, nuclear war, or even such mundane things as refined sugar or fat in their diet. Some even go so far as to define themselves to others in terms of particular people in the public eye who are irritating to us.

Why do we have so much trouble following in the footsteps of Jesus more closely? Most of the time Jesus tried to be "pro-active" instead of "re-active." As we listen to Jesus speaking to us through the Gospels, Jesus defines who He is in terms of what He favors rather than in terms of what He abhors. "I came that you may have life and have it abundantly." "I am the good shepherd, and a good shepherd is willing to lay down his life for his sheep." "Blessed are the poor in spirit . . . they who mourn . . . the pure in heart . . . the meek . . . the peacemakers . . . ."

The challenge coming from Jesus is, "Take the risk, and let yourself be defined in terms of what you are for and in terms of who you love, because no matter what I love you!"

Investing Our Gifts

When people start telling me about their talents or about their spiritual gifts, I think about someone I often see at national church gatherings. I went to seminary with her. In addition to being attractive, intelligent, and an excellent musician, I also appreciate her style of ministry. What I appreciate most about her, however, is her stewardship of the gifts God has given her. She is a fantastic woman, not merely because she is multi-talented, but rather because of her stewardship of her talents. While she is not the only multi-talented and obviously blessed person I have met, I do think of her when I read Jesus' parable of the talents. I see the parable as one about stewardship and gifts in general.

There are three ways gifts or talents can be used: They can be invested, buried, or exploited. Good stewardship calls for investment of talents, even if one must do it at a low rate of interest or return. When greed takes over, all of that return is taken for personal gain, and that is the heart of exploitation. It is not the rate of return that makes the difference between investment and exploitation, but rather the way in which that return is used. Admittedly, that is a fine line of distinction, but it is also the reason why it is so easy to go wrong. One of the fascinating developments of the last couple of decades is the ethic of exploitation that has developed in the various modern media. Leaders even talk of positive versus negative exploitation. What they do not realize is that this distortion of traditional values is part of the poison that is so detrimental to our modern society.

Jesus was not so much concerned with exploitation of talents and gifts as he was with burial. Out and out waste of talent or ignoring it is by far the worst course of action of all. God gives us gifts that we might use them for abundant living and loving. That is why I appreciate good stewards like that woman I knew in seminary. They make the most of the gifts God have given them. By so doing, they are an effective witness to God's limitless love and grace. Are you a good steward of your talents?

Precious Trust

There are several definitions of trust, but for at least today, it is the firm belief or confidence in the honesty, integrity, and reliability of another person or thing. Trust seems to be a major problem, whether trust in friends, those who are supposed to serve us, or God and God's Son. In the past, trust was a common commodity. It was freely exchanged between people. We were not as skeptical, either of individuals or of institutions. Trust was cherished as something of great value. Trust was guarded as essential to worthwhile relationships whether those relationships were business or personal in nature.

Today, trust is even more valuable, but for a different reason. It is more rare. Every public statement is treated with skepticism. Trust is frequently abused. A common malady of relationships is a loss of trust in the other person. When we treat others as if we do not trust them, there is a tendency for others not to trust us. We tend to fall into the pattern of not trusting something or someone until and unless we have to do so. As a result, relationships are often shallow, lifeless, and lacking in joy.

Until recently, I was naive in my trust of people, cautious in my trust of things, and hesitant in my trust of God. I wanted God to do it my way, right when requested. Without knowing it, I was saying to God that I trusted my judgment more than I trusted God's judgment.

My attitude towards people and towards God has changed. I tend to trust people at a very early stage, but I let them know of my trust and thus give them the responsibility. I seldom hear people say they do not trust me, and I believe that this is partly due to my open trust of them.

My trust in God is becoming more child-like. God's wisdom is much greater than my foolish ideas. God's sense of timing is far better than my patience can otherwise tolerate. I seldom ask God why. I almost never ask when. My relationship with Jesus no longer seems as shallow. That relationship seems to have a life of its own. I experience more joy and laughter because of that richer relationship.

What about you? How much do you trust God?

Faith Fuel

A Big Birthday

Each year, Christians around the world celebrate Pentecost, the so-called birthday of the church. Pentecost is a turning point in Christian history. In the Old Testament, the Spirit is seen in a number of different ways. Primarily, the Spirit is seen as the source of mental and spiritual perception, along with the capabilities of its leaders. Prophecy is the primary manifestation of the activity of the Holy Spirit in the Old Testament.

The phenomenon of ecstasy is not the most important effect of Spirit possession, nor is it necessarily a proof. The Spirit is the source of all intellectual and spiritual gifts, whether they are the artistry of Bezalel or the understanding and wisdom with which Daniel interpreted dreams. Most importantly, the Spirit is the activity of God that sanctifies both the people of God as a whole and the individual.

By the time of John the Baptist, Israel had been waiting for a long time in hope for a general renewal of the Holy Spirit, and John saw that day rapidly approaching. The primary turning point for the Holy Spirit in the Bible is the Baptism of Jesus, when the Spirit descended upon Jesus the Savior. Following His works, death, resurrection, and ascension at Pentecost, Jesus passed on the Holy Spirit to all those who believed in Him. Those of us who believe in Jesus as the Christ, our personal savior and Lord, also have the spirit passed on to us.

God Provides Abundance

Memorial Day weekend in 1980 was very busy. On Saturday, I united a couple in marriage. The wedding party was unusual in that it consisted of the bride's three daughters from her previous marriage, joined with the groom's three sons from his previous marriage. The children joined in vowing to support their parents in the new union. I was close to the whole united family in that I had dated the bride just a few months earlier!

On Sunday morning, we celebrated Pentecost, the birthday of the church. That afternoon we celebrated the life of a wonderful man who had gone on to the larger life. His memorial service was very well attended. One verse from the Gospel of John was appropriately used at all three gatherings: "I came that they may have life, and have it abundantly." (John 10:10b)

106

Faith Fuel

Such abundant life obviously present in the couple and their children, with the source of their love obviously coming from Our Lord. The gift of the Holy Spirit bestowed on all who accept Jesus as the Christ is an abundant gift indeed. That presence of the Spirit makes the abundant life possible to all. The memorial service was a time in which we celebrated an abundant life that the departed saint had shared with his friends and loved ones.

There does not seem to be any relationship between material wealth and the abundant life that Jesus describes. Jesus seems to say that the abundant life is more accessible to the poor than to the rich! It is a matter of counting blessings instead of pennies. The Lord is supplying our every need. That is the essence of the abundant life of which Jesus speaks. Celebrate the joy and peace of the abundant life. Include God in the celebration!

Growing Christians in Growing Churches

Many want their church to grow, but they do not understand what it takes to achieve that goal. The growth process begins with immersing ourselves in Jesus Christ, doing daily devotions of Bible study and prayer. It is quite natural to focus on spiritual growth and the leadership of the pastor. Physical growth of the church is not a separate issue. Growth happens simply because God provides it when we are doing our spiritual homework. A great deal of research has been done to document what happens in growing churches.

For those with a hunger for statistics, eighty percent of all church growth is the result of members bringing friends and family. In a declining church, about a fifth of its members are focused inward, concentrating on what happens in programs within the church. In a truly stable church, that number rises to about a third. In a growing and reproducing church, that number rises towards half.

In a declining congregation, less than one in ten members has an outward focus, visiting prospective members, or reaching out into the community. In the growing and reproducing congregation, at least one in five members are reaching out, making new friends outside of their congregation and bringing them to church.

The rest of the members of congregations are simply consumers. They may or may not give money to the church that compensates for their consumption. Our Lord said that the greatest among us is the servant of all. Growing congregations have their focus on serving people beyond themselves and bringing them to Jesus.

Faith Fuel

Ah! A Mystery!

According to a typical dictionary, the word 'mystery' applies to what cannot be fully understood by human reason. It also refers to those things that attract curiosity and speculation while resisting or defying explanation. There is an old saying: "The Lord moves in mysterious ways!" In other words, God's movements cannot be fully understood by human reason. What God does attracts curiosity and speculation. The Lord's movements seem to resist or defy any explanation we try to make.

People react to mysteries in various ways but mostly in one of three ways. There are those who, when confronted by a mystery, give up trying to understand and walk away from it. There are those who just stare in awe and wonder, enjoying the experience of the mystery, but not particularly moved to do anything about it. Then there are those people who feel uncomfortable in the presence of a mystery, and do their level best to try to solve it.

When someone says, "The Lord moves in mysterious ways," they may be saying that they find God's ways illogical or unreasonable. If they are saying that they give up, and want to turn their back on the mystery in order to try to forget it, they may end up turning their back on God as well. Sometimes these are the ones who say that God is distant and unreachable.

"The Lord moves in mysterious ways" can also be said by someone who is willing to spend a lifetime studying God's movements and God's will in order to learn more both for themselves and for those that will follow.

Finally, "The Lord moves in mysterious ways" can be said by a person who simply loves to bask in the warm presence of God. They allow themselves to be filled with wonder and awe and peace. How do YOU react to the mysteries of our Creator?

Healing Spiritual Pain

I was once involved in a seminar for singles in which I shared in the leadership with a rabbi who was very progressive and liberal. He made it plain that one of his primary purposes in ministry was to eliminate all guilt. If possible, he wanted to teach people how to live so

Faith Fuel

as to feel never guilty about anything. From his perspective, all guilt was both useless and destructive.

This approach to guilt is not Biblical. Unfortunately, many people reject Christ and His Church because they are afraid to be confronted with their guilt and sins, despite intuitively knowing that they need forgiveness and redemption.

From a Christian psychologist's perspective, guilt can be described as a kind of spiritual pain. While mentally healthy people do not like pain, of itself pain is not normally bad. It is an indication that something is wrong. Physical pain is an indication of disease, damage, or stress. In a similar way, spiritual pain is an indication of disease, damage (to feelings), or stress (relating to ourselves, others, or God). Pain is therefore redemptive when it leads us to changed living, changed thinking, and other remedial action.

Jesus ministered to all kinds of pain. Healing was obvious when he helped the blind to see and the lame to walk. More subtle were his ministries to those feeling guilt, fear, anger, and anxiety. We as a church and as individuals need to be watchful and sensitive to the pain of others. More importantly, we need to help them find the healing they need. It is a very logical extension of "Do unto others as you would have others do unto you."

The Antidote to Sin

Our basic nature as children of God is a combination of potential for good and propensity for evil. While one side of us can be described as the image of God, the other side can be described in terms of sin. The term sin is largely misunderstood. This misunderstanding is grounded in two misconceptions about our lives.

People confuse 'sin,' which is a condition of the spirit, with 'sins,' which are bad deeds. When we are trying to live a Christ-like life, and when we are living out acceptance of Him as Savior, our spiritual condition is no longer that of 'sin.' To be a true disciple of Jesus, we are walking 'in the Spirit' instead of 'in sin.' Although we continue to do bad deeds, those sins are not counted because of God's grace through Jesus' sacrifice on the cross. So long as we live with Christ in our hearts, we live by God's grace and love.

People often also perceive the relationship of sinners to their sins backwards. Most say we are sinners because we sin. The Bible teaches us the opposite! We commit sins because we are sinners!

Seeing ourselves this way keeps our relationship with Christ in the proper perspective.

Sin is complete self-interest. We are 'in sin' when we trust entirely in ourselves and turn away from God. Today we have actually regressed in terms of sin because we tend to believe in our science and our technology rather than God. We have become polytheistic, worshipping such gods as drugs, money, success, power, sex, nationalism, and personal self-esteem. Sin means separation from God: That separation becomes permanent when we die in sin. The greatest thanksgiving for a Christian is for the opportunity to live eternally with God because of Christ's gift of His life.

Resurrections

Most people celebrate Easter only once a year. People become aware of resurrection and new life just once each spring. If we look closer, there are always resurrections all around us. Some resurrections are not tangible or physical. Many have watched programs die, only to revive and thrive again. Old churches have been revitalized from the liquidated assets of congregations that have dissolved. People have died inside when their spouse moved on to the larger life, and they have later found new life with a new spouse.

Considering the resurrections recorded in the New Testament, some of us faithlessly respond by saying they did not die, and they were only asleep. When we talk with people who have died on the operating table during surgery and have been revived (resurrected), some argue that they were not medically and legally dead yet.

We observe congregations having life, vitality, growth, and an exciting future, even though some debated the life of those congregations only a short time previously. It is not important whether those congregations were dead, or dormant, or "not-living-but-merely-existing." Individuals or groups cannot be "born again" unless they put to death their past. This is done symbolically by being buried in the waters of baptism.

Resurrection for a congregation often means leaving behind the seven last words of a dying church, "We've never done it that way before." Instead, a congregation has to adopt the seven first words for a living church, "God is leading us this way today."

Faith Fuel

Our Spiritual Diet

Through most of its history, Christian leaders have emphasized the importance of prayer. A significant percentage of Christians have come to see prayer as some kind of medicine we must take if we are to be "good" Christians. Prayer is not so much a medicine as it is a food. Neither is it a vitamin supplement that is to be taken when we feel a bit malnourished. It is an essential part of life's diet.

We should not wait until we are spiritually hungry to feed on the bread of life, any more than we should wait until we are starving before we decide to eat. We do not wait until malnutrition is ravaging our bodies before we eat a balanced diet. In addition, we should not just eat one big meal per week on Sunday morning, and then spiritually snack the rest of the week.

If we decide we must be spiritually fed regularly, our spiritual diet should not consist entirely of Twinkies® and Cokes® memorized rituals and formula prayers designed to make God like us. Our diet should be balanced with good spiritual nutrition. Junk-food prayers may satisfy our spiritual hunger for a time, but they will not provide long-term spiritual nutrition.

Dieting requires discipline, whether we are trying to lose weight, gain weight, or adjust our body chemistry and health. Discipline coupled with a good authority for guidance leads to success. The same is true in terms of our spiritual diet. If we need help in improving our spiritual nutrition, one way is to start a daily devotional series. Daily devotional books can be ordered on the internet, or we can get them at a Christian bookstore. Reading a devotional each morning is not a substitute for reading the Bible, but it is a good start. Growth can proceed from there.

Party Poopers

All of us from time to time become discouraged. Discouragement can strike anyone, whether we are children, teens, working adults, or retired clerks, carpenters, comptrollers, or clergy. Discouragement seems to strike all of us from time to time. Jesus never directly discusses discouragement. In the book of Colossians, fathers are told not to provoke their children, lest they become discouraged. This is the only reference to discouragement in the New Testament.

Faith Fuel

In the Old Testament, discouragement seems to run rampant at times. In the Psalms, we often see the writer discouraged to the point of despair. Jesus was not insensitive to this! Actions speak louder than words. In His every word and deed, Jesus demonstrated courage rather than discouragement. Certainly, Jesus had cause to be discouraged. Matthew, Mark, and Luke all record Jesus asking, "'How long am I to be with you? How long am I to bear with you?" In the Gospel of John, Jesus says to Philip, "Have I been with you so long, and yet you do not know me, Philip?" Jesus suffered the frustration and anger that go hand in hand with discouragement. The shortest verse in the Bible reflects discouragement as well as sadness: "Jesus wept."

Sometimes, we clergy come close to crying over well intentioned but insensitive people who bring negative words and actions into otherwise joyous occasions. We find hope in reading the words of another pastor, the Apostle Paul. The same man who spoke of "... danger from known people, danger from Gentiles, danger in the city, danger in the wilderness, danger at sea, danger from false brethren..." also wrote, "... whatever is true, whatever is honorable, whatever is just, whatever is pure, whatever is lovely, whatever is gracious, if there is any excellence, if there is anything worthy of praise, think about these things...and, the God of peace will be with you."

In Jesus' Arms

There are beautiful stained glass windows in the sanctuary of First Christian Church in Oakland, California. Along the north side there are portraits of rather expressionless saints. As beautiful as the glass is, I do not find the mood of those portraits particularly inspiring. The window at the back of the sanctuary, on the east wall above the balcony, is another story. Jesus is in the picture, along with a woman and three children. One child is in the woman's arms, with a rather shy or coy expression. The second child is on his knees, at the feet of Jesus, tugging, at his tunic. The third child is being held in the arms of Jesus, with the child's head resting on Jesus' shoulder, with the child's eyes closed and at peace. The viewer can be particularly taken with this third child.

Try to imagine yourself embracing and being embraced by Jesus, with your head on His shoulder, with your eyes closed; feeling the warmth of his embrace and the comfort of his presence. In that stance, you simply would like to enjoy the intimacy. You would like to enjoy the comfort of crying on His shoulder. You would like to enjoy the sense of peace and wholeness that comes from being in His presence. You sense that these children in the stained glass picture will go forth and tackle the world with gusto because they have been intimate with their hero, Jesus.

Are we expressionless saints who stare out at the world and do not get involved, or are we the brash children of God, ready to tackle anything? Teddy Roosevelt said: "Far better it is to dare mighty things, to win glorious triumphs even though checkered with failure, than to take rank with those poor souls who neither enjoy much nor suffer much, but live in that cold grey twilight that knows not victory nor defeat."

Jesus said, "I came that you might have life and have it abundantly."

Truth Is Appropriate

One of the most practical pieces of advice that Jesus has ever given to his disciples is "You will know them by their fruits. Grapes are not gathered from thorn *bushes* nor figs from thistles, are they?" [Matthew 7:16 (NASB)] Jesus is talking about hard evidence. Instead of making our evaluations about people based upon what others say about them, or upon what we think we see in them, we are to evaluate them on the basis of what they do and say.

A celebrity was going through her fan mail late one night, and when she opened one letter, she knew that God was speaking to her through the writer. She wrote back to say her spirit had been fed thoroughly and, was nourished by the "fruit" of the letter. After several months of letters and phone conversations, they were able to meet, and the Holy Spirit moved among them. About a month later, she suddenly did not like "the taste of the fruit." Was a good tree yielding bad fruit? Jesus says this does not happen. Had the tree become "diseased?" There was no evidence of this. Had the woman become "allergic" to the fruit that God was providing though this "tree?" She called and said, "Please don't call any more."

Jesus also said, "You shall know the truth, and the truth shall make you free." When the truth suggests that our wisdom has been faulty, the pain of that truth may spoil a beautiful friendship, unless the hearer of that painful truth knows how to love unconditionally as Jesus teaches us to do. If we are to love our neighbors as ourselves, we must love unconditionally!

113

Faith Fuel

Speak with Love

A long time ago, I read on my tea bag tag, "Gossip is a waterfall of words without a drop of common sense." When we share our faith with someone, it should not be simply a "waterfall of words." Spreading the gospel does not mean we have to say a lot. Good communication is not measured by the number of words we speak. Gossiping about life at our church is certainly not a good way to spread the good news.

The quality of the vocabulary is not important either. Pretty prose does not even sell books anymore. All it takes is simple words like love, joy, hope, and faith. Simple eloquence such as, "Jesus is alive in my heart" says it best. What really spreads the gospel is the depth of the way we communicate. Chitchat about the church over coffee does not impress anyone. Mere facts about the faith do not win people to Christ. Opinions do a little better, but everybody has opinions about religion. No, the best communication of the gospel involves our feelings about what we believe, and about the intimacy we have with our God through Jesus.

It takes practice and trust to communicate at a "feelings" level, but then that is the best way to express the caring love that Jesus teaches us. In addition, if we know someone very well, and if our relationship involves the regular sharing of feelings in both directions, we may be cheating that person out of their salvation. It is cheating them by not sharing with them something that is really important, what is actually vitally important to them even if they do not know it. It means we are cheating a good friend out of what they need to hear. Some friend!

Through Jesus' Eyes

Vision is basic to Christian spiritual health. Vision simply means trying to see everything that happens from Christ's perspective. Jews and Moslems hope what they do is pleasing in God' sight. Christians can go one step further however, because Jesus walked this Earth just as we do.

Seeing things through the eyes of Jesus does not simply mean having good intentions. It does not mean having a super religious point of view either. Jesus was often criticized for not being religious enough!

114

Faith Fuel

Jesus observed Jewish festivals and fulfilled the law, and He also liked to go to weddings, wakes, and other parties. Being part of God's plan meant being away from the Temple most of the time. Instead, He was healing, comforting, and sharing the good news that the kingdom of God is at hand.

It is important for Christians to go to church, just as it was important for Jesus to go to the Temple and synagogues. Going to church flexes our spiritual muscles and keeps us spiritually fit. It keeps us in tune with the whole body of Christ so we do not end up arrogantly doing our own thing. Praying in the midst of God's people helped Jesus recharge his spiritual batteries. Meeting with people both in their homes and in their synagogues helped Him keep his perspective.

Have you ever noticed how often Jesus withdrew to pray? When we open our eyes after praying, it is important to remember that Jesus sees through our eyes just as He works through our hands. Those without an intimate relationship with Jesus miss out on the power that flows in such a relationship. When we are aware of Jesus seeing things through our eyes, we begin to see things as He does. Our spiritual vitality depends upon our maintaining a vision of that larger perspective. I am working on it.

Be Uncommon

A popular quote circulating all over the world on the Internet is a quote by Glen Bland, from his book, *Success: The Glen Bland Method.* This is what he says:

I do not choose to be a common man. It is my right to be uncommon if I can.

I seek opportunity, not security. I do not wish to be a kept citizen, humbled and dulled by having the state look after me. I want to take the calculated risk, to dream and to build, to fail and to succeed.

I refuse to barter incentive for a dole. I prefer the challenges of life to a guaranteed existence, the thrill of fulfillment to the stale calm of Utopia. I will not trade freedom for beneficence, nor dignity for a handout.

It is my heritage to think and to act for myself, to enjoy the benefits of my creations, and to face the world boldly and say:

With God's help, this I have done.

Faith Fuel

Let us express parallel thoughts from a Christian's perspective:

I do not choose to be a common Christian, simply talking the talk. God calls me to be uncommonly His, glorifying Him.

I seek to be obedient, not necessarily to be secure in terms of life on Earth. I do not wish to be a slave to people or possessions–self-centered and dulled by seeking only to have my own needs met and my own desires fulfilled. I want to take the leap of faith, to catch God's vision, to build up the kingdom of God–to fail perhaps in the eyes of others, but to gain eternal life.

I refuse to barter God's gifts for temporary satisfaction. I prefer to pursue joyously the "impossible" dreams of God rather than to have mere existence. I prefer the joyous thrill of divine fulfillment over the stale calm of the status quo. I will not trade freedom in Christ for approval of friends, nor trade compassion for pride.

It is my heritage to be a child of God who lives in the divine abundance of God's grace. It is my heritage to enjoy the glories of God's creation and the benefits of God's mercies. It is my heritage to face the world boldly and say:

"The kingdom of God is at hand: I repent! I am letting God be my God, and I am letting Jesus Christ be my King!"

The Jesus Challenge

"Be perfect!"

This sounds like an impossible command. In the Sermon on the Mount, Jesus says, "Be perfect, therefore, as your heavenly Father is perfect." [Matthew 5:48 (NRSV)] Many people have been perplexed or confused by this verse. Over the years, it has also undoubtedly been the source of some well-intentioned but misguided Bible lessons.

The Greek word for perfect is *teleios*. It can be translated *complete, perfect,* or even *mature.* Unfortunately, all too many people think of *teleios* simply as comparitive to Jesus or to Our Heavenly Father. None of us will ever live the perfect life as Jesus did. Only God, Jesus, and the Holy Spirit are perfect in the divine sense. This is not what Jesus is asking of us when He says, "Be perfect." Jesus wants us to be perfect in the human sense.

Faith Fuel

We currently live in a "me" focused society. Millions of people are focused upon being perfect in one or more areas. A person may focus on perfect health or perfect fitness. Some focus on having a perfect or ideal family. Others focus on their work. Those with no opportunity to seek perfection in the workplace may seek perfection in their recreational activities. Still others may seek perfection through plastic surgery, through drugs, or both. Some use caffeine, nicotine, alcohol, and other drugs to make their world at least *seem* closer to perfection. In contrast, some seek perfection through returning to a more natural life through natural foods and herbs. Still others seek counsel from books, tapes, or professionals to improve themselves and move at least a little closer to perfection.

The primary problem with most of these quests for perfection is with what they choose as a point of reference. In most cases, they are trying to be perfect in their own eyes, or in the eyes of those people they respect. Max Ehrman said, "If you compare yourself with others, you may become vain and bitter, for always there will be greater and lesser persons than yourself." When we try to be perfect in our own eyes, the result is often a distortion of what God intended us to be. When we try to be perfect in the eyes of other people, it almost always leads to frustration, because for some we cannot do anything right, and others will not criticize us to our face.

Some time ago, I decided that the only one I truly have to please is God, and the only person I want even to try to imitate is Jesus. Earlier in my life, I had other heroes. My first hero was my Dad. As the years went on, I added a bit of hero status to a music teacher, a preacher, several professors, and a few friends. As I have read the gospels over and over again, Jesus has become much more real to me. He is the ultimate hero. I try to walk in His steps, but I keep stumbling. I am trying to treat other people as Jesus would, but my shyness often gets in the way. I try to live out His commands, but my hungers and needs often get in the way. I am not going to stop trying! The more I try to plumb the depths of Jesus' teachings, the more I discover the overall simplicity of His lessons. Looking back, I like to consider my efforts at walking in His steps. As I consider past failures in the midst of His forgiveness, He seems to add just a bit more to my life to make me better next time.

I like to think that there is *teleios* in our efforts to be like Jesus. Our honest efforts to be like Jesus give us moments of completeness— little pointers of accomplishment. They add a measure of maturity to life's journey. Our honest efforts to be like Jesus bring us perfection for those moments, and that is what Jesus wants of us.

Faith Fuel

Evidence of the Spirit

It is important to understand why Pentecost is a turning point in Christian history. In the Old Testament, the Spirit is seen in a number of different ways. Primarily the Spirit is seen as the source of mental and spiritual perception and the abilities exhibited in its rulers. Prophecy is the primary manifestation of the activity of the Spirit in the Old Testament.

The phenomenon of ecstatic speech (tongues) and/or ecstasy are not the most important effects of Spirit possession. They are not necessarily proof of possession either. The Spirit is the source of all intellectual and spiritual gifts, whether they are the artistry of Bezalel or the understanding and wisdom with which Daniel interpreted dreams. The Spirit is the activity of God within us, which sanctifies both the people of God as a whole, as well as the individual.

By the time of John the Baptist, Israel had been waiting for a long time in hope for a general renewal of the Holy Spirit. John saw that day rapidly approaching. The primary turning point for the Holy Spirit in the Bible is the Baptism of Jesus, when the Spirit descended upon Jesus as Savior. Following His works, death, resurrection, and ascension, it was at Pentecost Jesus passed on the Holy Spirit to all those who believe in Him and receive Him into their hearts. It is the basis for believing that we are *born again*. Thus, Pentecost is the birthday of the church.

One of the sources of controversy within the church is speaking in tongues. The Greek term for it is γλῶσσα–*glôssa*, which means *tongue* or *tongues*. Speaking in tongues consists of fluent speech-like syllables. Some consider it meaningless, while others consider them to be a holy language. Some consider it a miracle. The term occurs mostly in the Book of Acts and in I Corinthians. A majority of Christians consider it to be a gift of the Holy Spirit. Some consider it a real unlearned language or the language of angels. Others believe that speaking in tongues includes many languages. They point out that one can very realistically imitate tongues, a fact that the Apostle Paul acknowledges in I Corinthians. Skeptics believe that the "gift" is therefore learned and meaningless.

Mark 16:17 says, "They will speak with new tongues." The problem is that many scholars believe that Mark originally ended at verse 8. Perhaps verses 9-16 were added at a later date. All of it was written after Pentecost. There are implied references to speaking in tongues in two other places. "Likewise the Spirit helps us in our weakness; for we do not know how to pray as we ought, but that very Spirit intercedes with sighs too deep for words." [Romans 8:26 (NRSV)] "But you, beloved, build yourselves up on your most holy faith; pray in the Holy Spirit..." [Jude 1:20 (NRSV)]

I have a friend who loves to pray in the Holy Spirit. Some years ago, she prayed over me in the Holy Spirit. I felt warmth flowing over me. I have since identified this through other experiences as the presence of the Holy Spirit. The closest comparison I can offer is that of being held in gently warm loving arms. I pray that every Christian can experience God's presence and power in this way.

Commitment Shy

In recent years, we have been repeatedly hearing the lament that people are commitment shy. Single men and women are said to complain that members of the opposite sex are afraid to make a commitment. Married couples contemplate divorce either because one or both of them lack a sense of commitment. The clergy often complain that church members fail to fulfill their commitments, and the same lament is heard in the business world as well.

Commitment requires self-discipline. In a society highly valuing leisure and freedom, commitment tends to be placed low on priority lists. To many, a sense of freedom and a sense of commitment are opposites. Such is not the case however. Personal freedom is most highly valued in the context of powerful commitments in other parts of life. Moreover, we must carefully divide up our lives and keep the various parts separate in a disciplined way in order to maintain that freedom.

The Apostle Paul was a truly free man. In more than one of his letters, he speaks of being a slave to Jesus Christ, and yet in his letter to the people of Galatia he said, "For freedom Christ has set us free." (Galatians 5:1 NRSV) In 1970, Fred Craddock preached a sermon about Paul's freedom, in which he said, "To be free one must of course have alternatives, but to be truly free one must be able to continue to function in the face of those alternatives without being frozen by choices."

The Apostle Paul made a total commitment to Jesus. In so doing, he set himself free from other things that had enslaved him. He no longer had to worry about impressing other people. He set himself free from worrying about money, hunger, thirst, clothing, freedom, his rights, and even life itself. In making himself a committed slave for Christ, he found the freedom to be all that God had called him to be.

For those who have never allowed themselves the privilege of knowing Jesus, making a commitment to someone who lived two thousand years ago seems nearly impossible. For those who have difficulty making simple commitments in daily living, making a commitment to Jesus seems like an impossible dream. Ironically, those who step out in faith to make a commitment discover more than simply new freedom. They also discover the ease of maintaining other commitments in the shadow of their commitment to Christ.

The psalmist says more however. After making our commitment, we are to trust in God, and trust that God will act. Christians that step out in faith with Jesus discover the actions that Christ takes in their lives. They discover new joy and new vitality that comes from a commitment to Christ in simple trust.

Where's Your Focus?

What we are doing, what we have, and what we want are, are of little importance in comparison to who we are, what we share, and where we are going. This applies to groups as well as to individuals! There are three fundamental ways that we can journey through life. We can journey backwards, seeing all that we have accomplished, and seeing the distance we have traveled. Another way is to journey forwards, looking down, seeing only what and where we are in the present moment. The third alternative is to journey through life walking with our eyes on the horizon, seeing where we are going and seeing what goals are being approached. All of us engage in a mixture of these three walks.

Jesus encourages us to keep our eyes on the horizon and to stay aware of our potential. Jesus accepts us the way we are, and He loves us without conditions or limits. He tells us to be the salt of the earth and the light of the world. Jesus constantly calls attention to what we are doing and where we are going.

God does not require that we be perfect or that we achieve perfection on the first try, for God keeps on redeeming us–and redeeming our mistakes. What God does want us to do is to keep on growing. We never grow old–we just stop growing. Perfection is in being all that we can be and doing the best we can each day. God wants us to move creatively from where we are to where we should be. We can ask, "Where am I growing?"

Faith Fuel

Free Will

When God gave each of us free will, The Creator gave us both a gift and a burden. God could have set us up so we would only know how to do His Divine intentions, but instead we have been given the opportunity to make choices. The burden is that decision making always involves some degree of risk, and it requires us to exercise some kind of trust in some area related to the decision. Free will has a price.

Since our Lord Christ was fully human as well as fully divine, we must assume that He made decisions of His own free will like the rest of us. Jesus took risks just like we take risks, and Jesus had to exercise trust just as we do. He chose to have twelve close friends, and one of them betrayed him, while another later denied ever knowing him. Was it worth it? Should He have risked betrayal and denial? If he did it all over again, do you think He would do the same things the same way? Do you think He would have chosen the same friends?

There is a rather familiar sacred song entitled "I walked Today Where Jesus Walked," and the singer of the song takes us on an imaginary trip to where the walk takes place. Setting up our imaginations in that way is romantic, but it is not very practical! How about our daily living? Can we, at the end of our day say, "I walked today where Jesus walked...?" Do we begin our day by taking the risk of inviting the companionship of Jesus in that day? When we go to a party, do we take the risk of inviting Him along? Is our trust level in Him high enough that we feel comfortable having Him along wherever we go? Perhaps we are afraid that we will end up being like Peter (who denied Him) or Judas (who betrayed Him). Even so, we know that Jesus loved them both just as they were. Jesus loves you and me just as we are! Is not that the best news the world has ever had?

Thinking Straight

It is said that the most common spiritual ailment is guilt, that the most common physical ailment is the "common" cold, and that the most common mental ailment is depression. In the case of the cold, all we can do is drink many fluids, get enough rest, and control the symptoms. In the case of guilt, the best cure is an honest conversation with Our Savior.

121

Faith Fuel

In the case of depression, a fairly recent development has been the emergence of Cognitive Therapy. Unlike the previous treatments for depression, it is highly successful in terms of lasting results. Cognitive Therapy has arisen from the discovery that most depressions are not caused by "wrong thoughts" or by physiological problems. Instead, we have discovered that our blue moods are caused by faulty habit patterns in our thinking. In musical terms, it would be like music for the piano mistakenly written in a different key for the left hand than for the right. In a painter's terms, it would be like an artist trying to paint a scenic portrait without knowing that he is color-blind. It also might be likened to playing solitaire with one card missing, or trying to use a computer program that has an unknown glitch.

In seminary, I was told the common cold of the local congregations was faulty theology. Most people base their Christian faith on what people tell them the Bible says rather than basing their faith on what the Bible actually says. The New Testament is available inexpensively in many translations. Some churches order 1000 at a time with information about their congregation printed on the back, and they give them away as a church growth tool. What if people do not read what you give them? It has been proven countless times that people who read their Bibles daily live healthier and happier lives. It is the best therapy around–physically, mentally, and spiritually–both in terms of preventative medicine and effective treatment. It is not that hard to swallow.

Finding Real Joy

My favorite book of devotions is very short and entitled *$3.00 Worth of God*, by Wilbur Rees. It says in one part, "'Make it drip-dry,' they are telling you, Lord. The whole world wants it slick and easy. Put your presence in a pill. Seal the abundant life in a vacuum can so it will be there with the instant coffee. ..." Real joy for a Christian requires a close relationship with the Lord. Such a relationship, like any relationship that is worthwhile, takes effort and work as well as time. Some people try to divorce themselves from the Lord because the joy takes too much effort. In even more cases, it is simply a separation instead of a divorce. One of the great wonders is that no matter how much we ignore the Lord or try to push Him away, He is still there and never ignores us.

Faith Fuel

If your faith seems to be "drip-dry," then it is unlikely you have discovered the joy that is possible in really knowing the Lord. The Lord has all kinds of time for you–do you have some time for the Lord? Either our faith is an abridged edition, or it is full-blown! If you find it easy to describe your faith in a capsule, maybe you need to do some more thinking. Any relationship, whether with God or anyone else, needs to be growing always. If it is not growing, it is stagnant. One of the images of hell is that it is stagnant. My prayer for the church is that we may never stop growing!

The Call to Mission

As disciples of Jesus Christ, He calls upon each of us to develop loving relationships with persons outside of the church. There are a few people who are fearful enough to relate only to those within the church, but most have no problem with this first part of Christ's call upon our lives. The part that follows is logical: through those relationships, we are to discover people's specific needs and situations. Again, there are a few people who are so hardened and self-absorbed that they cannot be this compassionate. Most of us find that developing a friendship involves being sensitive to those needs and conditions that we discover.

The third part of Christ's call upon our lives is not really subject to debate even though some try to argue about it. We are called to help those people outside the church experience God's love manifest in Jesus Christ, and we are to do it by relating Christ's love to their needs and conditions.

Contrast this with our painfully common attitude as a church. We cannot wait for persons to come to us–instead of our going out to them. Jesus commands us intentionally to reach out and touch others' lives. We have to spend the time to get to know people well enough and love them enough to discover their needs.

It is not loving and or Christ-like to accost a stranger and offer him a type of religious salve before we determine what his hurts and situation are. We are not here to peddle panaceas and offer easy solutions to serious problems. Doing things right means effort and discipline, although we can state it simply: we must listen carefully, and then respond lovingly.

When some people listen, they are merely waiting until they can get in another word. Some of us have the habit of concentrating on what we have to say next, rather than concentrating on what the

123

person is saying. Sometimes it helps to feed back to the person what you are hearing as a way of telling them you are really listening. Another thing we can do is to probe for details, asking who, what, when, where, how, and why. Coupled with this should be questions about the person's feelings, as well as about their thoughts.

When we respond in love, it means doing so with patience, kindness, humility, and compassion. If we are going to witness, we should do so out of our own experience, not merely quoting Bible passages. From there we get on with our witness and mission!

Vacations

When the season for vacations rolls around, I think of a pastor who was serving a church in Texas in the early 1970's. While some in his flock did not like the season, he looked forward to it. If you talked with him, you would understand why.

He knew there would be Sundays when the pews would be less filled than usual. due to the absences of those on vacations. He would miss those who were gone. To some this meant something negative, but to that Texas pastor, it meant that soon there would be people in those pews who would be returning refreshed and ready to tackle new challenges that God would throw at them. Vacations are Biblical! Vacations are a natural reflection of the Old Testament idea of the Sabbath. Every so often, it is good to be refreshed by a restful change. Even if the change is not so restful, it still seems to be refreshing.

Although people will go on vacation, the church never takes a vacation. Consequently, everyone has to pray for their church and give it their spiritual and financial support even if they are gone. Steady financial support for the church has always been important. Look around you when people are on vacation. Pray for those who are sick, that they may be healed and returned to active duty in the Christian community. Pray for those who for any reason find that they choose not to be in church on a given Sunday that they may be tuned in to the guidance and power of the Holy Spirit. Pray for those on vacation, that they may be refreshed and empowered to do God's will after their extended Sabbath.

Faith Fuel

What's Your View?

My hobby is photography. As a child, I took delight in using my Brownie Hawkeye camera to take snapshots of everything large and small. Part of the time, I even used my Dad's Zeiss Contaflex with close up lenses to take pictures of small flowers. Most of the pictures I take today involve the use of a wide-angle lens. Most of my award-winning pictures are scenic scenes. I love to photograph the broad expanse of God's creation. My shift in this direction took a long time.

I have a similar approach to the Bible. Seminary classes tended to emphasize the use of a telephoto approach to the Bible's portraits of characters and stories. My earliest sermons reflected close examinations of the details of scripture, taking a close-up view of people, places, and themes. I used to enjoy digging out the meaning of the original texts, particularly of the New Testament. As I have grown older, I have had a shift in emphasis in Bible study similar to my shift in photography. As I read the scriptures daily, I try to see God's Word from the perspective of whole chapters, or even from the vantage point of entire books.

Have you ever put a piece of steak in your mouth that was a little too large? The size and shape of that piece of meat determines how we chew and swallow it. In a similar way, "chunks" of scripture can cause us to think about passages differently. When we consider the Bible in larger portions, the Bible has a better chance of expressing its own agenda over ours. We are less likely to bend the Bible to fit our own agenda.

An excellent example is found in I Corinthians 15. The overall chapter is about the meaning of death, the meaning of resurrection, and the nature of eternal life in Jesus Christ. When we break down the chapter into smaller portions, we see each as an answer to a variety of our own questions. In verse 29, for example, the Apostle Paul mentions a superstitious practice that grew out of the pagan environment of the church in Corinth–baptizing on behalf of the dead. The Church of Jesus Christ of the Latter Day Saints (Mormon) reads this half verse as a direction to practice baptism on behalf of the dead. Pro-Life groups like to quote Exodus 20:13 in the Old Testament as a Biblical argument against abortion. Seen in the larger context that includes the next chapter, the perspective is quite different, neither condemning nor endorsing the procedure. The more we study the scriptures in big bites, the bigger is our appetite.

Faith Fuel

Being the Church

When you hear the word "church," what does the word mean to you? Is it a particular place? Does it refer to Sunday morning worship? Does it refer to a group of people? It is all of these things! The Bible says that the church is the body of Christ, made up of people who have accepted Christ as their Lord and Savior.

If someone is simply observing a worship service, that person is not a part of the church! Believing that Jesus was born, lived, died, and was resurrected from the dead does not mean that such a believer is a Christian or is part of the church. There are literally millions of people who believe that because they embrace the celebrations of Christmas and Easter that they are Christians. As Garrison Kiellor said, "Going to church no more makes you a Christian than standing in a garage makes you a car."

One of the best ways that the church can distinctively not be just a religious social club is to emphasize one basic truth package. To be a fully functional Christian, a person must accept that Jesus died for our sins on the cross, that He was buried, that He was raised from the dead on Easter, and that He lives forever alive as our Savior. Having accepted all this, each person must surrender his life to Jesus as his Lord.

Without this basic truth, the result can be called at best "Christianity Lite." Without this basic truth, a person may have the flavor of being a Christian, but they will have none of the substance. To be a good and loving person is not enough - a Christian is a servant of The Master who is alive forever.

To be a servant or "thrall" of Jesus Christ is at the core of the meaning of the word "enthralled." Once we decide to do everything to please The Master, we are liberated from being concerned with what others would consider good or bad, right or wrong. Christ sets us free from the slavish adhesion to rules and regulations. The second verse of the old Mennonite hymn, "I Bind My Heart This Tide," by Lauchlan Watt says it best:

> I bind my heart in thrall
> To the God the Lord of all -
> To the God, the poor man's friend,
> And the Christ whom He did send.
> I bind myself to peace -
> To make strife and envy cease.

126

Faith Fuel

God, knit Thou sure the cord
Of my thrall-dom to my Lord!

Seeing Through Jesus' Eyes

Do you see what I see? Probably not! Even if we were standing right in the same spot and looking at the same thing, we would probably see things differently. When traveling, I often look at a scene in terms of the picture I want to project on a screen for others to see. I have learned to be quite careful when looking through my camera's viewfinder to notice everything that appears there. Even then, I end up throwing away about half of the pictures I take!

When looking at people, I try to see what is best in them. I want to see people through Jesus' eyes. Early one summer I met the granddaughter of one of the members of the congregation I was serving. I got a fantastic impression of her. Someone standing next to me would have seen a very attractive young woman. What impressed me that day, however, was a glimpse I got of the spiritual power God had placed within her. Coming out of worship with the joy of the day radiating on her face, I got a glimpse of the bright hopes and fantastic plans God has laid out for her. I hope I will have the privilege of witnessing some of that future God has laid within her.

One spring, I talked with a man who was living out that kind of joyous life. He was struggling with serious issues in his life, but the joy of Christ's presence was radiating from his own face and from the faces of his wife and daughters. As he talked, I could sense the confidence and joy he felt as he faced the future with Christ.

I frequently see others that seem to be living out the fantastic life that God wants for them. What is it that is different? Their occupation or age does not matter. Their ethnic background, sex, our physical makeup does not matter either. Contrary to the rest of the world's values, intelligence, education, creativity, talent, and beauty do not matter either. The difference is the presence of the Christ who walks with them and within them. No matter how big their workload, their stress level is manageable. No matter what "brand" of Christianity they embrace, they are not shackled by the particular methodology of being the church. Their relationship with Christ is more important than doctrines, traditions, practices, or anything else. They are indeed free to be all that God created them to be.

Faith Fuel

Sharing Our Hope

When we hardly know someone, the talk is often superficial. Moving beyond chitchat, we exchange a few facts. Then as the relationship continues to develop, we begin to delve into our opinions. If the relationship becomes even more solid, we begin to share our feelings, and once in awhile, we might even go a bit deeper into each other's hearts. In the Christian community, there is a type of dialogue that seems to defy the simple categories of chitchat, facts, opinions, and feelings. These dialogues begin with someone talking about their hopes. Hope is certainly not unique to Christian circles, but the subject gets sticky when we talk about moving beyond hope into faith.

No one enjoys appearing foolish. One cannot avoid sounding like a fool, however, when claiming to believe that his hopes are about to be fulfilled. To paint pictures of one's dreams is an accepted creative pastime. To claim with conviction that a dream is about to come true is another matter altogether. It appears foolish indeed! Faith is the substance of things hoped for, but that substance cannot be weighed, measured, or detected in the usual way. Faith is the evidence of things unseen, but such evidence is not admissible in the court of common logic. It is like this:

Hope

Living in fear we can't cope.
Living unhappy we mope.
Trusting in God
Is the path that we trod
Because hope that is seen is not hope.

Living in joy we can cope -
Faith conquers our steepest slope!
Trusting in God
Is the path that we trod,
For we are living in joy, faith and hope.

How can we keep our mouths shut when we have hope? Might we appear to be foolish? The Apostle Paul says, "We are fools for Christ's sake."

Faith Fuel

God's Real World

Like virtually everyone else, I get excited about the Olympics. When it is over, I ponder the values that all have been embracing over those two weeks. There are several catchwords and catch phrases used throughout the Olympics. We hear the words *fitness, training, dedication,* and *discipline* over and over again. We also hear phrases like *hard work, dedication to the ideal,* and *striving for perfection.*

It is gratifying to see people pursuing their goals with vigor. When they reach those goals, they rightfully enjoy their victories and achievements. We all share their joy in the thrill of victory, and we share their agony in defeat. Most of us appreciate the striving for excellence we see in others, and some of us perhaps feel a bit of envy that we have never achieved such excellence, or had it recognized.

We also notice, however, that many of these athletic heroes are rather one-sided individuals. These are young athletes who, for a large part of their childhood and adolescence, have likely been devoid of family life and opportunities for unstructured play. The result may be poor personality development. There are athletes whose obsession with winning leaves little room for the sheer joy of competition. There are also many athletes who know little else of life except for what they experienced in competition. They therefore may develop the distorted view that everything in life must involve some sort of competition.

The Olympics and other competitions raise nagging questions. What good is physical fitness without emotional and spiritual fitness? What good is learning discipline, if one cannot apply it in other areas of life? What good is hard work, if there is so much of it that one hardly has time to enjoy the life God has given? Some may have achieved "perfection" in their Olympic scores, but when the competition is over, the most they may have to show for it is elusive fame, trophies, aching bones, and distorted lives. For a few brief shining moments, while we watch these events, we have dreams of being athletes. Then, we come back to the real world. We can find lasting joy in having the physical, emotional, and spiritual tools to be able to enjoy the abundant life that God has given us.

Faith Fuel

"Absence is to love what wind is to fire–it extinguishes the small, but it enkindles the great." This is a centuries-old Chinese proverb. The relationship between love and fire has been known for thousands of years. On Pentecost, Christians come to church to deal with the relationship of fire, God's love, and our faith. Pentecost is not entirely a Christian celebration. It began as an event on the Jewish calendar. Seven weeks after Passover, Jews come together on the fiftieth day and make a special offering in thanks for the harvest. One particular time, fifty days after the Passover, men were gathered in a room as the followers of Christ. Jesus had said that He would send the Holy Comforter after He was gone but a little while.

During Jesus' ministry, His disciples knew the presence of the Holy Spirit, so the coming of the Holy Spirit on Pentecost was not entirely new. We only have a small amount of information in the book of Acts to tell us what happened at Pentecost. We have a small picture. What does all of this have to do with an ancient Chinese proverb?

Jesus begins his ministry with a great deal of expectation. We see someone who is truly filled with enthusiasm for what was to be accomplished. Jesus would go through a period of time when he would do a lot of healing and ministering, and then He would have to retire in prayer to recharge his spiritual batteries. His humanity is something we can identify with. He is the son of God, but as He also described Himself, the "Son of Man."

About half way through Jesus' ministry, He told the parable of the sower. The parable says that as the sower goes out to sow, some seed fell on shallow soil, some fell on good soil, some fell on thorny soil, and some fell on the rocks. In three out of four areas of sowing, there is utter failure. However, the fourth area brings forth a bountiful harvest. There is a great deal of hope in that! Let us look to the batting average of a typical professional baseball player. Only one time in four he gets a hit. With the greatest batters, for every success there are two failures. The work of the Holy Spirit turns all our failures into something inconsequential, so that our successes can mean so very much more.

We cannot imagine anyone in lower spirits than Jesus' disciples on the day after the crucifixion. They were utterly crushed. Out of the "failure" of the cross came the triumph of that same cross, when the tomb was found empty on Easter Sunday morning. Then there came a period when again they had that empty feeling. They

Faith Fuel

were told to go to Jerusalem and wait.

"Absence is to love what wind is to fire." In this case, instead of extinguishing the small, absence enkindled the great. Love was a raging forest fire by the time Pentecost came. No wonder tongues of fire appeared on their heads! We can look at this as a simple miracle, but that fails to reach the point of realizing what power we are talking about, the power of love that came to its peak and its focus at Pentecost.

"Absence is to love what wind is to fire." Many of us fall away from the Lord, and we get farther and farther away until we really feel there is a huge gulf between our Lord and us. Then suddenly something happens, and that fire suddenly overwhelms us. We have anew what some people call a new conversion experience. We are reborn. Our faith has a new surge of vitality. That absence from the Lord, though it was not truly an absence, is like a breeze fanning the flames in that relationship.

"Absence is to love what wind is to fire." Pentecost reminds us of the importance of the Holy Spirit in our lives, but that Holy Spirit is always with us. Many of us are afraid to let the fire of the Holy Spirit fill us. We see the tremendous power there, and we want to be in control of ourselves at all times. We are afraid to turn that control over to the Holy Spirit. When we turn our control over to God, we have far more freedom and far more control over what goes on in our lives. Most of us have a batting average of about .250 with regard to our faith, and we have many strikeouts behind us. Praise God, the Holy Spirit is there, and when we need to, we can hit a home run. Our faith can transform us into the people that God intended us to be.

Faith Fuel

Marching Orders

When I was in the Cub Scouts, my family went to Yosemite the first time. My parents bought me a Kodak *Brownie Hawkeye* camera, and soon I was an avid amateur photographer. When someone offered to finance a trip to the Holy Land for me, I bought my first camera with interchangeable lenses. One of those lenses was a wide-angle lens, and for some reason it became my favorite. A few years later, I was part of a monthly color slide competition, and most of the slides I submitted that received winning ribbons were taken with that wide-angle lens.

As I look back, it appears that looking through the wide-angle lens affected how I see all of life. Most people see their lives on an hour-by-hour or day-by-day basis, but I tend to see things more broadly, seeing our country's progress in terms of decades, and seeing the larger church in terms of centuries. When I was a younger adult, I looked at my professional and spiritual life in terms of 3-5 year blocks of time. It has been a little over a half century since I accepted Christ and was baptized. It is amazing at how patient God has been with me. It has been necessary to seek forgiveness for many things. God's grace and mercy are amazing. I hope that I keep growing and improving.

God has called me to a challenging and fulfilling profession. Now I am doing more writing. Most of all, God has given me a heart for Him and for His Son Jesus. His final marching orders are in Matthew 28:19-20: "Go therefore and make disciples of all the nations, baptizing them in the name of the Father and of the Son and of the Holy Spirit, teaching them to observe all things that I have commanded you; and lo, I am with you always, even to the end of the age." These are our marching orders too!

133
Watching
Each one of us that walks this earth finds brilliant times we love.
We see our lives so clearly strong and blessed by God above.
At first we stop with awe and thanks, but then proceed with zest.
Inspired, there's nothing small or great that keeps us from our best.

Faith Fuel

At other times our way seems dark—we strive to keep awake.
Our zest's been tapped, our best's been tried
—no path seems ours to take.
Our ears are pricked, our eyes are focused out beyond our scope.
Our watching's ache's just bearable with faith that's fueled with hope.

Our watching's painful when we wait as loved ones fade and die.
Our watching's painful when the truth is scorned with someone's lie.
Our watching's mad when scheming foes don't care what conflict costs.
Our watching's sad when dreams are dashed
or when our love's been lost.

Some watching's easy on the eyes, when beauty comes our way.
Some watching's fun when laughter fills another fertile day.
Some watching's entertainment as we root for favorite teams.
Some watching's preparation for a quest to fill our dreams.

We watch because we're human, and
we've learned that patience pays.
It's not enough to wait and hope—we watch for better days.
We watch because instinctively we know that God's above.
We watch because our world's a gift
that's wrapped with grace and love.

Following the Spirit's Leading

I began thinking one day about one of my former professors from seminary. He was a truly brilliant man named Jack Suggs. During my Master of Divinity program, he was Dr. Suggs to me, but I did not take any classes from him. During the last year of my Doctor of Ministry Degree program, he announced to all of us that from then on we should feel comfortable being on a first name basis with our professors. We were scholastic *equals*. That statement was an unexpected gift! It really felt good!

The full impact of that change in status took place gradually. Two years later, I took a tour of the Holy Land with Gentry Shelton and Jack Stewart. Gentry Shelton had been my professor of Christian Education, and Jack Stewart had been my professor of Old Testament. Jack Suggs was to have gone with us, but two months before we left, Jack Suggs became acting dean after Dean Elmer Henson went on to the larger life.

133

Faith Fuel

After graduation, I attended TCU/Ministers week each February. The lectures were superb, and the music was truly memorable. The best part however was seeing old friends, particularly Jack Suggs. On one memorable Tuesday, Jack and I had lunch together in the basement of the seminary. We were talking about how we had gotten to know one another more closely during my doctoral studies. I remembered one particular statement he had made. He said, "You're the first man I have ever known to take advantage of Jesus' statements in Matthew to teach discipleship. I think you're a closet pietist." At that luncheon several years later, I asked him why he had given me that label. Jack said, "I do not remember saying that, but I probably said it because I am a pietist myself." Jack? A pietist?

For those not familiar with the term, a pietist is a person whose life is centered on Bible study and personal religious experience. More simply, a pietist is a person who lives life as a devotional experience. The maximum pursuit of pietism leads to a monastic life of devotion and prayer in a retreat setting like a monastery. Most pietists lead a more normal life, at least by outward appearances.

In his prime, Jack was considered one of the world's foremost experts in the gospels of Matthew, Mark, and Luke. When Jack identified himself as a pietist, I realized that while in that theologically liberal seminary setting, he was not a liberal. Most people did not know it. Jack was a rather orthodox man who loved Jesus as much as anyone I have ever known.

Several years later, some of the mainline denominations encouraged their leaders to pursue spiritual renewal, hoping that this would reverse the decline of the numbers in their ranks. I participated in a spiritual retreat at Bethany College in West Virginia. It was a profoundly moving experience. As time went on, it became evident that the denominational leaders wanted the Holy Spirit to conform to their agenda. You guessed it. It did not happen. The program floundered and died. Jack would have said, "Of course!" It is essential that we truly want God to set the agenda. We have to be willing to let God be God, and to let Jesus be our King. We have to be truly willing to go wherever the Holy Spirit leads us.

Lectio Divina

"He who has ears to hear, let him hear!" The gospels of Matthew, Mark, and Luke, quote Jesus as saying these words on several occasions. This is an excellent reminder that long before our scriptures became words written and read, these same words were spoken and heard. These words were first spoken by those actually participating in God's activity and experiencing God's revelation. Simply put, before God's revelation became written in The Bible, it was experienced and reported.

This is incredibly important! While Jesus lived and moved among us, the Torah, the Prophets, and the Writings of the Old Testament were simply words on scrolls that were analyzed and interpreted. The scriptures had become lifeless documents to those who tried to live by them. The words in the books had become separated from the Holy Spirit that had propelled them into existence. The Holy was not being experienced by those who read and heard God's Word. Jesus came upon the scene and turned that world upside down!

In the tenth chapter of Luke's gospel, a lawyer asks Jesus about the requirements to obtain eternal life. The lawyer wants to discuss the subject scripturally. He even tells Jesus what he thinks is the answer. Wanting to push Jesus further, he asks Jesus to define the term *neighbor*. The lawyer is accustomed to debating the scriptures in this manner. Jesus sidesteps the lawyer by telling the Parable of the Good Samaritan. Then Jesus asks the lawyer which man in the parable was a neighbor. The lawyer wanted a sterile academic answer, but Jesus gave the question life by making the answer a life application. Then as now, there are three ways we can approach scripture.

A scholar's work is to glean as much information as possible out of the material available. Approaching scriptures as a scholar means analyzing the words, grammar, and historical context, and then reporting the results for others to ponder. This kind of work tends to reduce the scriptures to words on a page. The Bible gives us all kinds of information we can use, but it does not always give us the information we seek.

When we read the Bible for inspiration, we are not really looking for information. We are looking for emotional and spiritual support. In Bible times, men frequently recited favorite scriptures as touch points in their daily living. The same is true today, and there is a large industry of devotional materials centered upon this approach to the Bible.

Still another way is to approach the Bible for transformation. This approach is called *lectio divina*. If the Bible is read, not for information or inspiration, but read for its own sake, the Bible gradually changes the person reading it. Because the Bible has its own agenda, the person reading it begins to see life differently. Such people become more positive, peaceful, and joyful. They also become more productive.

Faith Fuel

Life becomes fuller, deeper, and more satisfying. The simple reason is that the Bible can lead us to a place where we stop living just for ourselves. Those transformed by the Bible have a larger sense of purpose and direction. All that God does, God does well!

Transitions

Springtime is the season of graduations. There is a sense of things being final or finished. There are celebrations of accomplishments. For many there is a sense of wonder about the future, but most see the season in terms of endings–the ending of the school year in particular. Very few people stop to think of all of this as being a time of transition. As Moses led the people of God out of Egypt, we can be sure that most of them were saying to themselves and each other, "Free at last!" They were leaving their lifetime homes to follow a God that seemed new to them. They were finally out from under the yoke of Egyptian slavery. They hoped that this Moses they were following knew what He was doing.

Picture a scene hundreds of years later, when Jesus rose from the grave: "Free at last!" We can almost hear Him say it. When astronauts return to Earth after a sojourn in space, we can imagine them saying to themselves, "Home at last!" We can only wonder what goes through the minds of those on Air Force One, when it touches down on our American soil after a trip overseas.

What if we take each one of these endings and look at them as transitions? Graduation from high school becomes a transition from childhood to adulthood. The exodus becomes a transition from slavery to great adventure and miracles. Jesus' resurrection becomes a transition from Earth-bound life unto life eternal. The ends of journeys on Earth become transitions to new challenges and new adventures.

When I graduated from high school, I had hoped to earn a good living after four years of college. After five and a half years, I was looking forward to a career of teaching music. God had another idea. After three years of seminary, I thought I was finished with education at last. God then led me to get a doctorate in Theology and Pastoral Counseling. Was I done? Heavens no! A decade later, I was getting training to be a consultant in church growth and evangelism. It was also the time when God began using the scriptures to transform me. One could easily argue that all of life is a series of transitions until we make that final transition to eternal life with God.

136

Faith Fuel

Every moment of our lives, no matter how precious, is unique and will not be repeated. Every day is a gift of God's grace to be savored and fulfilled. Yes, for everything, there is a season, and each season stands on its own. The constant between this life and the next is our spirit. This is why our spiritual development is so important. One of the reasons I can never fully retire is because I want my spiritual life to constantly develop and grow. I do not want to stand on the past. When I preach and teach, I want to be always directed by the Holy Spirit, so that my spirit can grow with those of others. God keeps surprising me with things to share in worship that I cannot imagine on my own. The life of serving God is exciting. I would not have it any other way.

Flags of Faith

Sunday, June 14, is designated as "Flag Day" by the United States government. The intention of course is to honor "Old Glory," the 50-star American flag. When I first entered seminary in 1970, I made the conscious decision never to mix religion and politics. I designated my voter registration in Texas as Non-Partisan, and I have been politically non-partisan ever since. In terms of faith and practice however, I am extremely partisan. My Master, best friend, and constant companion is Jesus.

Because of this, if I choose to talk about Flag Day, I will not discuss any kind of political flag. The Christian Flag was first conceived in 1897 by Charles Overton, when he was forced to give an impromptu lecture in place of a scheduled speaker. Overton saw a flag of the United States, and drawing on the flag for inspiration, he gave a speech asking the students what a flag representing Christianity would look like. In 1907, he and Ralph Diffendorfer, secretary of the Methodist Young People's Missionary Movement, designed and began promoting a flag. Currently it is accepted by most Protestants in North America, Latin America, and Africa. The red cross in the upper left represents Christ's blood, the blue box that contains it represents His royalty, and the white of the flag represents His purity. Roman Catholics do not have a flag as such, but if occasion arises, the Vatican Flag is used. It is technically the "national" flag of Vatican City, an independent nation within Rome, Italy. The Pope is the Chief of State.

The Anglican Communion is an international association of Anglican Churches. It is a loose association that looks to the Church of England as its "mother" church. Currently, Anglican Churches tend to

137

be evangelical or conservative. The exceptions are the Episcopal Churches of the United States, which tend to be very liberal, and the Church of England, which tends to be moderate. The Copts of Egypt, along with a few Coptic Churches in other countries, fly the Coptic Flag. They have fairly close ties to the Roman Catholic Church, but their history is not closely tied to either the Roman Catholics or the Eastern Orthodox churches.

The Eastern Orthodox Church is the second largest Christian communion in the world. The Church is composed of numerous self-governing church bodies, each geographically and nationally distinct but theologically unified. Each self-governing body is shepherded by a Synod of independent bishops whose duty is, among other things, to preserve and teach their Church practices. If they fly a flag, it is that of the Ecumenical Patriarch in Constantinople (Istanbul), Turkey. He is roughly equivalent to the Pope of the Roman Catholic Church in the symbolic sense.

Each of these flags is a symbol of allegiance. There are a handful of pledges of allegiance used by churches towards the Christian flag. For example:

> I pledge allegiance to the Christian flag
> and to the Savior for whose kingdom it
> stands; one brotherhood, uniting all
> Christians in service and in love.

How strong is your allegiance to Christ and His church?

Prayer Warriors

There is so much for which to pray! It has often been pointed out that peace is not simply the absence of war. Today's newspaper provides us with so much information about war in the Middle East. We are caught up in the tragedy and the horror of it all. In the midst of all of this, it is easy to lose sight of the wars going on at home. These are wars on a different scale but not on a smaller scale.

The Christian warfare against evil of all kinds goes on throughout the world. The problem is not that we shift our prayers to the women and men in the Middle East, but it is rather a matter of adding many more to our prayer lists that may not have been there previously. In fact, the women and men of the armed forces need our prayers even when they are not facing a crisis. We are just now aware of their need because of our own sensitivities with regard to war.

138

Faith Fuel

Must we face war to be reminded to pray for those who defend us? Must we face sickness to pray for those in the healing professions? Must we see pictures of starving children in order to prick our consciences to the point of wanting to give to organized compassion efforts?

Must we be confronted with injustice that we may work and pray for peace with justice? Must we be confronted with hatred and violence that we may work and pray for love, mercy, compassion, and understanding? Must a church be confronted with the possibility of death before it can desire to do evangelism?

Just as surely as evil finds ways to disguise itself, when evil is discovered it has a way of distorting our values and ruining our perspective. In the story of the Garden of Eden, evil in its obvious form was disobedience. The story also tells us that Eve and Adam were tricked into not trusting God, God's decisions, or God's motives. Evil tricked them into trusting in their own logic rather than in the Divine Will. Their story continues to be our story, whether we like it or not. Hunger, injustice, and war continue to be the by-products of our own folly.

In the midst of all of this is the living Christ, who in stark reality has been through all that we have been through, and through all that, we will ever face—including death. We have a guide through the pitfalls of our world. We have a voice we can listen to, when our frail logic always seems to get us into more trouble. Those of us who walk with the living Christ have much to share with those who suffer from hungers, injustices, and Sin of all kinds. Compassion demands that we share.

The Gift of Singularity

Throughout a large segment of Christianity, the laity assumes that their clergy will remain celibate throughout their lives. Sometimes there are scandals with regard to the relationships between priests and nuns, and at other times, there are simply whispers about a priest that has "gotten out of line." There is a powerful movement among the priests in the United States these days to abolish the celibacy requirement, and there is strong support in the midst of the laity.

Throughout Christian history, there has been strong support for those who have given up the privileges of matrimony and parenthood for the sake of Christ and Christ's church. That support however is almost totally absent among Protestants. Protestants in the United

Faith Fuel

States often grudgingly admit to their clergy's "right" not to marry. In precise opposition to Roman Catholics, however, there is widespread "feeling" that clergy cannot fully minister to all of the needs of families without being married. Roman Catholics often "feel" that marriage impedes one's ability fully to minister to families.

A small percentage of Roman Catholic clergy are indeed married, and their bishops find extreme difficulty in placing these priests in a parish setting. While approximately 20% of Protestant clergy are not married, it is also true that those who try to place them in a parish setting often have difficulty.

All of this represents a very dangerous type of vicious prejudice. One could even go so far as to call this kind of thinking a subtle form of bigotry. For lack of a better term, it can be called "The Pigeonhole Effect." Let us label it as a disease in this case and call it "PHE."

A person applying for a job can be a victim of PHE. If the applicant is wearing a red dress for the interview, and the person doing the interview had a fight with a person in a red dress a short time before, the job applicant may unintentionally make a bad impression because of PHE.

A young mortician may have difficulty getting a date with the woman he wants because of PHE. Certain motorists will get pulled over on the highway on "suspicion" because of PHE. Physicians may not admit to their occupations in certain public gatherings because of PHE.

The effects of PHE can even be more insidious. The children of violent or alcoholic parents have a very strong tendency to marry someone like their worst parent. "Pigeonholes" are often very comfortable because they are a known quantity. Unconsciously we seek someone whose behavior we can predict, even when those predictions are very negative, rather than seeking someone who is a totally unknown quantity.

There is hope! All of us have a tendency to place people in pigeonholes–judging them by our assumptions rather than by experience. In Christ, there is the way to avoid all of that. In Christ, there is the possibility to find forgiveness, to find redemption, and to begin again.

Faith Fuel

Good Intentions

It has been said by many a theologian that we should be careful about what we pray for because we may just get it. On another level, we often talk with zeal about things that we would like to have when in truth we are not prepared for the consequences that come with getting what we want. Countless stories have been told to illustrate this basic idea, but let us look at an illustration out of the changing life of many churches.

There once was a church that was truly blessed. Early in its history, it had received a large sum of money for its business district property. A large new facility was built out beyond the business area of town, modeled after a cathedral in another country. The church had several periods of good growth, and during one of those periods it even help found another congregation in a nearby community. Like so many well-established churches, the congregation began to see itself as an institution, and consequently it lost its sense of movement and sense of mission. In the early years of the decline of this church, they were not at all concerned because they had always recovered before. As the decline of their numbers became serious, they began to think in terms of survival. They began asking some destructive questions. What must we do to survive? What must we do to attract young couples? How can we build a youth program so as to have a future for this church? How can we get more people to come so as to have the money to pay our bills?

All of these questions were logical and business-like, but they were among the most destructive questions a church can ask. They failed to remember that although the church uses business principles, the church is not a business. They were thinking in terms of survival as an institution rather than thinking in terms of their loss of movement. They were thinking in terms of nurturing what was already established. They were not thinking in terms of the mission to which God had called them. They were unwilling to risk their life as an institution for the sake of those who needed the church as much as they did.

They told their pastor how much they wanted to grow. They indicated a willingness to do what was necessary to achieve their goal. As their pastor began to lead them into a life of evangelism, they began to realize what would happen when they began to get results. They began to realize that as they grew, the old members would lose much of their power and control over "their" church. They told their pastor what they wanted, they praised him for what he was doing, and then

141

later they criticized him for having done what they wanted. As they continued to struggle for money to keep themselves going, they told their pastor that if he "would just cut out this evangelism nonsense" that everyone would get along a lot better.

The saddest part of this story is that those who were being critical were a very small minority. Even though many of them have now moved to other churches hoping to find more people who will agree with them, the church that they have left behind is succumbing to this tyranny of the few. Behind the scenes, there is a happy ending to all of this. Even though that congregation will probably cease to exist soon, the church of Jesus Christ will continue and thrive. The church is much bigger than its people, whether the group is large or small. The congregations that are happiest and healthiest are those whose people have the humility to recognize whose they are.

No Worries!

Think about all of your mistakes made in the past and say, "What, me worry?" Think of all of the problems that you face in the present and say, "What, me worry?" Contemplate the best and worst possibilities of your future and say, "What, me worry?" That does not mean becoming like *Mad Magazine*'s leader, Alfred E. Newman. It does mean Christians can say this in obedience to Christ.

We admire those of robust faith who put all their sins and problems in God's hands and refuse to worry. We sometimes shudder when people refuse to consider dangerous possibilities and insist that they will take things as they come. We wonder about the sanity of those who say they do not care what happens to them so long as they are happy right now. Yet there is a common thread of logic in all of these attitudes. These people are all different in the ways that they care and handle fear.

When we stop caring we stop loving, and we also stop living—we merely exist. People of robust faith care most of all about their relationship with God. They do whatever is necessary to please God, to nurture that relationship, and to trust God completely. Their fear of failing to maintain that relationship overshadows any other fear.

People who take things as they come have rational fears but control them in favor of enjoying life to the fullest. They care about the relationship they have with life itself and place their trust in themselves.

142

Faith Fuel

The people who say, "I do not care so long as I am happy" also trust only themselves. They are afraid of getting involved with life and trust no one.

Faith in God means more than trusting in God's ability to achieve God's will and our dreams. Faith is trusting God enough to know that God will do it. Whom do you trust?

Cheap Grace Sometimes Isn't

When Christians are truly Christian, what they do very well is care. One of the most important ingredients of caring is listening, but it is important to hear as well as listen. Jesus often remarked that those who have the ears to listen should hear.

An unknown author said: "James Shott and John Nott fought a duel. Nott was shot, and Shott was not. In this case, it was better to be Shott than Nott. There was a rumor that Nott was not shot, but Shott himself insists that he was not shot. It may be that the shot Shott shot shot Nott, but the shot that Nott shot shot not Shott."

Trying to read this aloud can bring a chuckle or two, but it is easy to become both careless and uncaring when we talk with one another.

Parents tell of children who "understand" what they want to hear by "filling in the gaps" with their own logic. When the hearing impaired do not hear all that a person is saying, their natural tendency is to "fill in the gaps" with their own logic. They do this because they want to avoid the embarrassment of admitting that they did not hear everything that was said. The result is sometimes humorous. Tragically, however, the result often is painful for the person wanting to be understood.

The same principles apply to children who are the losers in a classroom vote. It is at best insensitive (and often boorish) for them not to hear, to accept and to support the results of a democratic vote. Some of these children grouse for months about "the way it should have been done"–often sowing the seeds of doubt with rumors like the one in the quote. They did not hear the majority when they lost the vote. These children use their egocentric logic to "fill in the gaps" of their loss. There is tremendous pain and suffering brought to the other children who are trying to move ahead into the future, by these losers grumbling about not getting their way.

143

In any case, it is very insensitive and uncaring to assume that we must be excused for our behavior. We should not demand to be excused because we are old, hard of hearing, or the loser of a vote, any more than because we are young, a gossip, or lacking in social graces. It is not a matter of making excuses but humbly accepting ourselves for what we are and accepting the path of those we love. That is the loving way. That is the caring way. That is the Christian way.

It's Personal

I had an uncle who was a chaplain during World War II. He was highly intelligent and artistically talented. While pastor of a church in California, he let college age men pose for him for a series of pastel portraits of Christ and the Apostles. Gossip forced him to leave the pastoral ministry for a time, but he loved his Lord so much he returned several years later, having changed denominations. He acquired Parkinson's disease before there were drugs to treat it, forcing him once again to leave the parish ministry. He went into real estate in a lovely community, but the disease took its toll. He went on to be with his Lord before ever completing the series of portraits.

I was privileged to have that portrait of Christ hanging in my home or office for a long time. Each time I looked at it, I had mixed feelings. On the one hand, I remembered the joy that filled my uncle throughout most of his life. For him, Christianity was a religion of joy and laughter. His oldest daughter had a tendency to see most vividly the darker side of the church–its problems and its struggles. In the course of her growing up, somehow she missed the most crucial point about the Christian faith. She failed to get into her heart the idea that Christianity is different because it involves a personal relationship with Jesus Christ.

A continuing wonder for me as a pastor is the number of people that share my cousin's mistake. It is amazing how many people both inside and outside the church has missed this most important point. My cousin does not even want to sing hymns about Jesus. She says she and God get along just fine, without confusing things with talk about Jesus.

The temple leaders in Jesus' time made the same mistake. In their eyes, they knew how to live because they had the Torah–the law. When they could not find happiness in their living, they did one of two things. They sometimes sat down and worked out a logical explanation

144

based upon their own interpretation of the way they saw things. When that did not work, they sought temporary pleasures to take their mind off their troubles.

People in the church who are like these follow similar patterns. If things are not going well, sometimes they blame the pastor. The vast majority of pastoral changes happen because a minority looks for a scapegoat. If the pastor is too popular to be vulnerable to such nonsense, the next most popular target is the monthly financial report. Those with feeble faith often blame spending patterns on the church's trouble—even when their logic is obviously faulty to everyone else.

For those who do not have an intimate and vital relationship with Jesus, their ultimate cry for help with their pain is to say, "Let us give up!" They honestly believe that if everyone else will go along with them and give up the ship, everything will work out just fine. Wilbur Rees said it best in his little book, *$3.00 Worth of God*. "I'll take that plastic Christ, please. No! No! Not the flesh and blood one! He is a dirty little Jew that smells of the barn…."

Does this sound like anyone you know?

Saying Yes to Jesus

I like the line art graphic that shows a cross rising out of the Bible. Some people speak of finding Jesus in the Bible. I think to be more precise we can say that Jesus rises above the Bible. It is my understanding from scriptures that God always wants to say yes to us. Jesus seems to communicate so clearly that God wants to bless us. More than one theologian has said that God can be spoken of as "The Eternal Yes." God is the embodiment of all that is good, positive, and affirmative.

The Bible does not explain why there is evil in the world. We do know however that there is evil in the midst of God's creation. We are creatures of God. We are created in the image of God. Unlike God, however, our lives are not always good, positive, and affirmative. We are sinners. Unlike God, "The Eternal Yes," we are "Yes/No" creatures. We make choices, and consequently we make mistakes.

We cannot avoid making mistakes by always saying no, anymore than we can by always saying yes. We are living in the midst

Faith Fuel

of the "me" generation. It is easy to make decisions based upon what is good for ourselves alone. It is also easy to make decisions based upon what we believe is right in our own eyes. Jesus tells us that there is a better way. He gives us a better way–the only way that is ultimately and consistently right. Jesus says that we are to base our decisions upon God's will, rather than upon our won consciences.

When we become Christians, we cannot stop making decisions. Unlike other people, however, our decision-making is not based upon "ought," "must," or "should." Jesus said, "If you love me you will keep my commandments." He did not say, "If you do not do what I tell you, you will go to hell!" That is what the scribes and Pharisees were saying.

To put it another way, being a Christian is not a matter of saying "yes" to blessings and "no" to sins. Being a Christian is simply saying "yes" to Jesus. When we surrender our will and our pride to Jesus, He becomes Lord of our lives. When Jesus is Lord of our lives, we have the power to say "No" as well as the power to say "Yes." The difference is in the consequences of our decisions.

Jesus does not expect us to say "Yes" to everyone who asks for our help, to everyone who asks us to give, or to everyone who demands that we "be more Christ-like." Neither does Jesus expect us to say "No" every time we think we have to–or even to say "No" to everything that we think might possibly be sinful! When we are in Christ we are given the power to say "Yes" in His name, and we are given the power to say "No" in His name.

Out in that secular world of ours there are many temptations to say "yes" to things we should not. The same is true within the church. Just because the church asks us to do something, it does not mean that we are obligated. We need to consider well questions of the availability of time, resources, and God given ability. Out in that secular world of ours there are many temptations to say "no" to things that we do not want to do that should be done. The same is true within the church. Once again, we need to consider well the questions as above– whether we have the time and resources, and whether God has given us the ability. God shows us His will for our lives when God gives us the ability to do a task within a window of opportunity.

Whenever a church faces the possibilities of another year of ministry to its community, each member of a congregation must face some basic questions: Does your life truly reflect the fact that I have said "Yes" to Jesus Christ? What abilities, large or small, do you have right now that can be used by His church? What abilities, no longer mine, can you help others find within themselves? How can you best affirm and encourage your sisters and brothers in Christ? What is your "call?"

Be a Child

Jesus told his disciples that unless they became like children they could not enter the kingdom of heaven. Like so much of the truth that Jesus preached, this saying that has been passed down to us is like a double-edged sword–it cuts both ways. On the surface, Jesus seemed to be talking about the innocence found in children. A truth cutting in the same direction says we need to approach life with a child's sense of simplicity.

When this simple truth of Jesus cuts in the other direction, we have to abandon our seriousness! This other side of the truth is identified by a child's sense of joy and fun! Accepting Christ as our Savior is a serious decision. That decision however should not bind us into somber slavery or legalistic fundamentalism. Rather, being in Christ should set us free into fun and a child-like joy!

Picture this: Jesus is as near to you as your next breath. In your prayers, you are pouring out your soul in serious contemplation of the suffering around you and your own personal suffering. You are saying to Jesus, "Look here! Do not you see how we are suffering? Cannot you do something about this? It looks like you are not going to do anything about our suffering right now! Will not you just SAY something–will not you just give me some word out of your experience that will help me through this?"

We can imagine Jesus saying, "Lighten up! I am suffering with you! You know that! You also know that I am with you! Supporting you! Encouraging you! I am helping you to see beyond your current suffering to the wonders around you and the glory that will be revealed to you! This current situation may not be fun, but you can still have My joy!"

Dreams and Visions

A natural part of childhood is dreaming. Children do not usually remember nightmares, but sometimes they remember other dreams. The dreams children remember the most easily are daydreams. During those innocent years, we feel free to dream truly big dreams, but as we get older, we get inhibited.

When I was in high school, my favorite teacher had a quotation on the bulletin board which he attributed to Teddy Roosevelt: "Far better is it to dare mighty things, to win glorious triumphs even though checkered with failure, than to take rank with those poor souls who neither enjoy much nor suffer much–but live in that cold gray twilight that knows not victory nor defeat!"

The prophet Joel spoke of old men dreaming dreams in the final days. Zechariah had a dream about John the Baptist. Pilate's wife had a dream about Jesus when Our Lord stood accused before her husband. A responsible Christian adult must not be afraid to dream. Indeed, dreams are legitimate forms of prophecy when those dreams are provided by God. It is important not to be a false prophet–pushing our dreams for the church when the dreams are not provided by God!

How can we know that our dream comes from God? First, we should examine the worthiness of the dream. Would it bring out the best in the people involved? Is it inspiring? Would it help hurting people or fulfill the needs of deprived people? Is it in keeping with God's will?

Can the potential results be clearly seen? God does not provide us with vague goals of faintly possible results! Are you determined to fulfill God's dream for you? Are you willing to put the fulfillment of this dream ahead of literally everything else in your life? Are you willing to sacrifice other goals and commitments for the sake of Christ's church?

Spreading the Word

In recent years, the word *evangelism* has gotten a bad reputation. The word simply means, "sharing the Good News." When most people today hear the word evangelism today, they think of the confrontational model, where the evangelist confronts the person needing conversion with the Gospel. That confrontation may be low-key or high pressure. The confrontation may be one to one or to a group. It may take the form of personal witness, Bible quotation, or both. It may be in the context of worship or in the context of everyday living. In any case, the person who has not been saved is confronted with the Gospel and challenged to turn over his or her life to Jesus Christ. Under some circumstances, this model of evangelism is still valid, and it may be the only way to get through to some people.

148

Faith Fuel

The second model of evangelism is called lifestyle evangelism, which has been advocated since World War II by many churches in North America. In a climate where the church is seen as vital to the life of the community by church members and nonmembers alike, this model of witnessing by our lifestyle has some degree of success. As churches have experienced a diminishing role in the eyes of the community, those churches following this model have been shrinking.

The third model of evangelism has several names, the most common being 'discipling' evangelism. It is currently achieving the greatest success in western culture. It eliminates the less attractive features of the first two models while keeping the best. Church members disciple non-members simply by inviting people to share in what you enjoy about the church, making them feel like a welcome part of your life in the church community. The Holy Spirit does the witnessing, confronting, and converting. It works! We plant, the church waters, and God gives the growth! Evangelism means sowing the seed of the Good News (inviting), that the church can water (welcome), so that God will bring a harvest (growth in spirit and ministry).

Being Really Free

"For freedom Christ has set us free . . . ." That statement marks the beginning of the fifth chapter of the Apostle Paul's letter to the people of Galatia. He writes about the responsible use of freedom. On the Sunday prior to the Fourth of July in the United States, many churches observe "Freedom Sunday." They casually do a bit of mixing of church and state. Freedom is a Biblical issue!

In a sermon preached in February of 1970, Fred Craddock made a statement about freedom that is burned into my memory: "To be free one must of course have alternatives; but to be really free, one must be able to continue to function in the face of those alternatives, without being frozen by choices."

Since Christ sets us free, we always have alternatives. When we really know Christ, we never have trouble making the right choices. The right choice might be painful however. Religion and politics are the two most volatile subjects in the human vocabulary. Mixing these two subjects involves great risks. It is not a good idea to mix politics and religion without recognizing those risks. A Christian must speak out on moral and ethical issues when those issues become political. It is important to maintain one's moral and ethical stance without being swayed by politics.

149

Faith Fuel

One basic problem all governments face is that leaders tend to shy away from hard moral and ethical choices. They choose instead the choices that are politically expedient. Interest groups and lobbies compound the problem. It used to be said that we cannot legislate morality, but the history of the civil rights movement shows that legislation can certainly help. One has to be willing to endure the pain of enforcement however.

Trust and Peace

One of the more popular movements in recent years is the concept of "pulling your own strings. It is by no means a new idea, but in this increasingly troubled world of ours, people are trusting less in outside authority and more on themselves. It is a major theme of the 'me' generation. People are becoming more and more self-centered, as they think they cannot trust anyone but themselves for decisions. It is pathetic to see people fearful of the wisdom of others. It is also an extremely difficult habit to break. The saddest thing of all is, without trust there is no real peace.

Many people tell their pastor that trusting in God completely is a real challenge. In fact, many people talk about trusting God, but most put rather severe limits on how much they trust God. I was very moved several years ago to hear author Käaren Witte speak of promises and possibilities. She spoke of trusting God to keep God's promises, and of trusting God to bring us the most exciting possibilities. She issued some very real challenges. What can happen when we trust God that way? How do we respond to that challenge to trust?

I like to be in control of a situation. I am willing to accept responsibility for my own actions, and partly for the actions of those around me. With more experience, I have been putting more trust in the leading of the Holy Spirit. I experienced more than a little fear with doing it at first, but gradually that fear has turned into excitement. I can hardly wait to see where the Lord is going to lead me. Try it! You will like it! It is fun!

Spectators

A well-known Christian thinker and writer expressed the idea few years ago that too many people go to church. On any given

150

Faith Fuel

Sunday in any typical worship setting, he said too many people sit in the audience. The man who expressed these unusual ideas was by no means a heretic. He was Elton Trueblood. Admittedly, I am quoting him out of context in order to get your attention! Sometimes the words we use do not communicate what we intend to say. Sometimes our words betray a hidden truth that we are reluctant to admit.

We speak of going to a game, a concert, or a play, and when we do, we have a particular function in mind for ourselves at these events. With our attendance and our applause, we express our support for these performances. We function as spectators. We offer our cheers or jeers. In the same way, we say, "I go to such-and-such church." We do not often hear people say, "I worship at such-and-such-church." We do not often hear, "I am learning to minister to people in the name of Jesus Christ at such-and-such church." Remember, Jesus did not say, "Go and watch the priests do the work of God." Jesus did say, "Take my yoke upon you and learn of me...."

When at worship, it is important that we be not just in the audience, but rather communing with God. Our worship does not consist of listening to prayers, scriptures, and sermons. We are not to simply go to church. We are to take His Yoke, tend His sheep, take up our cross, and follow Him.

Being a Christian means more than going to church on Sunday, more than supporting a particular congregation with money, time, and talent. Being a follower of Jesus Christ means being a minister in common life, meeting the needs of our sisters and brothers everywhere.

Losing Our Bearings

When large numbers of people gather, individuals often act differently than they do otherwise. Inhibitions are relaxed at least somewhat. Inhibitions are also relaxed when we are far from our usual environment. Away from "home" in a new environment, interacting with people in a new context, people's behavior can be and often is a bit crazy. Our behavior changes in a change of environment.

When I was working for Disneyland, I observed a tendency for people to lose track of their basic points of reference. Adults get lost at Disneyland and Disney World far more easily than do the children. At Disneyland, there is a place for lost parents to go, so that their children can find them. I was taking tickets at a turnstile once, when the Disneyland operator began paging a doctor to take an emergency call.

151

Faith Fuel

I had a long line waiting to get in to the ride. Suddenly, a man I had been talking to for more than ten minutes looked up at the speaker in the tree above his head. "May I borrow your phone? I think I heard the Disneyland operator paging me." She had been paging that doctor's name for nearly ten minutes!

During large gatherings, there are sometimes giant video screens on either side of the stage so that all can see what is going on. Sometimes cameras pan the audience. When people see themselves on the video screens, they often scream, yell, and wave at the camera, even if they make fools of themselves. They are in a new environment, regular points of reference are lost, and these people lose some of the inhibitions they might otherwise have.

Too often, our "church" speech and behavior patterns are limited to Sundays. Outside of the church environment, religious points of reference are lost, and inhibitions often take over. A person's faith grows remarkably, when the faith and witness of their Sundays wash over into the rest of the week!

Models

While we often think of models as people employed to display clothing or other merchandise, the term model has much greater meanings. In the most critical sense, model applies to someone or something that is worthy of imitation. The person could be a model to be imitated, or they can serve as a reference to be avoided. A model could point to the best in behavior or the worst.

Today's models, even the so-called supermodels, are seen by their employers as little more than animated mannequins, serving as clothes racks. They work very hard. Unfortunately, they are often models only in that very limited sense. Behind the scenes, their egos are often out of control, and their lives are distorted to near destruction by the fame and attention they seek. They seldom serve as examples that the rest of us should emulate.

Celebrities in the past were often models in the much larger sense. They were heroes. Their lives stood out as those to be admired. In today's world, we do not have a shortage of heroes, but a shortage of journalists who are willing to tell the stories of those real heroes. The stories that put food on media's tables are those that tell of people who stumble and fall. Journalists are all too seldom attracted to stories of people who pick themselves up after they fall. They seldom tell stories of those who rise up from the rubble. Tarnished lives are more

152

newsworthy than burnished heroes are. God sees differently. God redeems tarnished lives that are willing to submit to His polishing influence.

Jesus is the greatest hero of all, but giving God bad press gets more attention. It is easy to call disasters "acts of God." It is easy to label a miracle as "good luck." It is harder to put those events into more appropriate and larger perspective. Asking ourselves what God is doing in our lives—and trying to do what Jesus would do—keeps all of that bad press in perspective. God is tougher than bad press!

The next time you see a celebrity in the news, ask yourself how God sees that person. Ask yourself what mighty works God might do in that life if that person was willing to let God be God and to let Christ be King. God can and does do great things in our lives. All things are possible because our hero, Jesus Christ, strengthens us.

Important Foolishness

The Holy Spirit empowers our prayer life. Sometimes we get unexpectedly positive results. Although I have witnessed miracles countless times, I seldom pray as though I am expecting a miracle. Sometimes, hours after I have prayed with someone I see that I had a missed opportunity. We do not pray as though expecting a miracle very often. It is not because God is not prompting me to tap into His Holy Power. As the son of a scientist, I used to be skeptical of the power that I knew was available to me. That knowledge was not in my heart, but just in my head.

When studying Acts, we are constantly struck with comparisons between the first century churches and our own in the 21st century. It is instructive to compare our prayer life today with that of the early church. A few years ago, I wrote a poem about prayer that expresses part of my struggle.

Prayer

A scientific age proclaims the foolishness of prayer.
The media just lusts for facts and people's points of view.
We live our lives with stumbling steps and struggle, still aware
That things do not always come by chance or scientific cue.
So mysticism has its place and superstition too,
And luck is less a threat than facing power out of sight.
So we want power we can understand and keep in view,
And we want gods to be controlled with scientific might.

153

Faith Fuel

A humble person gathers scorn by those who relish strength,
And kneeling just is not a stance for those who want control.
When chaos reigns, as people struggle, keeping fear at length,
Their comfort's sought in facts and trends, or in opinion polls.
The ease with which a life of prayer is lived seems odd to some.
Unlike the lives of those who offer prayers when times seem right,
A life of prayer is one that lives each moment with the Son.
We pray and love the power found just walking in God's light.

There always will be some who do not seek the living God.
To focus on one's self is always easier for most.
To shift away from self-control, the concept must seem odd,
But life's a prayer for those who live to join the heavenly hosts,
And prayer is so much more than giving thanks to God above.
A prayer is even more than calling out in pain or fear.
Our God is waiting to forgive, relating just with love.
The bonding starts with prayer fulfilled, with God forever near.

Mysteries of the Day

Every day is a divine mystery. Each day is the same twenty-four hours for billions of people, yet for each person the day plays out differently. For some the day is dominated by sadness, and for some the day is played out in laughter. For some, the day is an adventure in pleasure, and for others the day is a torture of tears. Some people will find the day to be one of discovery and answers. For others, that same day will be a day of questions and confusion.

Yes, each day is a mystery for those who are curious, as well as for those who are not. Since sunrise, this is the same day for the pastor and the plumber, the teacher and the truck driver, and the doctor and the dogcatcher. There are an equal number of hours for the butterflies and the bulldogs, the deer and the dahlias, the robins and the rhododendrons. For babies, this will be their first day of experiencing life with their custom-made robe of flesh. For some others, this will be the last day they occupy their Earth-bound body.

The child in each of us wants to find all the joy and fun we can. Some of us will succeed in that quest, and we will find smiles, giggles, and the good joyful feelings God wants for His children. Some will fail in their quest but find their joy on another day. There are some who will not try to find the joys and possibilities offered by the day because they

154

think it is not worth the effort, but without that effort, they may never find their sublime rewards.

Thomas Jefferson said, "We hold these truths to be self-evident, that all men are created equal, that they are endowed by their Creator with certain unalienable rights; that among these are life, liberty and the pursuit of happiness." Jefferson understood the value of pursuing joy each and every day. Wilbur Rees once described each day as "God's gift, wrapped in the tissue of expectancy." When we awaken from sleep, we have three choices. We can ponder the gifts of days past, we can wish for better gifts in the future, or we can "unwrap" our day while looking for what joys and possibilities it may hold.

These twenty-four hours at our disposal are not intended for observation. These hours invite our participation in the endless stream of days that are a mixture of possibilities, limitations, joys, tears, pains, and pleasures. While the Bible provides Basic Instructions Before Leaving Earth, there are no other instruction manuals of comparable worth. Each day is a miracle, because God creates each day to be unique–it will never be repeated.

Best of all, each moment of each day comes with choices. Some believe that being free simply means having alternatives. God makes His children truly free because He does not lock us into particular choices. Instead, God loves us so much that He teaches us the best choices, yet He still gives us the freedom to make bad choices. Today is another day made for rejoicing. Yes, there are many who will not feel like rejoicing today. Some are in sorrow, and some are in pain. Some are lonely, and some are angry. In the midst of it all, God has given us life–this day–as a gift. I believe this gift is good.

Rules of Thumb

A few years ago, a book was published entitled **Rules of Thumb**. A rule of thumb is defined as being true most of the time. The book is still popular. There is an internet web site with that title which invites contributions from others. Here are some general rules of thumb:

- Odd numbers are more believable than even.
- Green cars are involved in more accidents than any other color.
- When ants travel in a straight line, it will rain soon.

- To get the most out of your car, treat it like your favorite dog or cat.
- When traveling, the more parked big rig trucks, the better the food.
- If your feet are cold, put on a hat.

There are rules of thumb for churches too. Some of them I learned as a consultant in church growth and evangelism. Some are humorous.

As we consider lists like these, we immediately can see that there are always exceptions. Not all of these rules of thumb for churches apply to every congregation. Some rules of thumb, regardless of subject, never apply. Nevertheless, these rules make us think, even when they are wrong.

When Moses came down from Mount Sinai, he started out presenting ten simple rules that God wants us to obey. As a rule of thumb, most of us believe we are consistently obedient to all ten. The truth is that we sin:

- When we make anything or anyone more important than God.
- When we obsess over anyone or anything.
- When we inappropriately use God's name.
- When we exert ourselves physically on the Sabbath except when preparing food.
- When we do not honor our parents.
- When we hate someone.
- When we violate the covenant we have with our spouse.
- When we take something that is not rightfully ours.
- When we fail to tell the whole truth.
- When we desire something or someone that is not or should not be ours.

Part of the genius of Jesus is that He asks us to focus on what we really should do, and on who we really should be. Most people in our society today define their life in terms of what they do, what they have, and what they want. A joy-filled Christian is not defined in terms of what they do, but in terms of who they are. Such a Christian is defined not in terms of what they have, but in terms of what they share. Joy-filled Christians do not define themselves in terms of what they want, but in terms of where they are going. Does this describe you?

Don't Just Try

Faith Fuel

During the Independence Day weekend, cable and satellite channels battle for viewers by showing favorite episodes of popular series along with favorite and classic movies. In a dark scene of George Lucas' *The Empire Strikes Back* the hero, Luke Skywalker is taught by his teacher, Yoda, how to use the power of "The Force" for his benefit and that of others. Unlike "The Force," God cannot be controlled and manipulated to our benefit. Instead, Christians can allow themselves to be used by God for His glory and His agenda. In this memorable scene, Yoda instructs Luke to raise his space ship out of a swamp where it had sunk. Luke says he will try. Yoda says, "No! Not try! Do, or do not. There is no try!" Luke makes an effort, but fails. He tells Yoda that he is asking the impossible, and that it cannot be done. As Luke walks away, little Yoda quietly raises the space ship out of the water and moves it to dry land. Luke walks around the ship, exclaiming how he cannot believe it. Yoda responds quietly, "That is why you fail."

Although *Star Wars* is based upon fantasy New Age beliefs, Christians can make the same kind of point about authentic Christian faith. We often fail to see God glorified with miracles in our presence because we will not "believe it." Repeatedly Jesus makes the point in His teachings that we are to ask God with centered faith–to ask while fully believing that God wants us to ask–and that God wants to do what we ask. In the Gospel of John, Jesus says this:

> Truly, truly, I say to you, he who believes in Me, the works that I do, he will do also; and greater works than these he will do; because I go to the Father. Whatever you ask in My name, that will I do, so that the Father may be glorified in the Son. If you ask Me anything in My name, I will do it. [John 14:12-14 (NASB)]

Most of us, when we pray, ask the Father "in Jesus name." I began full-time ministry in 1973. I have very seldom heard anyone–layperson or clergy–talk about the power that is in Jesus' name. If we truly respect the power that is in Jesus' name, we never use it casually. If we take the passage quoted above seriously enough, it seems logical that we would never speak it except when we are invoking its power and when the Holy Spirit is provoking us. To approach God in this way requires a level of respect and awe that few of us practice. To make our spiritual journey with this kind of respect and awe requires a sense of discipline that those in the military might envy.

Those with a desire to enter into this level of spiritual discipline often employ the services of a spiritual director. Their director keeps them accountable and helps them maintain their chosen spiritual disciplines. There are many classical spiritual disciplines to choose from, including confession, devotion, fasting, friendship, journal keeping, leadership, meditation, pilgrimage, intercessory prayer, purity, Sabbath keeping, service, simplicity, small groups, solitude, spiritual direction, stewardship, study, submission, witness, work, and worship. It is both logical and Biblical to say that those who engage in the spiritual disciplines have a more satisfying prayer life. Those who pray with the most power lead a spiritually disciplined life. Unlike Luke Skywalker, I do not want to *try*. I want to do what God calls me to *do*.

Sins Versus Virtues

Most of us have heard of the seven deadly sins, but few of us can name them. That is no great loss of course, but the traditional list includes lust, gluttony, greed, sloth, wrath, envy, and pride. It is tempting to ignore this old list totally, but knowledge is power.

Originally, the sin of lust did not simply designate sexual passion. Before the church began making modifications to its official position on the subject, this first sin on the list was designated as extravagance. It referred to frequent purchase of luxury goods and services, particularly those associated with decadence and corruption. American society in the 21st century is definitely extravagant. During the Renaissance, the church found it more politically correct to limit their interpretation of this sin to sexual lust. Our media's advertising patterns illustrate this very well.

The sin of gluttony refers to the over consumption of anything to the point of waste. In some cultures, it is seen as a sign of status, or as simply a vice. Regardless, American society has increased its health care costs significantly due to obesity. An early saint of the church said gluttony means one of six things: eating too soon, eating too expensively, eating too much, eating too eagerly, eating too daintily, or eating wildly or boringly.

Greed is also a sin of excess. The acquisition of excess wealth is a sin against God because it means total focus on the temporary life we have on this Earth over the eternal life God offers. Greed is not simply financial. It includes the hoarding of all kinds of material things.

The sin known as sloth means laziness and apathy. The Greek term for it is *acedia*. Almost literally it means, "I do not care" or "It does not matter to me." It describes someone totally without joy or desire. It can also mean despair. It is probably the biggest temptation of those physically ill. In contrast, we have all known sick people who were cracking jokes and anxious to get back to life as it was before they

Faith Fuel

were afflicted. They make do with what energy they have.

Wrath or rage is a sin because it means anger without reason or righteousness. It often results from impatience with how that person sees their life. With wrath or rage, justice becomes vengeance, which leads to assaults, murders, and, in rare cases, genocide.

The sin of envy is similar to greed in that both stem from insatiable desire. It is also called coveting. Envy differs from greed because envy means wanting that which is already in the possession of someone else. Envious people do not simply want many possessions. They do not want others to have them.

Of the seven deadly sins, the one considered the most destructive and dangerous is pride, sometimes called *hubris*. Taking pride in how God has made us is normal. When pride is sinful however, it means not acknowledging other people's accomplishments, even if theirs is less than our own. Sinful pride also means our natural self-love becomes perverted into contempt or hatred of others. The sin of pride means, in essence, trying to compete with God! Over the centuries, many saints have considered pride to be the root of all evil.

In contrast to the seven deadly sins are the seven cardinal virtues: chastity (fidelity), temperance (restraint), charity (generosity), diligence (attentiveness), patience (tolerance), kindness (compassion), and humility (modesty). I have placed in parentheses some alternate words for the same virtues.

The seven deadly sins are often encouraged by the media in our modern society. In contrast, the church encourages the seven cardinal virtues. We can all be stained by any of the deadly sins any day. This is even more reason why we need the blood of Christ to cleanse us, and to set us free from our bondage to deadly sins.

Faith Fuel

Different Witnesses

Anyone who is a fan of murder mysteries knows that eyewitnesses to a murder can tell completely different but truthful stories. A police officer doing the interrogations often gets the truth not from a single witness, but rather assembles it like a jigsaw puzzle.

This can be true of anything to which we witness! When we witness to our faith, each of us has a different version of our experience of Jesus Christ. Each of us has a different story to tell, yet each of us is a witness to the same event–the life, death, and resurrection of Jesus Christ. This is also true of the New Testament writers. Only the writers of Matthew and Luke include stories of Jesus' birth. The other writers take his birth for granted and do not mention it.

Even Matthew and Luke tell differing stories about Jesus' birth. We will never know the "complete" story, but between these two writers, we have a sketch. History is always a sketch. Even with the aid of video tape or film, it is virtually impossible to assemble an absolutely complete record of an event of any magnitude.

The problems of completely witnessing the present are almost as great. Even when we share experiences with others, we find that at the moment of an event the others see things that we do not. We also see things that others do not. Truly understanding what is happening is a lot easier with group effort.

Witnessing to the future is even more difficult. If a person has a charismatic personality, sometimes that person can sway others to share a vision of the future. As with the past and present however, sharing a vision of the future by its nature invites alternative voices to speak. In any forum, whether in the church or elsewhere, the person with the most charismatic personality or with the loudest voice is usually the one who convinces others. How then do we decide who has the best vision of the future, that a person or group may have the best sense of direction?

Some say that those with the loudest voices are often wrong. This is half-true! Those with soft voices and those who choose not to speak at all are often wrong also! In Bible times, those who wanted others to believe their vision often amplified their arguments with attempted connections with astrology, fortune telling, mysticism, and superstition. Then as now, there was an abundance of false prophets. Today, in addition to all of this, we have people who claim to be psychic, those who claim direct modern revelation from God, and those who use the power of the electronic media to sell their vision.

160

Faith Fuel

Historically the church has always been slow to embrace new visions of the future. The church has always been skeptical of those who claim to be witnesses to future history. The church has been particularly skeptical of those who seem to have practically run all the way around God while taking pictures. This is as it should be.

Having admitted all of this we must also admit that the church cannot truly be the church without vision. The church must have both a sense of direction and a sense of movement. God cannot guide this vehicle we call the church unless we have our foot off the brake pedal and on the gas! God can only guide us if we have our hands on the steering wheel and our eyes on the road ahead! For the church to proceed it cannot spend all of its time admiring its new paint job, listening for rattles, or fiddling with the radio! Realistically the church can only be watching the road immediately ahead. At the same time however, it can be planning where next to buy gas, which way to turn at the next junction, and what is available in the next town. I am enjoying the scenery as we go along, but I am also asking God to help me have an idea of what lies ahead. I hope that you are doing the same.

I see churches filled to overflowing again and again with people praising God. I see churches as having a powerful ministry again in their current locations. I am praying that God will multiply the churches' puny efforts for His glory. In short, I am asking God for miracles. I want our churches to be prepared to receive these blessings according to the richness and mercy of God.

Faith Fuel

AUGUST

Facing Challenges

Have you ever set out to climb a mountain? I did once! I suppose one could accuse me of stretching the idea of mountain climbing in this case. I was in high school when five of us decided to climb Half Dome in Yosemite National Park. It is a mountain climbed by tourists, and the climb did not require special equipment. Nonetheless, our climb required determination, stamina, and more than a little courage.

From the time I was a little boy I have enjoyed hiking. This particular hike was the biggest challenge I had ever faced. The same could be said for the rest of my family and my friend who was with us. It was a sixteen-mile hike. Some of it was quite steep. The final climb up the peak itself was as steep as possible without special equipment. The hike began at 4034 feet. After traveling only three and a third miles, we were at 5950 feet elevation. The top of the dome is 7000 feet, eight miles and five hours each way of rigorous hiking from the beginning point. We did not have to climb Half Dome. We could have gone all of our lives without making even the attempt, but it was great experience. As I look back, I think that the experience did much to prepare me for what I often face in doing full time Christian ministry. When doing church work we are often faced with the equivalent of climbing a mountain.

For a moment however, let us get back to Half Dome. In Yosemite, they sell sweatshirts depicting Half Dome, and there are two versions. One version has an image of the Dome with the words, "I made it to the top." The other version says, "I ALMOST made it to the top." My cousin was ten years younger than my parents were when she and her husband made the attempt and did not make it to the top. My parents have never been what you would call athletes. In August of 2007, a 92 year-old man climbed to the top with his children, grandchildren, and one great grandchild. They took their time over three days, but they made it to the top.

Overcoming a challenge of any kind is often not simply a matter of physical preparedness or age. Those of us in the church can always look to the wisdom of Isaiah at the end of chapter 40, which says, "Even youths shall faint and grow weary, and the young shall fall exhausted; but they who wait for the Lord shall renew their strength, they shall mount up with wings as eagles, they shall run and not grow weary, they shall walk and not faint."

162

Faith Fuel

Geunther Gabel-Williams was one of the most famous wild animal trainer of the twentieth century. On one occasion he was doing his act with some Bengal Tigers when there was a power failure. Inside that circus tent, the audience could hear Mr. Gabel-Williams continuing to crack his whip and shouting his commands. When the lights came back on, the act was going on just as though nothing had happened.

Afterward in a press conference, the tiger tamer was asked what had happened in the darkness. He said that when the lights went out he knew he had two choices. If he ran for the door of the cage the tigers would smell his fear, and he probably would not have made it. He knew that the cats could see quite well in the darkness of the tent even if he could not. The cats however did not know that he could not see when the lights went out. He went on with the act, and the tigers never knew that there was a problem.

This teaches us how to face our church problems! This instructs us on how to face challenges! We face them together! We keep trying!

Royal Visitors

Some may know about the attitude towards visitors at Coptic monasteries. When visitors arrive, they are treated like royalty. More than that, they are treated as though those in the monastery had been anticipating their arrival. The visitors are treated lovingly and generously. They can literally ask for anything, and if it is in the power of those there at the monastery, the wish will be granted.

If you ask the monks why this is so, they will tell you that their reason is a simple one. They expect that Jesus will return to earth at any time. Since they do not know what Jesus looks like, or even what form he will take when he comes, the monks treat every one who arrives as though that person were Jesus himself.

Every church for whom I have ever consulted in evangelism has told me that they are a loving and friendly church. They have told me how warmly they treat their visitors. Every one of those churches has honestly believed that because of the way they treat their visitors, there is absolutely no reason why those visitors should not return and join their fellowship. The fact is however, none of these churches has ever been as warm and friendly as they thought they were! Each of us should think carefully how we see a visitor. Each of us should consider whether or not the friendship we offer is momentary. Do you follow up our warmth and friendliness later that day with a phone call? Do we call

Faith Fuel

them again later that week? Have we made any effort this past year to nurture a friendship with our visitors?

More than four out of five members of every church are members because a friend or relative invited them! Friendship is the primary motivating factor of church growth. Many of us have voted for church growth. Most of us have approved spending money to bring visitors to our doors. Each of us must consider carefully. "What have I done personally to generate friendship with one of our visitors?"

From Quest to Quest

Back in 1969, I decided to end my quest to be a great choral conductor and to serve Christ and His church instead. At the time, I did not want to become a preacher. I was sure that there must be other ways to serve our Lord productively and successfully. Even as I made the decision to go into the ministry, I realized that I was stepping into a different world. I looked at missionary work and decided that, since I am weak in foreign language skills, I would not want to serve Christ in a jungle somewhere! Having decided to remain on my native soil, I pondered what parts of the country I would be willing to go to in order to serve.

I still had a great deal of fear of the unknown. I was confident of my call to the ministry, but I was scared. Motivated by that fear I set my limits. I did not want to serve in a small town. I did not want to serve where it was too hot or too cold. I wanted to be close enough to a major airport that I could go "home" if I got homesick. What a bowl of jelly I was!

Immediately, God began to challenge those limitations I had set for myself. I found myself driving nearly fifteen hundred miles to go to seminary. When I arrived, I was humbled by not being able to move in at the University for two weeks. I was further humbled by an adult case of the chicken pox. While still nursing my scabs from the pox along with three weeks' growth of beard, I discovered that God had called me to preach. I also discovered that same evening that God would provide for me whatever I needed as I responded to that call.

First, I was put in a student church where I would learn how to pray effectively. Then I was put in a church where I learned how to deal with illness in the midst of ministry. My first full-time parish was a wealthy one, where I learned how to take orders from a senior pastor. Then, returning to seminary, I was called to my first small town church. God has always challenged me to push my limits. Going to Florida, a state I had not previously considered, was one such challenge. I learned to deal with heat and humidity. Could I deal with the bone-numbing cold of Alaska? I am quite sure that if God called me there I would learn to deal with those new challenges.

Would I be willing to accept a position overseas? I do not know! That still scares me! Besides, I am not ready to leave where I am. I am not ready to give up on the idea that God still has plans for me ahead. The best is yet to come! I do feel however a sense of challenge that I have never felt before. I have tried tools that have worked in the past, and I have tried new tools. I am still challenged by the possibilities.

Grace Under Pressure

Problems that demand our immediate attention have a tendency to make us feel that we must find immediate answers or face failure. This leads to impatience with ourselves as well as with God. We are very accustomed to having advertising agencies give us the perfect answers to problems we did not know we had! When we approach God in prayer, we also have a tendency to expect answers within thirty seconds of our questions.

Organized prayer often is not as fulfilling as it can be. People join organized prayer efforts for differing reasons. Some people join prayer efforts simply because of the experience of intimacy with the Holy Spirit. They recognize the power that is available to them. They want to rekindle that experience of great joy. Their humble approach to prayer leads to the joy that they seek. Their prayer lives are recognized as the most consistently effective. The spiritual health of a church depends upon these people taking the most active part in the planning process. The future of the church depends upon these people being vocal about what the Holy Spirit is doing in their midst.

Others join a prayer effort because of the secular concept of teamwork. They approach prayer based upon a limited understanding of Matthew 18:20 (NRSV): "For where two or three are gathered in my name, I am there among them." Their secular approach and interpretation of this scripture limits the effectiveness of their prayer life, which is often frustrating. The spiritual health of a congregation depends upon these people doing a lot of listening while being supportive of the first group. They must be very careful to limit their vocal contributions to the planning process.

Still others approach being in a prayer effort from purely secular motives–they like the fellowship and gossip. Their involvement in the power of the Holy Spirit is merely indirect. Praying for the same things as the first group, these people bask in the glow of the effectiveness of the prayers of others. They smugly give themselves credit when in fact they have experienced little or no communion with the Holy Spirit. The spiritual health of a church depends upon this last group of people keeping out of the planning process of the congregation. Anything they have to say about the future direction of the church is of little or no value! As you think about your future and that of the spiritual community that you love, how much thinking grows out of prayer?

The Blessing of Quiet

In Psalm 46 we read, "Be still and know that I am God." For some that seems like an impossible command! Be still? How can we be still while racing down the highway? How can we be still when we must answer nervously chattering people? How can we be still when we left our stomach three floors below in that elevator? How can we be still when we are already late to half of everything that we do? How can we be still amid all of this chaos?

"Be still and know that I am God." In this highly stressed and hurried world of ours, the call to be still seems like a call to a luxury that we cannot afford. Does not God know how much there is to do? Does not God realize that what we really need is more energy to get done what we want to do? Does not God realize that if we stop and be still our reflexes may not be able to save us from disaster? Does not God realize that we just do not have time to be still when there is little enough time for sleep?

God does know what we are up against! God's Son shared our common lot through Jesus! We read, "Jesus wept," "Jesus withdrew to pray," and "Jesus slept on the cushion in the back of the boat;" but we never read, "Jesus hurried . . . Jesus felt compelled . . . Jesus was late . . . ."

A pat response might be that Jesus did not live in this century, but if we read the gospels carefully, we find that Jesus accomplished a great deal in the brief time that he was on Earth. We have a very real paradox here. It seems that Jesus, by taking the time to commune with Our Creator, had more time to heal, teach, love and reconcile.

If we begin our day with the proper preparation. communing with God, we will not have to race down the freeway. If we are at peace with ourselves, we will not have to feel compelled to respond to the nervous chatter of everyone we meet. Empowered by God we can actually enjoy that elevator ride. When we properly begin our day, our mind is so organized that we need not be late for anything. When there is peace, shalom, within us, chaos around us does not disturb us.

Now
Impatiently we want things now, the time for waiting's never been.
It seems that everything we do is sensitive to timing's pen.
This pen's a cage without a door, and nothing's right outside its bars.
Yet from the vantage point of God there are no bars, there's only stars.

The now of God is never caged or bound by circumstance of law.
The thought of God is polished substance even though created raw.
The word of God is now and whole, created without timing's cage.
The now of God is flawless joy, without the need to turn a page.

Tomorrow's needs will come in time, and yesterday's will always press.
The needs of yesterday were either solved or added to our mess.
The needs of now are quicker solved when yesterday is in the past.
The now with which we work at last cannot be measured slow or fast.

Impatiently we want things now, not hearing "no" or even "slow."
With time there's opportunity to wait for now and simply grow.
When wisdom comes, the now gives way to slowly finding what has been.
Such wisdom finds such strength for now that future's joy looks back at "then."

When life on earth is done and there is simply no more now to face,
I think the loss of time's firm bars will edify God's holy grace.
When death is passed and life's set free to soar through all eternity,
I think I'll see the now of God as love fulfilled with joyful glee.

Whom Do You Trust?

Until recently, people both inside and outside the Christian faith had a tendency to relate their needs to God. Many prayed about their problems, took their problems to clergy, or lit a candle in church. Though people did not understand our world, they believed God controlled everything, particularly in times of crisis. Witnessing and evangelism was relatively easy.

167

Since that time, humankind has become more oriented toward science and technology, believing in self-reliance. Rather than employing faith and prayer, humans seek answers in knowledge and money. Outside of churches, fewer and fewer problems are seen to be God-related, and humankind thinks less in theological terms.

Despite this, the rates of suicide and divorce rise, institutions for the physically and emotionally crippled are overloaded, and society's problems intensify and increase. Those outside the Christian community are asking theological questions, though not identified as such. "Who am I?" "Why am I here?" "What is the purpose of all of this?" "Why can't I cope?" "Why am I lonely and unhappy?"

There is a kind of spiritual curiosity in such things as ghosts, ESP, parapsychology, and astrology. Eastern mystical religions are gaining adherents, while within the Christian faith there is renewed interest in spiritual gifts and prayer. Effective witnessing and evangelism simply have new approaches!

Today, people have a renewed interest in the transcendent and in the mysteries of life, for which science and technology have no ready answers. Christians can effectively respond to this interest. The Gospel of Jesus Christ is a great gift to give.

Controlling Pride

Pride often gets in the way of our best intentions. Many say pride is the root of all sin. It is the difference between justified self-respect and conceit. Luke 18: 11-12 displays one proud Pharisee: "The Pharisee stood apart by himself and prayed, 'I thank you, God, that I am not greedy, dishonest, or an adulterer, like everybody else. I thank you that I am not like that tax collector over there. I fast two days a week, and I give you one tenth of all my income.'"

A more humble person might have prayed the same prayer a little differently: "I thank you, God, that you are guiding me away from being greedy, dishonest, or an adulterer, and I pray that you will continue to save us all from these things. Please use the discipline of fasting to help me to grow in wisdom, in stature, and in favor with you, and please accept one tenth of my income as I humbly return unto you what is rightfully yours."

Our pride is out of control when we believe our cause is righteous simply because it is our cause. Our pride is out of control when we assume that God sees the same differences between good and evil that we do.

Those familiar with the musical, "Camelot," may remember that when Sir Lancelot first makes his appearance, he does so singing a song entitled "C'est Moi!" He had every virtue except humility! Most of us do not display such extremes, but we do let our pride get out of control at times. We get smugly satisfied that we are doing our part ("enough") for the furtherance of the kingdom. We are often smugly satisfied with our levels of loving and giving. The only way to be sure? Honestly pray about it, and check it out with God.

Loving and Using

I once saw a thought provoking sign that read, "Love people and use things–not vice versa!" The sign made an impression on me: we have a tendency to treat people like things, and then we attach "personality" to objects, pets, and other things.

When we buy gas, does "Gaylord" help us, or is the attendant a faceless thing that we have no desire to communicate with or to love? When we talk with that person who gives us business, is she a person named "Diane" or just a customer? Not long ago, Cheryl Teigs was modeling some of the latest fashions. The designer spoke of the fashions as though they had personality, and he spoke of Cheryl as though she were a clothes rack! Another prime example is the athlete who is treated like a machine that makes money for the owners.

There are less obvious examples as well. Speaking of a new possession, how often have we said, "Isn't she beautiful?" When speaking of something that has been around for a long time, we say, "That old thing really has personality!" A telling sign in this area is our priorities. We often place the welfare of the possessions of a business ahead of the people who run the business.

It seems important to examine ourselves, and our dealings with others. Do we love things and possessions more than we love people? Do we spend our money on things before we spend it on people? Do we manipulate or use people to get ahead or to get what we want? Do we place ourselves ahead of the people with whom we deal, work, and play? The answers to these questions may not come easy. We may find it heard to be truthful with ourselves and with God!

Faith Fuel

Measuring Importance

While a student at Long Beach City College, I knew someone named Steve. He had heard about the Surgeon General's report on the effect of smoking upon one's health, but he still smoked quite a bit and did not worry about it. He provided some interesting rationale. First, he was going to die anyway eventually, and since he enjoyed smoking so much, he might as well die of lung cancer as anything else. Second, he believed he could quit anytime he wanted to, but he was enjoying himself too much to quit. Steve had a nasty perpetual cough which he said he did not mind.

When I was serving as a Minister of Christian Education and Youth, I knew a woman I will call "Jane." She had heard that regular Bible study had a tremendous effect upon one's spiritual health, but she refused to try some systematic Bible study. Jane gave two reasons. First, she was not going to die for lack of Bible study, at least not physically, and since she enjoyed life without Bible study so much, why should she start? Second, she could start studying her Bible anytime she wanted to, but she did not want to since she was having such fun without it. She perpetually complained that her prayer life was poor, but she said it was okay. Many of us know people like this. They believe they have legitimate reasons for not working on the most important relationship of all–the one with Jesus Christ.

I used to drink Salada tea, and it had epigrams on the tea bag tags. One said, "You never grow old, you just stop growing." I believe the converse of this is also true. You will not grow old if you keep on growing. Growth requires work! When we are tired, sick, or lacking in energy, the one thing we always have the energy for is nurturing or relationship with Jesus Christ. Doing disciplined Bible study, having a disciplined prayer life, or having disciplined giving of time and talent to the kingdom will rub off on other areas of life.

Unthinking Bias

Most of us go through life believing we have a clear idea of what we are doing. We try to think before we act and speak. It is shocking when we discover we have unconscious prejudice or bias. It hurts to discover our unconscious bias is hurting someone. Ethnic bias and sexual bias are very important, and our politicians pass laws

170

dealing with obvious biases and prejudices. When does bias or prejudice hurt enough people to make us willing to make an effort to stop?

If two people apply for a job, where both people have equal qualifications in terms of training, talent, and experience:

- A tall person will be given preference over a short person.
- A slender person will be given preference over an overweight person.
- A younger person will be given preference over an older person.
- A married person will be given preference over a single person.
- Someone with children will be given preference over someone childless.
- With women, a blonde-haired woman or redhead will be given preference over a brown-haired woman.
- With men, a brown-haired man or red-haired man will be given preference over a blonde-haired man.

Even the church has problems handing out responsibilities and electing persons to positions of leadership. When choosing clergy, Protestant congregations choose men over women and married persons over single persons. Within the laity, there is a tendency to resist letting "'little-Johnnie-who-I-taught-in-Sunday-School," who is now an adult, be Chairman of the Board even if he/she is otherwise qualified.

Our congregations are finally beginning to become aware of a couples oriented attitude, and singles are less often made to feel like a "fifth wheel." Nearly half of our population is single, but only a few churches do singles ministries. The times are continuing to change, and I hope that the church will keep up.

Faith Fuel

SEPTEMBER

Lonely Beauty

I had a phone conversation one evening with an old friend who went to Texas Christian University with me. Among other things, we talked about the man she almost married, the man she married but divorced, and the man to whom she was then happily married. She was a completely committed Christian who loves her Lord very much. For a long time, she suffered from what psychologists call "Beautiful Woman Syndrome." Beginning in high school, she was caught up in the beauty contest machinery of her state. She often felt insecure and lonely because she felt people were friendly only because she was extraordinarily attractive. Sadly, too many men used her instead of loved her. Despite her Christian faith, and despite the unconditional love of her parents and siblings, it took her a long time to realize her prejudicial distrust of all men. It was both making her unhappy and wreaking destruction on many facets of her life. Before she married the second time, she got that part of her life's act together. God gave her beauty, and she got it into perspective.

Sometimes that source of all beauty is avoided. Children of alcoholic parents, children raised solely by their mothers, and sexually abused children often suffer from the "Masculine God Syndrome." Subconsciously, many people stay away from church because we refer to God as "Father." There are times when we need to help people find a healthy view of God, before they can fully embrace God's family. That's when real beauty begins to shine from within.

The Critical Ingredient

Years ago, I began reading material by Norman Vincent Peale. I always had trouble putting what he taught into practice. The challenge was trying to be positive, realistic, upbeat and practical, and all without being excessively optimistic. Positive thinking can accomplish a great deal. Excessive optimism, though, can lead to frustration. There was a missing ingredient, but for a long time I could not identify it.

It should have been obvious, but I was riding an elephant searching for an elephant. Deciding what that missing ingredient was, I decided to test this ingredient in the recipe for happiness, joy, and peace. The potency of this ingredient turned out to be incredible. When

172

Faith Fuel

I felt under the weather, it worked as powerfully as some "wonder" drug. When I was tired and lacking in energy, it renewed my zest for doing things. When I awakened in the middle of the night, it helped me get back to sleep.

What was this fabulous ingredient? It was a genuinely thankful spirit! I find that the more I say genuine prayers of thanksgiving, the better I feel and the happier I am. Genuine thanksgiving relieves tension and stress. Genuine thanksgiving is a catalyst that makes positive thinking work wonders.

If you are skeptical, I do not blame you. I have been involved in this experiment for years, and it works. Do not take my word for it. Give it a try! Genuine prayers of thanksgiving make life easier. Genuine thanksgiving is noticed by others, and there are positive results in terms of relationships. The Apostle Paul's letters all begin with thanksgiving. There is nothing to lose!

Motivations

I do not understand my own actions. For I do not do what I want, but I do the very thing I hate. [Romans 7:15 (NRSV)]

We human beings are full of contradictions. We often desire the things (or people) we cannot have or should not have. We also tend to reject what we need. Jesus was not the only person who recognized this. Being fully human, Jesus experienced this phenomenon, and being divine, He did not succumb to it. Those of us in the Christian community can cling to Him for guidance and encouragement, as we seek to grow in His wisdom. Growth means change, and that requires motivation.

People have things that motivate them one way or another. Apart from survival instincts, studies have shown that there are five major things that motive us towards positive change:

Dedication
Commitment
Compassion
Community
Education

There are generational differences with regard to how most people are motivated towards positive change. Those born prior to

173

1935 have had a tendency to be motivated primarily by dedication. Those born between 1925 and 1955 have tended to be motivated primarily by commitment. Those born between 1945 and 1970 have had a tendency to be motivated by compassion. Those born between 1960 and 1985 have tended to be motivated by a sense of community. Those born after 1985 are usually motivated by compassion. In communities where there is a college or university, education can be a primary motivator, regardless of age.

Thirty-five to fifty years ago, most stewardship campaigns and evangelism efforts were motivated by dedication and commitment. All programs, approaches, and techniques were oriented towards dedication and commitment, and understandably so. There are many success stories from that period of history. Stewardship campaigns could depend upon results based upon dedication and commitment. Door-to-door evangelism and revivals followed the same pattern. Today however, few people are motivated by dedication and commitment.

Lyle Schaller compiled an abundance of data to indicate that there have been more changes in society and church life between 1960 and 2000 than in the previous 400 years. The church is creating new tools to deal with these changes. Many of us are uncomfortable with change, but change is an automatic byproduct of growth. Both society and the church are growing into a new era. What are the best motivators for us in this new age?

In rapidly growing churches of North America, there are some common things that cross previous church boundaries. Nearly all growing churches promote taking the Bible seriously and practicing authentic orthodox Christianity. There is a tendency to focus on contemporary music and contemporized interpretation of traditional music. The vast majority of these churches are focused primarily on compassion and community towards those outside their congregational circle. To be honorable and faithful Christians, we have to let the Holy Spirit lead us to new ways to spread the good news and support the church.

Filling Needs

Before church one Sunday morning, some people were discussing the price of gasoline. That led to talking about the price of gasoline in other countries, and we talked our economy. Within our borders, there are many resources for energy. Some are adequately utilized, but many are not. For the last half-century or so, leaders have not had the courage to move forward in energy development for a number of reasons. One thing is certain: God provides the abundance, and we need to be better stewards of that abundance.

The church is a reflection of the rest of society. Sometimes we have had to stop helping people in need who came to our doors because we had tapped out the fund that supported those efforts. Sometimes, the congregation as a whole spent more money than they received in the offering plates. This has been a concern for all churches, and we have needed to pray about it. Each of us needs to be sure we are doing our part for God's kingdom!

When I first moved to Yosemite, I joined the congregation worshipping in the historic chapel. I would bring a check with me to put in the offering plate each Sunday. Since I was at the piano, the offering plate usually did not come to me. I would sometimes forget to put the check in the offering plate after church, and the checks accumulated. Then I had an idea! God wants us to give from the first fruits of our abundance. We need to make our gifts to the church before we start paying our bills. I contacted my bank and arranged for my account to be debited each week for the church. I have done that ever since.

There will always be people in need. Part of being the church means responding to needs as they come. I hate saying no to a real need. In Bible times, the people of God used to divide their harvests into equal portions corresponding to the ten fingers on their hands. One of those portions belonged to God. It was "from the first fruits" or, as we put it today, "off the top." There was no question. If you are not in the habit, it seems like a lot. When I started tithing, I discovered I had more money for the things that I needed.

Growing in Faith

One of the fastest growing areas of evangelism and church growth is in small groups. New types of groups are forming constantly. Quite often, people in the community who do not have a church home find it easier to join an informal group than to attend a Sunday service for the first time. One of the ways we can bring more people into the life of the church is through special events, fellowship activities, and small groups.

In seminary, one of my favorite professors discovered a gift in me during a small group session. It has been very useful in working with people over the years. When we are growing spiritually, we sometimes discover strengths and gifts that we had not previously detected. Spiritual maturity is not a goal to be achieved. It is a lifelong journey. We many times experience spurts in our own spiritual growth when in small groups.

Every once in awhile, pastors find people in their congregations who are looking for a deeper spiritual pilgrimage. These people are not critical, guilt-ridden, neurotic, or maladjusted. They go to church regularly, are good stewards, and are active in church life. They are involved in either the mission efforts or nurturing efforts of the church— sometimes both. They are looking for greater personal awareness and a greater sense of fulfillment. In essence, they need to participate in a spiritual growth group. They usually can admit most people in the congregation do not sense this need. We never grow old unless we stop growing. The potential of the mind and spirit is unlimited.

About 70 years ago, therapists began experimenting with poetry therapy, and quickly they discovered significant successes. In the 1960s, the first books were written on the subject. In the church, as pastoral counseling began to become a more disciplined field, bibliotherapy began to become popular. I took a course in bibliotherapy in 1974, and I have had a number of occasions to use it over the years since then.

Spiritual growth groups are different, even though they seem to be an outgrowth of therapy. It is not a social group, nor is it an educational group or a therapy group. Yes, these factors are present in a spiritual growth group, but the focus is on unused or under-used potential in each individual. Although the pastor is often the leader, he or she is also a participant. The prayers of saints of the past provide the seed material. Spiritual growth groups do not "study" prayers nor pray them. Members of the group react to these prayers and reflect upon them.

There are advantages to seeking spiritual growth in a group setting rather than as individuals. In a group, participants have opportunities to reflect off others' comments as well as off the prayers themselves. In addition, members of the group begin to hold each other accountable for one another's participation and growth. Spiritual growth helps the whole church.

Accepting Ourselves

Any time there is competition, it is important to have a referee present to make sure everything is fair. If one team is not allowed to lose, neither team is really allowed to win. The same principle can be applied to individuals. If someone is not allowed to fail, their "win" is worthless. It is basic to human nature for us to be able to learn from our failures and mistakes. If we do not learn from our failures, we never have the opportunity to achieve great success. Charles Baudelaire said, "Every man who refuses to accept the conditions of life sells his soul." When we allow others to do for us what we can do for ourselves, we are surrendering our souls. True faithfulness begins when we accept ourselves as we are, making the most of what we have.

When we accept ourselves as who we are as sisters and brothers in Christ, we come face to face with certain realities.

- Jesus is alive and loves us.
- God has the best agenda for our lives beginning before we are born and continuing through eternity.
- Heaven is real.
- Hell is real.
- The Bible is the place where we connect with God in an accurate and tangible way.
- We are forgiven when we humbly ask.
- We are redeemed as we let God be God.
- God supplies what we need to do His will.
- The Holy Spirit empowers us to do what is necessary and pleasing in God's sight.
- Our only marching orders are to love one another as Christ loves us and to share Him with others.
- If we get people to church, they will hear about Jesus. The Holy Spirit will do the rest.

Since we are all responsible for getting people introduced to Jesus, all of us be open to trying new things in that effort. Let us learn from our past failures and find greater success. That way, with God's help, we all win!

Worldly Justice

It was nearly twenty years ago when I first heard the expression, "What goes around comes around." If we think about it, this expression is a modern rendition of what farmers have said for thousands of years: we reap what we sow. Up until the United States got ensnared in the war in Vietnam, this ancient wisdom was considered common sense. Since that war's era however, common

Faith Fuel

sense has been in increasingly short supply. Some bookstores still carry *The Death of Common Sense* by Philip K. Howard. It is good reading.

In the Apostle Paul's second letter to the people of Corinth, he offers some additional wisdom on this subject.

> But this I say: He who sows sparingly
> will also reap sparingly, and he who
> sows bountifully will also reap
> bountifully.
> [II Corinthians 9:6 (NKJV)]

Paul goes on to point out how God blesses our efforts in this way. The more willing we are to be generous with others, the more God will provide so that we can continue to be generous. Christians who walk the walk know this very well. Half-hearted efforts do not impress God. What goes around comes around!

Some additional less-common "common" sense dictates that we cannot harvest wheat where we have sown barley. Many a politician has failed to get re-elected when they assumed their constituents were too stupid to recognize their representative's bad behavior, and those constituents punished those politicians for their stupidity. Many parents fail to function as parents, and then they are disappointed when their kids become bad parents. Increasing numbers of people scorn the idea of worshiping God, yet they complain that God does not bless them as they think they should be blessed. What goes around comes around!

I can testify from personal experience that when we let God be God and let Christ be King, God graciously unleashes His blessings. What goes around comes around! God supplies the resources we need to help do His will for others. That is some uncommon "common" sense. God's wisdom is better than mine–even my own common sense.

Permanent Hope

In the church there is always hope! Sometimes it is necessary to remind people of this fact, but it is a reliable assumption. Churches in the so-called mainline denominations have been in decline for some time now, with the exception of the Southern Baptists. When a church is in decline over a long period of time it is easy for it to get discouraged.

Faith Fuel

Sometimes churches try to blame their problems on the pastor or on current programs. They think that a new program, the resurrection of an old program, or a change in the pastoral leadership will provide an easy solution. If these churches thoroughly investigate, they find that many growing churches have similar situations, similar pastors, and the same programs. Their hope is not focused in the right direction.

Some churches try to blame their problems on changes in demographics or shifting population. They blame changes in the neighborhood or perhaps changes within the church itself. They think that if they had more members of a certain age group their problems would be solved. If these churches thoroughly investigate, they find there are many similar congregations growing in similar neighborhoods. Again, their hope is focused in the wrong direction.

Some churches think that they have no choice but to relocate. They believe that if they sell their current property and move to a more attractive location, perhaps a growing neighborhood, their problems will be solved. Again, there is an abundance of statistical data that shows that the vast majority of these relocations do not yield the results they had hoped for. Again, there is misplaced hope. In a few churches, they have determined that their resources no longer could support a viable congregation. They liquidate their assets. The membership then either joins another church or disperses among several churches. They donate their assets to other churches in need, or they indicate that their assets are to be used to start churches where they are needed elsewhere. Their hope is focused upon the whole church, and they use their resources to renew the hope of others.

This is close to the most common solution to all of the problems described so far. Since there is always hope in the church, it is a matter of discovering where God wants us to look for hope. Some of the churches that have paid me to consult with them have decided to call in a consultant as a last resort. The vast majority do not wait that long, however, and they approach the consultation process with renewed hope. The churches that successfully turn their decline into growth do so by focusing upon their mission. By concentrating upon reaching others with the Good News of Jesus Christ, they discover that God supplies the resources for everything else.

When these churches stop thinking in terms of their own survival, they discover new health and new vitality. These churches begin to grow rapidly when they shift their thinking towards what Jesus would have them do. It is not just that Jesus is the hope of the church. Jesus has also suffered as we suffer, and he can show us the way to triumph. As the Apostle Paul says, hope does not disappoint us!

Faith Fuel

People of the Book

People's attitudes towards the Bible vary widely. We tend to notice when our own attitudes are in the process of change. While we try to deal with this change, we try to understand those whose attitudes are different from ours. There are those who almost worship the Bible itself instead of the God revealed therein. Some have acquired Bible-toter's shoulder from carrying a big Bible wherever they go. These are those who want a scripture to back up everything they do and say. Their Bible acts like a spiritual security blanket for them. They may feel hopeless when they have not the right verse to quote. While this behavior is not promoted in the churches that I have served, I must admit that it is disturbing to see too much of the opposite extreme.

There are people who go to great lengths to confirm their Christianity while avoiding contact with the Bible. They might feel a little guilty that they do not know the Bible better, but not enough do something about it. Sometimes they put their Bible out on a table or bookshelf and dust it rather regularly. Others stick it in the drawer of their nightstand. They are almost proud of their lack of knowledge of the Bible. Since they never study the Bible themselves, they do not consider the value of encouraging their children to read the Bible. This is parental neglect!

As a person of moderation, I tend shy away from both of these extremes. Which way should one lean? I would choose a sore shoulder rather than a sore conscience and an arid soul. The Bible can inspire, it can inform, and it can transform. How much we read the Bible is a reflection of our faith.

Power in the Book

It is amazing what Bible reading accomplishes–systematic Bible reading. It is habit forming. I am used to reading at least two chapters from the Old Testament and two chapters from the New Testament when I wake up in the morning. If I am in a hurry and cut down on the amount I read, I feel like I am missing out.

With daily Bible reading, I have noticed that I feel like my spiritual life is more in balance. It used to be that I did a lot of praying but little Bible study. My relationship with God was all in one direction. By doing more Bible reading, I feel that God is speaking to me. My

180

prayers are more responsive to what the scriptures say to me. My prayers are less a response to my day-by-day needs.

I have also discovered scripture means more when I read it aloud. When I read aloud, the words have more clarity. If I have someone's picture nearby as someone to read to, I find myself listening intently. My most powerful experience of scripture happens when I read it in worship. I can feel the power of God surging through me. It is a privilege for the word of God to come through me at that moment.

Scripture has a cleansing power for the mind. When I am tense and irritable, reading scripture helps clear away the debris of the day's events. When I wake up in the middle of the night and cannot get back to sleep, scripture reading has a way of putting past, present, and future into perspective. Sleep comes more easily. Psychologists call it bibliotherapy. It is good medicine indeed!

The Empty Chair

When I was in seminary, I was given a great deal of training in counseling and in psychotherapeutic techniques. One technique was called "The Empty Chair Technique." First, the man (or woman) with difficulty sat in one chair, facing another chair, and the he was asked to pretend that the person they had trouble with was sitting there in the other chair. While pretending, he re-enacted some of the things he used to say to that person. With the counselor encouraging him, he then began to say some of the things he had really wanted to say.

Then came the interesting part! He (or she) changed chairs and, pretending he was the other person, spoke back! He shifted back and forth between the two chairs, carrying on an imaginary conversation. The man (or woman) being counseled discovered that the imagery was very important. To be effective, he had to speak for himself only from his own chair, and he could speak for the other person only from the other chair. The effect was dramatic! He learned a lot about his own attitudes and about the other person's attitudes.

We can use this technique to improve our relationship with Jesus. Most are not ready to sit in Jesus' chair and talk with themselves, but we can talk with an empty chair the way some people pray to a cross or other symbol. It is useful to go into a room and imagine Jesus standing or sitting there, watching us, loving us, encouraging us, and guiding us. It is part of trying to make a conscious place for Jesus in our every waking moment.

Faith Fuel

No Goodbyes

C. S. Lewis once remarked, "Christians never say good-bye." A few summers ago, I went on a rather expansive tour of the western part of the United States. One morning at breakfast, I found myself in Zion National Park, emotionally lost in the wonders of God's creation. As I ate my eggs, I gazed out the window at the flaming red rock of the canyon walls, the morning sun streaming through the trees, and the sparkles of light shining up from the stream below. I was in somewhat of a trance as I went to the register to pay my bill. As I looked up at the very attractive girl who was taking my money I noticed a cross hanging at the base of her throat. We had a delightful but short conversation. As I walked away she said, "Have a nice forever!" Somehow, I felt as if we were not saying good-bye.

People who like to witness to their faith might miss the point. If an opportunity arises to share what we believe to a stranger on a bus or on a plane, many would talk as though this will be the only time this person will ever have to hear about Jesus. It makes the situation artificial, and this 'plastic' approach might close the ears of the listener.

There is a better approach! Christianity is built on relationships–relating to each other and to our God. The stranger in question, who needs to hear the gospel, will have the ears to hear if there is an opportunity to begin a relationship. The most obvious place to begin a relationship is with the person in the next seat. The approach should be as though one has all the time in the world because we want to build a friendship. If we can make a friend on that plane or bus, they just might discover another friend in Jesus. We can always avoid saying good-bye by telling them when we will see them again, even if it is, "I will see you in paradise."

The Unexpected

Few of us worry when wonderful things happen. Most of us often do worry when something strange happens. Being human, we feel quite uncomfortable when something does not fit into the patterns of our previous experiences. We have a natural human tendency to distrust something that is unusual. Sometimes we distrust our own senses - we have difficulty believing what we are seeing or hearing. At other times, we simply distrust the source of the unusual. Strange and

182

wonderful things often happen in a community of faith. Those who live a life of faith do not often distrust the strange because they live life with a sense of wonder. As a result, those who live outside the community of faith sometimes feel uncomfortable with our behavior.

It is simply a matter of logic. There are just two universal rules of human logic:

> Nothing can both be and not be
> at the same time.
> All conclusions are based upon
> a combination of facts and
> assumptions.

In all of human experience, one of our most frustrating experiences is to get into an argument where we agree on the facts but disagree about our conclusions. These disagreements happen because we have differing assumptions that we add to our facts. In the church, for instance, we assume the love of God along with God's grace, forgiveness, mercy, power, and omniscience. Those outside the church often do not understand our perspectives on situations because they do not share our assumptions about God. Our relationship with God strongly affects how we see our world. Our faith gives us a strength that amazes others. Our faith indeed seems both strange and wonderful.

Seeking Blessings

Do you want to be blessed? That may seem like a silly question. When Jesus met the crippled man at the well, He asked him if he wanted to be healed. Maybe this man enjoyed living off of the charity of others! It had been going on for many years, so the status quo may have been quite acceptable. God loves us enough not to assume what we want, even though The Holy One knows better than we do just what it is that we really need. God loves us and wants to bless us. God simply waits for us to finish our homework.

Are you willing to do what it takes to be blessed? This is a serious question! On several occasions, Jesus made it clear that those who wish to be considered as His disciples must take up their cross and follow him. In order to experience His complete joy, bearing our cross is necessary. In order to experience the success and fulfillment that He wants for us, bearing our cross is necessary. In order to experience the fullest measure of His love, bearing our cross is part of the process.

Faith Fuel

The cross that Christ gives us to bear is a far lighter burden than the one we design for ourselves. The difference is in letting Him choose the components of that burden, turning control over to Him. A fully functional Christian is one that knows when to surrender totally–at the beginning. This lesson is the most practical one a Christian ever learns, and it makes the Christian walk infinitely easier. Are you willing to surrender control to Jesus? Will you do what it takes to be blessed?

Faith Fuel

The Evolution of Worship

The flavor of Christian worship changes from generation to generation. During the first century, worship gatherings were centered mostly upon personal witnessing. There were people still living during the first century who had actually seen Jesus while he walked the earth in the flesh, and they repeated the things they had heard Him say.

As the church emerged from the Dark Ages, worship gatherings were centered upon plainsong, otherwise known as Gregorian chant, and upon a fixed liturgy. Worship was built around music that highlighted the scriptures and made them come alive.

During the Baroque era (1685-1750), worship was largely centered upon music that utilized established texts in the mass. The music helped people to remember the texts in a society where very few people had access to Bibles. Composers were simply craftsmen hired to write new music for every worship occasion. All music, both inside and outside of the church, conformed to rules of harmony established by the church. (Beethoven was the first composer to break out of these restrictions and to consider himself an artist.)

With the invention of moveable type (1450) and the rise of the Protestant movement after 1517, preaching and Bible teaching began to move church music into a more secondary role. In nineteenth-century American Protestant churches, there were sometimes worship experiences many hours long with little or no music!

The pendulum has now swung back in the other direction again, but the direction strongly emphasizes adult contemporary music, country & western music, and rock & roll. Traditional hymns are given new musical treatments. With the influence of television, there is a strong preference for interesting visual experiences that are coupled to both music and to Bible teaching. Video screens are becoming more common at the same rate that stained glass is becoming less common. Worship in the twenty-first century definitely is becoming a multimedia experience, and the surviving churches will adapt. They will adapt just as churches previously adapted to having stained glass, printed hymns, hymnals with music, and other innovations.

Faith Fuel

A Prayer of Wonder

Almighty, all-knowing, and everlasting God, you keep surprising me with blessings I did not ask for or expect. Whom will you fill with your spirit, power, and joy; that I may see it and give you praise? What will happen to inspire me to give you glory? Where will I be when you make yourself known to me in some new way?

Forgiving God, You have inspired me to accept your Son, Jesus, as the Savior who has died for my sins. How will you test me today so that I may know how well I am doing? What temptation will I be able to resist today, so that I may celebrate the spiritual growth you have given me? In the midst of the temptations, what opportunities will you give me to stand up for the faith you have given me?

Gracious and generous God, you keep showering me with blessings. What will you give me today that I may return it to you as my offering of joy? Who will you put in my path that I may show them your love? How will you open previously closed doors that I may tell others of your atoning grace in Jesus Christ?

Attentive and empathetic God, you have always listened to my prayers for others. Who would you have me pray for today? What would you have me ask for on behalf of those you call me to care about? Is this the best time to intercede for them? Where would you challenge me to be when you prompt me to pray? How can I be more sensitive to their needs? Why do you often prompt me to pray for people that I have not even met?

Encouraging and strengthening God, you know me better than I know myself. How can I be better in tune with your spirit? How can I best affirm the loving bond that you have established between us? How can I be the most receptive to The Savior's call upon my life to serve Him?

My Commander-in-Chief, you have never asked me to do anything that you have not already equipped me to do. I am not strong of body, yet you have strengthened me to do more than I ever dreamed of doing. I have often done very foolish things, yet you have lent me some of your wisdom when it has been important. My faith has sometimes quivered, yet you have strengthened my spirit and reminded me of your call upon my life. What else can I say?

In Jesus' name, Amen.

Faith Fuel

Home

In Bible times, Passover was a time of homecoming. All Jews within three days' walking distance traveled to Jerusalem for the party. The Jews living more than that distance away tried to get the entire extended family together in some way.

Robert Frost wrote, "Home is the place where, when you have to go there, they have to take you in." For the first half century of my life, home was located in Long Beach, California. When my parents moved out of that house to their retirement community, even some of my cousins felt the pangs of loss. It had been their home away from home as well.

Another image of home comes from a song I learned as a teenager. We loved to sing, "This World Is Not My Home, I am just a-Passin' Through." That old song came back to me when I was on one coast while most of my relatives were on the other. The song had particularly poignant meaning for me as I helped people rebuild their lives in the aftermath of Hurricane Andrew in Homestead, Florida.

When we talk about a church home, we have a different kind of image. For some it is the church in which they grew up. Until it dissolved, I considered East Side Christian Church in Long Beach my church home, even when I was pastoring other churches. For some their church home is simply a place they point to as where they attend on Christmas and Easter. Some point to a church as where they used to attend and might again someday. For most church attendees thinking about their church home, it is the place of an extended family. It is sometimes a better and more loving family than their genetic family. Some come back to church after not attending for a long time. Chances are their reason for leaving long since expired. They may have forgotten why they left in the first place.

Life-Changing Prayer

Sören Kierkegaard said, "Prayer does not change God, but it changes him who prays." Too often, we act as though it is not true. We pray as if we are giving orders to God. To use a common metaphor, we treat God like a cosmic flight attendant, ready to do our bidding when we press the prayer button.

Faith Fuel

We fail to pray effectively because we do not trust God to do what is best. We want to be in control, and we would like to take credit for the outcome of our prayers. This places limits on what we want God to do. Increasing numbers of Christians are discovering how much real power is unleashed when they surrender totally to God's will. When we let God be God, and let Christ be King, miracles occur with increasing frequency. There are three ingredients of effective and powerful prayer:

1. We trust God with the outcome, knowing that God knows what is best for us.
2. We surrender control to God, like Jesus did when surrendering to God's will in the Garden of Gethsemane.
3. We give credit, glory, thanksgiving, honor, and power to God in all things.

When God knows we recognize the role of the divine in our lives, more of that power is unleashed. The most amazing thing about the way prayer changes us lies in the consequences of intercessory prayer. Far more power is released in our lives when we pray for others than when we pray for ourselves. More power is consistently unleashed when we pray in the name of Jesus, than when we do not invoke His name. Christians have not made up that rule, but the Bible teaches us to do so, and experience bears it out. We will understand why when we have passed over to the other side of the mystery.

Fear

The Book of Proverbs says that the fear of God is the beginning of wisdom. Many people have irrational fears or phobias. Common phobias include:

- Acrophobia–dread of being at a great height
- Agoraphobia–dread of open spaces
- Arachnophobia–dread of spiders
- Claustrophobia–dread of closed or narrow spaces
- Ophidaphobia–dread of snakes

Of itself, fear is not a bad thing. It is part of our survival instinct. Sometimes fear is healthy and appropriate, and sometimes it is not. Soldiers learn to manage their fear. When we take precautions in our work or play, those precautions are a tool to manage possible danger. This too is a way of managing fear.

Many people are more afraid of public speaking than of dying. When we feel shy, it is our way of expressing our fear of rejection. Fear also motivates us when we do not want to try something new or do something a new way. There is a natural human tendency to continue

188

to do things that are useless, painful, or destructive. This is simply because not to do these things means doing something differently. Change can be very hard indeed.

While exiled on the island of Patmos, Jesus' beloved disciple John pondered these things. A much older and wiser man than when met Jesus, he spoke about fear directly. He said, "There is no fear in love, but perfect love casts out fear; for fear has to do with punishment, and whoever fears has not reached perfection in love. We love because he first loved us." [I John 4:18-19 (NRSV)]

Consider the implications of how God's perfect love casts out our fears. Since this is true, why is it that so often we refuse to do the very things God asks us to do? Do we not trust God? In our daily prayers, we need to remember to tell God how much we love Him and trust Him. God frequently challenges us to prove it. Even pastors struggle to live out what they pray and preach.

Most of us try hard to manage our fears. We usually succeed, but sometimes we do not. Christians do not fear tithing when they have learned to enjoy its rewards. Christians need to work on making friends among non-believers. It takes effort to lead non-believers to Christ. Most have had some small success, but we know we must do better. Some pastors do a better job teaching evangelism than doing it.

We need not fear heights if there are safety precautions taken. We need not fear open spaces if we recognize them as a bountiful gift in a crowded world. We need not fear spiders and snakes that are not poisonous or otherwise hostile to humans. We need not fear closed spaces when we know how to exit.

In the same way we need not fear being generous to God when we are confident that God is far more generous to us. We need not fear spreading the Good News when we are sure that it is a matter of eternal life with God or eternal isolation from all that is good, including life. It is a matter of managing our fears.

Generational Differences

It is interesting how people can pay attention differently when they really want to worship. Those born after 1960 or so, tend to like worship with a faster pace, contemporary music, and many rhythms. For these people, when things slow down or there is silence there is a tendency to get impatient or bored. For these younger generations, the *experience* of worship can be the first and most important consideration. The feelings they have after worship are extremely important to them as well. Critics want to say that these people approach worship as a form of entertainment. That is not necessarily true.

People born in previous generations see worship differently. They can begin to pay attention to worship before other people arrive, and before the music and visiting with others begin. It can happen again when there is a time for silent prayer. Unlike younger generations that use music to shut out other distractions, these older people say they hate it when there is music during silent prayer—it tends to make them focus on the music rather than upon God.

As they sit there in silence, they can become aware of the rhythm of their own breathing. They can sense the calming and slowing down of the beating of their hearts, as they begin to sense an envelope of warmth and peace. They can become aware of the still, small voice of God speaking to them in the quietness. They often find that one particular aspect of the presence and power of God may begin to rivet their attention. It is often about healing or other kinds of holy help that their friends and family need. While these folks' children may want the music and message to direct their worship, the older generations become more and more fascinated with how God is directing and focusing their prayers in the quiet times before, during, and after worship.

It is the way in which they focus their attention on worship that makes their worship different from that of their descendents. They enjoy the contemporary worship of their children, grandchildren, and great grandchildren, but they still hunger for and enjoy silence. They become enraptured with the power they experience when they totally surrender to the flood of the Holy Spirit enveloping them. It is in a different way their descendents tend to experience spiritual ecstasy, by letting music lift them higher and higher.

In both experiences of public worship, those in touch with God through Jesus experience what Harvey Cox calls "the seduction of the spirit." Whether the silent wafting of angel wings or the compelling sounds of music lift our spirits, the more we experience God's holy joy the more we want of it. Once we put our hand into the hand of The Master, we never want to turn back from the exhilaration of the saving power of Jesus. Some of us started putting our hands in His a long time ago, but others worshiping with us might be ready for the first time to give their lives to Him.

Regardless of physical age, we cannot ignore the fact that spiritual development and spiritual maturity both play significant roles in how different people approach worship. Some approach worship as spectators, seeing worship as a form of entertainment. Before, during, and after the worship service, those seeking more than entertainment may well be examining their feelings as well as their thoughts. As spiritual development matures however, worshipers focus less on themselves, their thoughts, and their feelings. Instead, they begin to seek Christ's presence in their hearts. When this happens, it is a major turning point in a person's spiritual journey. As we focus more and more on seeking Him, following Him, and trying to please Him, our spiritual growth is incredible. Eventually, the desire to surrender everything to Him and being at peace with that surrender transforms lives. We are never the same.

The Most Important Lesson

I first learned the importance of practice when I was in "junior first" grade. My piano teacher was a Mrs. Nelson, and learning for her mostly meant memorizing. Through a succession of piano teachers, I learned to memorize both the notes and the instructions for performance. In school, I had teachers who in a similar way wanted me simply to finish my assignments. Then I had teachers who taught me to look beyond the obvious. I had teachers who taught me how much fun learning and interpreting can be. At home, I found praise for doing well, and when I did not do well I was encouraged to do better.

It was not until I started to major in piano and voice in college that I found a piano teacher who encouraged me to think for myself, in terms of both how I memorized and how I performed. If some of my earlier teachers had taken this approach, my life might have been very different.

My faith journey has a similar story. In church school, I was encouraged to remember Bible stories, and I was encouraged to learn how to interpret those stories. I remember only one of my teachers encouraging me to get to know Jesus Christ. I cannot picture any of my later teachers encouraging me to develop that most important relationship of my life. It has been only fairly recently that this relationship has become vital to me. This has transformed both my professional life and my personal life.

In just the last few years, I have become interested in working hard to help others find what I have discovered in Jesus Christ. My interest in evangelism and church growth is a reflection of this. In previous efforts, my work in evangelism was mostly mechanical, following prescribed procedures in the form of rather precise packages.

Faith Fuel

I was particularly interested in doing the N.E.A. program entitled "Blueprints" because it provided a cut and dried procedure that virtually guaranteed success. I must confess however that I approached the program for the purposes of generating numbers in worship rather than a desire to share the Good News of Jesus Christ.

While I was in Detroit one week, I found that no matter how tired I was I had an enthusiasm for helping others get out the "news that is too good to keep." One of the churches I visited almost cancelled my visit because they were so discouraged and were ready to give up. I am praying for them. Another church was so wrapped up in itself and its own problems that it had little eye for the problems in the community around it. I hope I was able to change their thinking a bit. When my energy flags, my Lord energizes me!

All Hallow's Eve

In October of 1982, *Christianity Today* published an article entitled "Is Halloween a Witches' Brew?" by Harold L. Myra. Mr. Myra began by pointing out that many Christians find Halloween an uncomfortable topic. He asked the question, "Are there thoroughly Christian ways in which to view Halloween?"

Historically, the churches celebrated a festival honoring saints beginning in the fourth century. During the Middle Ages, all Christendom celebrated "All Saints' Day" in May. Eventually this festival was moved to November 1 and called All Hallow's Day. Soon it became customary to call the evening before All Hallow's Day "All-Hallow's Eve." While some may question supplanting the festivals of pagan religions by injecting them with Biblical values, the church has always found great value in "Christianizing" the calendar. With this introduction, it seems obvious that there are at least three themes that Christians can follow during the season of Halloween.

Since it all started with an intentional recognizing of all the saints of the past who now find their place in heaven, the church can continue to take advantage of this. We can recognize the great believers and saints of history. We can recognize those loved ones who have gone on to the larger life who nurtured us in our faith. The article pointed out both these themes. We can also talk about what it means to be a saint in the midst of an evil world today. We cannot gloss over the fact that evil exists, and to be a Christian means to be in opposition to evil by working with Our Savior.

Faith Fuel

On "All Hallow's Eve," we have children of all ages coming to our doors with the chant, "trick or treat!" Praise God, most of these children are *not* going to "trick" us if we do not "treat" them! In keeping with tradition, we give them something to eat and often praise them for their costumes. In addition to the praise, can we consider offering them a blessing? We might say, "May God deliver you from the evils that we recognize tonight!" Some of the children will mutter a "thank you" while others might only grunt or look at us as though we are crazy.

A Control Crisis

Who is in control of your life? Who has the permission and authority to direct or regulate your life? Who makes the decisions that affect the way in which you live? Whose will predominates your life? Are you satisfied, content, and at peace? That last question is the crucial one for most people, and many of us are not satisfied, content, and at peace. We are living in a time when there is an obvious crisis of control, and the answers to the opening questions are not as simple as one might think.

There are two extremes as models of control. First, there is control from within or self-control. The name for this is autonomy. A good example of this is in G. Gordon Liddy's book, *Will*. He describes taking rugged individualism to an extreme. He will not allow himself to be influenced by anyone except possibly the President of the United States due to his fanatic patriotism. A former leader of Iran stamped everything he did with God's approval. On the other extreme model of control is heteronomy. These people are easily influenced by others, particularly influenced by governmental or religious leaders. Those in the armed forces also experience heteronomy. Children who are under the control of their parents also experience heteronomy.

In between these two extremes are those who retain control over part of their lives. They voluntarily relinquish control over some areas to others. Even rugged individualists relinquish part of their control when they enter a hospital. Each model of control has advantages. It is not just a matter of where to place responsibility or blame. Psychologically it is a matter of ego and pride, coupled with our need for peace and happiness. In either model, if there is enough anxiety or unhappiness over a length of time, a crisis of control is the result.

Theonomy is a third alternative to these first two models of control. It means turning over control to God through Jesus Christ.

193

Faith Fuel

When we put everything in God's hands, God continues to give us our freedom to choose. It is the best of both worlds.

Fear Can Be Healthy

A former Miss America, Sue's behavior is at least partially controlled by her fear and distrust of men. Jack, a computer specialist, lashes out at people because of his fear of losing control. Marie, a personnel manager, often messes up her personal life because of her fear of being alone. Joe commits himself to more than he can handle, because he fears rejection if he says no.

Pharaoh and his people in Egypt were fearful of the increasing numbers of Jews, so the Jews were put into slavery. When Moses spent a lot of time on Mount Sinai, God's fearful people created the golden calf. King Saul, fearful of death, further angered God by consulting a psychic to tell him the future. Another (much later) Saul, fearful that a new Jewish sect was going to pollute the faith of God's people, persecuted the Christians until he met Jesus on the road to Damascus.

There is another side to fear. Healthy fears of things such as electricity and tornadoes keep us from being killed. Healthy fears of things that might threaten our survival have been a driving force to move humanity into the future. A healthy fear of our enemies has often fueled our creative juices. The solutions to these challenges have contributed to human progress.

Fear of punishment can help teach us appropriate behavior. Fear of shame can prod us into acting honorably. In our zealous efforts to portray God as loving, our striving for "theological correctness" emptied our Christian moral witness of its power. In a similar way, as we have tried to legislate loving behavior, the resulting sense of political correctness has emptied genuine love of it is meaning and its joy.

Some parents have made the mistake of constantly scolding their children. They believe if they exercise enough control, the children will turn out better. Short-changing their children's need for genuine and unconditional love, those parents do not recognize their mistake until it is too late.

Members of small churches sometimes respond fearfully to the financial cost of operating their church. There is a natural tendency to cling to what is being done at the moment or to try to revive what has

194

been done in the past. The challenge is to catch the vision of God's dreams for the church. With worship, we are challenged to have faith in the dreams that God gives us. As we leave the worship service, God hopes that we will have the courage to trust in His ability to achieve His dreams for our lives. The fear of God puts other fears into perspective, and then God's love casts out all of our fears.

Healing Prayer

For a long time I could never admit I had ever been angry with God. Since I felt it was wrong to be angry with God, I convinced myself I was angry with myself instead. Deep inside, I got really angry with myself because I could not allow myself to be angry with God.

I awoke in the middle of the night one night. When I could not get back to sleep, I began praying, which usually helps. If not, it brings me enough peace so that do not need any more sleep.

Suddenly I found myself expressing a lot of anger first at myself, then at God too. I really got vocal about it, and the only one to be disturbed was my cat because I am single. My anger got more heated, until suddenly I was exhausted! I was so drained of energy I did not want to crawl out of bed. I got on my knees while I patched things up with my Best Friend. All the harshness was gone from my voice. As I continued to pray quietly, God's peace enveloped me. I was grateful for the healing in progress. My negative thoughts tried to invade the progress of the healing. They were quickly displaced by the words and music of some old familiar hymns, including "Holy, Holy, Holy" and "Trust and Obey." When I got up the next morning, I felt as though a great load had been lifted from me. I had a much clearer idea regarding the direction in which God was leading me.

I tell this story to emphasize an often forgotten fact. Whether we pray for others or for ourselves, prayer can be very therapeutic for the person praying. As more than one Christian has observed, "Prayer does not change God—prayer changes me!" As for my anger towards God, the reasons were not legitimate, but the anger was no less real. God created me, and I know that God understands when one of His children throws a temper tantrum.

Faith Fuel

Dreams

One of the more famous songs associated with the late Walt Disney begins, "A dream is a wish your heart makes when you're fast asleep." In Bible times, dreams were considered a legitimate form of prophecy. If a leader had a dream, the first thing was to find a way to confirm this dream came from God, either through other prophecy or through prayer. In the 21st century, it is not considered rational or scientific to treat a dream as though it is a prophecy. Dreams are approached with great skepticism. There is nothing wrong with being skeptical about dreams. On the other hand, Christians should be wary of dismissing all dreams as fantasies, wishes, or nightmares.

There is a big difference between vision and goal setting! Goal setting simply organizes what we want to accomplish. Vision comes out of a fervent desire to accomplish God's will. Whereas goal setting projects our intentions, vision projects God's hopes. In the ancient world, prophets were often not very popular. If they had a reputation for accuracy however, they were taken seriously even if they were not liked. As Jesus put it, "A good tree cannot bear bad fruit, nor can a bad tree bear good fruit. Every tree that does not bear good fruit is cut down and thrown into the fire. Thus you will know them by their fruits." [Matthew 7:18-20 NRSV] The good fruit of accurate prophets was highly respected.

If a leader does not have a vision to pursue, that leader must depend upon someone who does have such vision. Church leaders cannot afford to assume the dreams they have are dreams God has given them. Leaders cannot even assume their own prayers alone confirm their dreams. Such confirmation must come from others who previously have born good fruit.

As a pastor, I have frequently heard from people regarding the hopes they have for their church. Very seldom do we hear from anyone regarding what they believe to be God's dreams for their church. It is an awesome responsibility to speak on behalf of God's dreams, for no sane person wants to be a false prophet. In every congregation I have served however, I have known a fully functional Christian whose prayer life bears good fruit. That is important! Let us pursue our goals in the context of God's dreams for us!

Faith Fuel

Waiting

Each one of us that walks this earth finds slower times we hate.
We find our lives suspended, stopped - directionless we wait.
At first we rest, relieved that life has made some time to breathe.
Too soon we're bored, fed up, and irked–our anger seems to seethe.

As those of faith we turn to prayer, we seek some holy skill
To energize our search for goals, or better still, God's will.
We want to give God orders, but we know that doesn't work.
Our patience thins, our egos droop, our vision's lost in murk.

We question why, we wonder how our lives can stand so still.
Around us yet the world moves on, our wait's a bitter pill.
Somewhere amidst all this we find there's more than time to think.
We realize there's time to heal, we're nowhere near the brink.

Some waiting's ours because we're wrong or having gone too far.
Some waiting's ours because we're not prepared or up to par.
Some waiting's ours because we've lost our bearings and our way.
Some waiting's ours because we're holding circumstance at bay.

Let waiting be a chance to heal some friendships torn and tossed.
Let waiting be a chance to nurture passions almost lost.
Let waiting be a time of growth, to nurture faith and love.
Let waiting be a time well spent in seeking God above.

Finding Forgiveness

In recent years, the importance of sin has been played down as an effort to alleviate guilt. Guilt is a major factor in mental illness when a person does not have a healthy relationship with God. Guilt and forgiveness were played down so heavily by psychologists, that in 1973 Karl Menninger upset the entire psychological community with a book entitled *Whatever Became of Sin?*

Sin is no less prevalent now than previously, but the attitude by society towards sin has changed. Even our universities are teaching the idea that there are no absolute values. They insist that everything is relative. If that is true, we have lost our reference points in life. Life itself has lost meaning. We see the results in the increased number of sociopathic and amoral people who make headlines with their crimes.

Faith Fuel

In the classic sense, sin is opposition or indifference to the will of God. Most of us realize that opposition to God is the essence of sin, but indifference to God's will is equally bad. In the Lord's Prayer, we ask God to forgive us. Those praying that prayer often do not attach any importance to that request for forgiveness. When we are indifferent to wrongdoing, forgiveness loses meaning and power.

If we are going to be fully Christian in the richest sense, then we must be aware of God's will, appreciate God's will, affirm God's will, and discipline ourselves to obey God's will. Being attentive to God's will means rejoicing in the right as well as condemning the wrong. Like God, we have to be ready to forgive. We have to be ready to acknowledge that all of us make mistakes. We are all sinners. We must be ready to return to Jesus the love he showed for us. After all, he died for our sins that we might be forgiven.

Foot in Mouth Disease

"Set a guard over my mouth, O Lord; keep watch over the door of my lips." (Psalm 141:3 NRSV)

An epigram is a single sentence conveying wisdom in a few words, often with humor. The popularity of epigrams comes and goes. In the 1960s, a popular epigram was, "Be sure that your brain is in gear before you start your mouth!" Another variation is the epigram that says, "Out of the mouths of babes come words we should never have said!"

Speaking rashly is sometimes part of being human. The Apostle Peter blurted things out, only to be admonished by Jesus. Sometimes we speak rashly because we want to appear more confident or knowledgeable than we really are. Sometimes we speak rashly because we feel insecure and want the attention of others.

Keeping watch can be just as much encouragement as prevention. Most Christians think Old Testament law mostly concerns itself with restricting or forbidding certain kinds of behavior. Actually, there is more material on how to do things right and well. In addition, there is far more material on when to celebrate than there is on when to punish.

As we get closer to Christmas, let us keep watch over our lips. Let us be sure that at every opportunity we affirm our love for God. Let us be sure that when there are opportunities to speak of God's so loving the world that He gave Jesus to us in the manger, let us say so!

Faith Fuel

When someone mentions "Peace on earth, goodwill towards men," let us affirm that such goodwill is also for women. Let us also affirm that real peace only comes from God.

Let us look for chances to mention that "Joy to the World" is not only a Christmas carol but a song that affirms the glory and grace of God any time. Let us look for chances to remind adults that Santa Claus did not rise from the dead. When people remind us that the Christmas tree was originally a fertility symbol, let us use it as an opportunity to talk about how God has redeemed the Christmas tree—and the rest of us in Jesus Christ.

Let us keep watch! Let God's praise be on our lips!

Faith Fuel

Prayer Instead of Carping

"They told me that if I voted for Barry Goldwater there would be wars, civil disorder, national strife, crime in the streets, and uncontrolled inflation. Well, I voted for Goldwater, and sure enough, all those things happened." [Barry Goldwater lost the election.]

That satirical statement was on the front page of the student newspaper at Cal-State Long Beach in 1968. It was during the unpopular war in Vietnam, and it pointedly spoke about our attitudes towards our leaders. Each November in the United States, each citizen has the privilege of going to the polls and voting for the candidates and issues of their choice. Then, with baited breath, people watch for the results and pray that their candidates win and issues get resolved as they have hoped. It usually includes a bout of Election Day fever, but soon this "disease" passes, and people all go back to life as usual.

"Life as usual" often means stopping prayer for our leaders, and people resume their carping. The complaining about the actions and policies of their leaders has little creative results, and it merely serves to increase their stress with its destructive eating away of their insides. What is needed is more constructive criticism and disciplined praying. Instead of grousing to their friends and relatives, they can write letters of suggestions and encouragement to their leaders. They can also pray for their leaders after the election, including those who won despite their vote.

In the New Testament, we are asked how we can claim to love a God we cannot see, when we do not love the brother or sister whom we do see. We can be more effective in our love for our leaders, even the ones with whom we disagree or those we dislike. We could then more effectively express our love for our Supreme Leader. Our worship could then be more thankful and honest!

Doing and Being

Yeas ago I read a magazine article by someone named Jean Gonick, in which she said, "I formulated a theory several years back that the world is divided into two types of people. ... Those who do, and those who are: the *'do-ers'* and the *'be-ers.'"* [Italics mine]

Both "do-ers" and "be-ers" do things. There is a difference. The "do-er" makes accomplishing things and achieving goals the center of his or her life. On the other hand, getting things done and achieving goals are side effects for the "be-er." A "do-er" goes to Golden Gate Park in San Francisco for a day of studying plants and animals. That "do-er" finds satisfaction in things like naming and listing more plants and animals than anyone. The "be-er" on the other hand goes to the same park for the same reason on the same day, and finds satisfaction in the variety to be found there, simply enjoying the shapes, sizes, colors, and movements, and learning a lot about God's creation in the process.

This is not a new idea! Jesus and the Apostle Paul made similar observations in their own time. The illustrations were just different. The prime example of "do-ers" in Jesus' time was the lifestyle of the Pharisees. Their lives were dedicated to the doing of The Law, doing exactly what The Law required. On the other hand, Jesus found opportunity to commend some "be-ers" people, who lived their lives in simple faith and trust in The Almighty, letting God be the "do-er" when it came to things important.

The Apostle Paul pointed out the importance of striking a balance between being and doing by putting them in perspective. He said faith without works is dead, that our works should reflect our faith. Paul said we should begin by being faithful. We should concentrate, said he, on being a *be-er*, a person of faith, and let doings be the result and side effect of our faith. When someone asks, "What do I do to be a better Christian?" we should simply suggest they begin by being a person of faith. A Christian is therefore a *be-er* first and foremost!

Thanksgiving–Period

Long ago, Habakkuk said, "Though the fig tree does not blossom, and no fruit is on the vines; though the produce of the olive fails, and the fields yield no food; though the flock is cut off from the fold, and there is no herd in the stalls, yet I will rejoice in the LORD; I will exult in the God of my salvation. [Habakkuk 3:17-18 (NRSV)]

If someone gives us an apple when we are hungry, we are thankful. If they were to give us the same apple when we are full, we are less thankful. If someone gives us an old battered sweater to wear when we are cold, we are grateful. When someone gives us such a sweater but if the day is not cold, we are less thankful. If God gives us rain after a year of drought, we are thankful. If God gives us rain, day after day for a month, we do not continue to be thankful for the rain.

When we have lived in the same place for a long time, we need to remember, without prodding, to be as thankful for that home after time has passed as we were at the beginning. We need to express our thanks to friends for their friendship, regardless of duration. We should thank God for God's loving-kindness, no matter what our circumstances. We need to tell our families what they mean to us. Other than on Sunday, we should praise God for the gift of God's Son, Jesus Christ. I love saying to friends, with the Apostle Paul, "I thank my God for all my remembrances of you...."

More or Less

More! More! More! We hear this cry from people who are genuinely hungry. We also hear this cry from people who were not hungry when they sat down to eat, but who simply like the taste. We hear the cry from those who really need to diet, and from the greedy those who just like any change in diet. Sometimes the cry grates on our ears, not pleasant to be heard. The cry seems so demanding of our time, our resources, and our energy. Our response is often "I do not *want* to give any more" or "I do not think I *can* give any more."

Less! Less! Less! We cry, "I am running out of resources." "There just is not enough to go around." "We will end up not being able to help anyone if we try to help everyone."

Waste! Waste! Waste! We hear the reminder but seldom see it applied to us. We see the speck in our neighbor's eye better than we see the log in our own.

We Christians hear another cry right out of the Bible but again the cry falls on ears just as deaf. Stewardship! We know that God provides enough of everything, and we have the responsibility for the best use and best distribution. What cry is loudest on our lips? What cry really needs to be heard?

From time to time, an old Chinese proverb comes to our attention: "There are three grand essentials to life—something to do, something to love, and something to hope for." Like most proverbs that have survived the test of time, this one is loaded with wisdom. We have something to do! We have to nurture what is here. We have to reach

202

out spiritually and physically. We have to make the most of what we have got.

We have something or someone to love. We have Christ and His Church to love, and we have our neighbors to love. Developing a loving-liking-trusting relationship with the Lord or with any neighbor can be a task really worth a lifetime of work,

We have something to hope for! Tomorrow always brings fresh opportunities, fresh challenges, and new blessings. We have a future as well as a past and present. We Christians have an unlimited future—in stewardship, in the legacy we leave behind, and in life eternal with our Lord Christ. We have the grand essentials. Let us make the most of them.

Double-Edged Truth

In his classic tragedy, *Macbeth*, William Shakespeare pointed out that the truth is a double-edged sword, cutting both ways. Macbeth had been told by the three "Weird Sisters" [witches] that no one born of a woman would slay Macbeth. In a fight to the death with his old friend MacDuff, Macbeth taunted his adversary with this truth. MacDuff then replied, confident in the knowledge he would win, saying that he was from his mother's womb "untimely ripped." The truth in which Macbeth had found protection was also a pronouncement of his doom—a truth that cut both ways.

In a verse from Psalm 37 we also find a truth that is like a two edged sword. "Take delight in the LORD, and he will give you the desires of your heart." [Psalms 37:4 (NRSV)] We can talk about taking delight in God from the aspect of getting the desires of our hearts. We can also talk about getting the desires of our hearts by taking delight in God.

It is relatively easy to take delight in God when such delight is born out of getting the desires of our hearts. Thanksgiving and praise focused upon God usually arises out of material blessings. Sometimes such thanks and praise arises out of a sense of deliverance, and such was the most frequent case in Bible times. For many years, a day has been set aside in the United States and some other countries for thanksgiving. The celebrations may or may not have a Judeo-Christian influence. Nonetheless, a great celebration begins the holiday season in the United States. In the context of the church, children are taught from an early age the old song that begins, "Count your many

203

Faith Fuel

blessings, name them one by one." Each Thanksgiving, children are told how counting their blessings leads them to be thankful.

According to Psalm 37, this is only part of the truth. It is one side of a two edged sword of truth. The other side is the challenge of taking delight in God for its own sake. Such delight is born out of a developing and growing relationship. Finding delight in a relationship with the Creator is possible, as evidenced by the great leaders in the Old Testament and by the Apostles in the New Testament. It is easier to develop a relationship with God's son, Jesus. Such is the reason for the incarnation. The desire of the human heart is born out of the desire of the heart of God. No wonder the psalmist says delight in God yields the desires of the heart.

Christians who draw close to Jesus learn that giving and thanksgiving are closely related. In the United States, to many people, Thanksgiving is just a holiday. To church folks, it is a time for thanking God for things we have and relationships we share. In the Bible, thanksgiving is seen differently. The people of God tend to thank God for what is not theirs! They thank God when God delivers them from danger and from the hands of their enemies. They thank God when God delivers them from sickness, hunger, and thirst. The focus in the Bible is more on God than on possessions.

How do they maintain that focus? They keep their minds on God by giving. They constantly make offerings to God as expressions of their thanksgiving. To start, they accept the idea that 1/10th of everything they have is God's anyway. They give 1/10 of their gross earnings to God, not as an offering but as a tithe. After they turn over to God what is rightfully God's, then they begin making sacrifices of their comforts and conveniences as ways of expressing their thanks to God. After that, they make further sacrifices as a way of saying to God that they are sorry for their sins. Jesus died on the cross and rose on Easter so that we no longer have to make sacrifices for our sins. We are thus set free to make greater use of all that is ours on loan from God. Christ gave on the cross, which leads to our tithing, which leads to giving, which leads to our giving thanks, which leads to Thanksgiving. Amazing!

Some Time Has Passed

Some time has passed since terror changed our sense of who we are.
As buildings fell and lives were lost, the news spread fast and far.
Our anger rose as innocence was lost in grief and pain,
Yet courage and compassion rose amidst destruction's gain.

Faith Fuel

Our world is not so civilized that madness can't emerge.
There're always those who bear a grudge with anger they can't purge.
There're those who cannot bear to see a smile upon a face –
They're jealous of the joy of others in our human race.

Some time has passed since people cried in terror "Oh, my God!"
Some time has passed since all shed tears as terror touched our sod.
Some time has passed since sickness claimed religion as its base.
Some time has passed, we've time to ponder what we really face.

The enemy we face is not a nation or a creed.
We face a threat to liberty and freedom's precious seed.
Such seed yields hope that burns and fuels our vict'ry and success.
Our progress as a people rests on working for the best.

The enemy we face is not a people, creed, or race.
We fight the crimes of infamy, it's justice we embrace.
There comes a time when morals count, when values light our trail.
Some time has passed, and with God's help, God's justice will prevail.

Faith Fuel
DECEMBER

Approaching Christmas

"So all the generations from Abraham to David are fourteen generations; and from David to the deportation to Babylon, fourteen generations; and from the deportation to Babylon to the Messiah, fourteen generations." (Matthew 1:17 NRSV)

Most of us do not take the time to read the genealogies of Jesus found in Matthew and Luke. With the exception of the Church of Jesus Christ of Latter Day Saints, Christians have little religious interest in genealogy. Biblical scholars have a lot of fun comparing the two genealogies, but there is one very interesting fact to be gleaned from Matthew's version.

Matthew's Gospel was addressed to a primarily Jewish audience. The audience being interested in lineage, Matthew puts the material first in his gospel. A Jewish audience would also be interested in numbers, particularly the number seven and its multiples. This is because of the historical emphasis on the Sabbath of course. In the verse quoted above, Matthew points out that there were six sets of seven generations between Abraham and Jesus. The implication is that there is no need for a seventh set of seven generations. Jesus completes God's creative plan for his people, and now God can have His Sabbath rest.

Theological and scholarly questions aside, the Advent of Jesus marks the fulfillment and completion of the Biblical saga that began with Abraham. The Advent of Jesus also marks the beginning of God's New Covenant with humankind. Jesus states it in all simplicity at the beginning of his earthly ministry, saying, "The Kingdom of God is at hand!" We are living in the acceptable year of Our Lord. Because the Kingdom of God is at hand, this year and every year is the "Year of Jubilee" as proclaimed in the Torah.

The joy of Christmas is just the icing on the cake. The cake was baked for the year 'round celebration of the Kingdom of God. During the National Evangelism Workshop held in Nashville in 1990, Anthony Campolo made an address entitled "The Kingdom of God as a Party." Available on video and audio tape, it is a marvelous resource for churches whose joy has dwindled to a few brief moments around Christmas and Easter. The tape in either version makes it clear that the Bible is full of abundant evidence that our traditionally somber worship services run contrary to God's will for worship experiences.

Faith Fuel

As the song goes, the joy of The Lord is our strength. Much of the zest that our churches claim they have lost has been lost because we do not allow ourselves the joy that God wants for us. Let us take back the sense of party from the secular world and show the un-churched what joy really means!

Mary's Cousin, Elizabeth

"All who heard them pondered them and said, 'hat then will this child become?' For, indeed, the hand of the Lord was with him."(Luke 1:66 NRSV)

Parents have a natural tendency to think that their child is special, particularly if it is their first. Sometimes the neighbors smile secretly when the parents are overly enthusiastic. After they get home they say, "They'll get over it!" Usually after a few weeks, or at most a few months, the parents "get over it" and get on with raising their child.

Sometimes the parents are religious. They spend as much or perhaps more time praising God for their child as they do praising the child. Folks sharing the same faith will smile and perhaps find the whole thing inspiring. Those not sharing the faith of the parents find the religious outpouring of the parents to be interesting, perhaps comical.

If the parents turn the birth of their child into a too-religious event, friends and neighbors become amazed. At the extreme, the friends and neighbors may even become frightened. Rumors begin to fly as gossip begins to flourish. There are whispers behind closed doors, out of the hearing of the parents.

If the parents are not aware of the whispers, their happiness may not be touched. If the parents hear about the whispers, they may have the confidence to ignore the gossip or not be troubled by it. Their first concern is their child. Then, in addition, their religion may so pervade their lives that the opinions of others will not matter.

Knowing this we look at our Biblical story, a part of the Christmas saga. The mother, Elizabeth, had not expected to be pregnant. The father, Zachariah, found it equally incredible. The father, however, had not been talking. At the birth, his joy was made complete. When his wife announced what they would call the baby, his friends and relatives protested. However, the old man confirmed, "His name is John." John?

Yes, John the Baptist had come out of a mysterious pregnancy, almost as mysterious as that of his cousin, Jesus. John had first experienced the presence of Jesus while they were both in the womb.

207

Faith Fuel

John had "leaped for joy" inside of the womb when a pregnant Mary had come to visit her sister Elizabeth, John's mother.

"What then will this child become?" asked the neighbors when John was born.

Living in a Dream

'Now the birth of Jesus the Messiah took place in this way. When his mother Mary had been engaged to Joseph, but before they lived together, she was found to be with child from the Holy Spirit." (Matthew 1:18 NRSV)

Since we live in a whole different culture, it is hard to picture the situation of Mary and Joseph—on their terms. In Biblical times, being married and being wedded were two very different things. Being married meant that a contract had been signed, a deal had been made. Sometimes these marriages took place before the bride and groom were born! It was often sealed with a glass of wine between the fathers of the children. Such a marriage we would now call an "engagement," only the contract was binding. A divorce was required to break this "engagement."

In the case of Mary and Joseph, the "wedding" was probably to be announced as soon as she was physically ready to start bearing children. It would be at that point that Mary and Joseph were to start living together, and there would be a huge celebration of the beginning of a new family unit. At the time our story begins, Joseph and Mary are married (engaged), but they are not living together (wedded) because Mary is not "ready."

All of this sounds so foreign to us! Where in today's world we speak of living together before marriage, in the Biblical world they spoke of extended marriage before living together! In today's world, women think about having children without a wedding, or having a wedding without having children. In the Biblical world, having a wedding signaled one's readiness to have children. Living together without having children brought shame upon the family.

When a man found out on the wedding night that his wife was not a virgin, he had two main choices. He could either cut his finger and put blood on the bedding to confirm his wife's virginity, or he could air the un-bloodied bedding for the community to see, and then have the marriage annulled. Joseph was an honorable man, and according to the scripture, he cared enough about Mary and Mary's family not to

Faith Fuel

bring them shame. He resolved to divorce her quietly. The Holy Spirit, however, intervened.

When we read about the Holy Spirit speaking to Joseph in a dream we once again feel unable to identify with the story. In a sense, we emotionally separate ourselves from identifying with Mary and Joseph because so much of the story seems like a different world, a dream world. Perhaps it is here that we can make the connection! It could be that Mary and Joseph both felt like they were living in a dream world. Would not we all like to live out God's dreams?

Humbled by the Spirit

"My soul magnifies the Lord, and my spirit rejoices in God my Savior." (Luke 1:47 NRSV)

We read that Mary said her soul "magnifies" the Lord. Taken at face value in English, her statement is full of interesting implications. Does she mean amplify? Enlarge? Increase? Augment? Intensify? Enhance? There are a lot of synonyms for "magnify!"

Does God need amplification? Does God need to be enhanced? Taken out of context, this would seem to be the musings of a very arrogant woman. The context of The Magnificat, however, is that of a young woman completely humbled. The Holy Spirit had not merely humbled her spirit. Mary's body had been humbled as well.

Outside of the Christmas narratives of Matthew and Luke, we know very little about Mary. In Matthew 13, she is named with Jesus' brothers; in John's Gospel, it is clear that one of the Mary's present at the crucifixion and resurrection is Jesus' mother; but at other times, it is not as clear. In Acts 1, Mary and Jesus' brothers are with the Apostles constantly as they are in prayer, just before Pentecost. We are told that Jesus' first miracle, recorded in John, was prompted by Mary. We are also told that during the course of Jesus' ministry Mary and Jesus' brothers went to see him.

Our only real glimpses of Mary's personality are in Luke. We see a young woman who accepted her subservient role in society. We see the same kind of humble acceptance in role as the mother of Jesus, the Son of God. One wonders if there would have been any difference if Jesus had been born to a twentieth century feminist. How would a "me-generation" feminist respond to being the mother of the Son of God?

Faith Fuel

"My soul magnifies the Lord," said Mary. She was an instrument of God's grace, a tool of God's salvation. Her role was a passive one, requiring total obedience and total servant-hood. There was no forum to question the sovereignty of God. There was no opportunity to object to the role thrust upon her. God's will and purpose were brought into focus in the Christ Child, "magnified" by Mary.

The Book of Acts records her being present with the Apostles, remembering Jesus in prayer. She was there for him during that final week of His earthly life, a supportive role on the sidelines. She was present at His death and in the effort to prepare his body for burial. Both Matthew and Luke record her as being rather traditionally present for His growth and early development. Her soul magnified.

An Honorable Man

"But just when he had resolved to do this, and angel of the Lord appeared to him in a dream and said, "Joseph, Son of David, do not be afraid to take Mary as your wife, for the child conceived in her is from the Holy Spirit." (Matthew 1:20 NRSV)

It was a question of possession! In our world today, we have different ideas about divorce and children than in Bible times. When we read in Exodus 20:14, "You shall not commit adultery," we assume today that God was referring to a sexual crime. In truth, however, adultery was seen as a crime of property. A woman was a field where a man planted his seed, hoping to harvest male children, to perpetuate his family. If a woman became pregnant by a man other than her husband, the other man stole the husband's property. The child born of such a union belonged to no one because he or she did not have a "legitimate" heritage. It was both a matter of legality and of family shame and embarrassment.

Joseph did not want embarrassment and shame for either his family or for Mary's. Community ridicule and pain could be devastating. At the same time, the pain of divorce has always been horrible, even when one is in the right. The choice was between ongoing daily pain, and the quick searing pain of divorce. Then, just as now, it was a difficult choice. Joseph made the painful resolve for divorce.

Those who make such a decision today do not have the complication of God's intervention. The angel's message to Joseph did not offer a quick solution to all of Joseph's problems. Rather, the message gave meaning to the struggles that they faced, making their struggles joyfully bearable.

Faith Fuel

There is inspiration here for all of those who face the question of whether or not their marriage should continue. God may have seemed overwhelmingly on Mary's side, but the angel's message told Joseph that God was on Joseph's side as well. God is lovingly present to all those who seek. God's love can overwhelm any earthly fear. God can provide us with alternatives or support that we never imagine.

God's word for Joseph was, "Do not be afraid." That is God's word for all those who seek to be obedient to God's will. Once Joseph had the confidence that comes with knowing that God was with him, he could face whatever the world might throw at him or at his family.

At Christmas, when we see that all was (and is) God's show, we are tempted to give up, "letting God do what God will do." Then we see that "the show" is not so much for God's glory as it is for our benefit. Later Jesus would confirm that he was sent that we might have life, the fullest possible life. When we see that Someone Else is in charge of the world's stage, we cannot walk off that stage in a huff. God is the producer and director, but we all have important parts to play in the drama. In life's stage, the applause goes to the actors, but the real credit belongs to The Director.

Homeward Bound?

"Joseph also went from the town of Nazareth in Galilee to Judea, to the city of David called Bethlehem, because he was descended from the house and family of David." (Luke 2:4 NRSV)

During the holiday season, we often hear a song entitled "I'll Be Home for Christmas." The song brings a sweet mood, a mood of remembering. I remember the first time I was away from home while in seminary. The phone call home on Thanksgiving gave me some strong feelings of homesickness. We began to talk around that time about how I would be home for Christmas. It gave me much to which I could look forward. I so much wanted to see old friends and family again.

We can be fairly certain that these were Joseph's feelings when he realized that he was going to Bethlehem for the census. There was the added excitement of having Mary with him—it was probably the first trip there for the young woman. She was pregnant, too, and only she and Joseph at this point knew that technically the baby was not Joseph's. The Bible does not tell us how much Mary and Joseph told their families during the early years of Jesus' life. We are not even sure just how much was known by the parents of John the Baptist, Zechariah and Elizabeth. We can be sure that, in the context of such a

211

census, going to Bethlehem was like going to a weeklong homecoming celebration.

In our common contemporary images of Bethlehem, we think in terms of snow and a foreboding cold, although it seldom snows there. We often think of their rejection at the end as being heartless, but undoubtedly the crowds forced the innkeepers to turn away many others. Such a homecoming would involve a huge celebration–King David no doubt had many descendents.

There was probably too much going on in the minds of Mary and Joseph for them really to get involved in the festivities. In that final few weeks of pregnancy, Mary may not have had the energy to do much in the way of celebrating. Joseph's sense of celebration was probably tempered by his sense of responsibility for his bride and the child about to be born.

If Joseph had kept with Jewish tradition, he would have hired some musicians to wait outside until the birth. In the Jewish mind, if a boy is born there must be music and dancing begun immediately. Joseph may not have had the resources for such an extra celebration to add to the homecoming, but he would have tried.

In the midst of the homecoming, Mary waited. If she was typical of young mothers, thoughts of celebration were constantly displaced by desires to eat and rest, eat and rest. We do not always have the time for the celebrations that are thrust upon us. We do not always have enough time to prepare for what is in store for us. On the other hand, Christmas as we know it comes every year at the same time. Knowing what we know, the celebration begins long before Christmas.

Naming a Child

"She will bear a son, and you are to name him Jesus, for he will save his people from their sins." (Matthew 1:21)

Joseph, son of David, was to be the father of a son. The son was to be known as Jesus, Son of Joseph, and Son of David. Jesus. Savior. Emmanuel. Messiah. Christ. Words can have power. Words have meanings. Names have meanings. Names can have power.

When parents find out that they are going to have a child, immediately they begin to think about names. When friends and relatives find out they begin to make suggestions. It can be a very frustrating process, particularly if there are one or more names that reoccur in the family's history. Zechariah and Elizabeth faced this kind

Faith Fuel

of controversy when they broke with family tradition and called the future baptist, *John*.

Some parents today go to a bookstore or library and get one or more books of names. The idea is to choose carefully and to consider all of the possibilities. Despite their relatively small size, many of these books tell us the meanings of names along with some history. In today's society, we consider such things only at the time of birth. We seldom consider the history and meaning of names after the child is born. Usually our children have no way of knowing how they came to have their name. Even less often do our children know the meanings of their names.

This was not so during Biblical times. Even as a boy, Jesus knew the meaning of his name. He knew that "Jesus" is a linguistic variant of the name "Joshua." He knew what "Joshua" means in Hebrew, and he knew what historically the name "Joshua" had meant. No doubt, he knew that another name had been given him: "Emmanuel," or "God with us." In carrying these names and that of his family, "David," he carried both a burden and a responsibility. Later in his life, Jesus would read from the prophet Isaiah while in the synagogue in Capernum. After reading the passage, he said that it was fulfilled in their hearing. In essence he was saying, "My name is Emmanuel, "God with us," this is the day of "God with us," and by reading this I am proclaiming the long awaited 'year of Jubilee.'"

As each of us looks at our own names, we too can ponder what they mean. It is possible that the literal meanings of our own names are significant to who we are and what kind of person we have become. It is also possible that the very processes by which our parents chose our names have affected our growth and development. It is very likely that our individual images of ourselves were shaped by the instances in which others have called us by name.

"Wonderful Counselor," "Mighty God," "Everlasting Father," and "Prince of Peace" are all names carried by the Manger Child. They are more than nicknames, and they are more than aliases. The names express the essence of the child we adore at Christmas.

A Child Is Born

"For a child has been born for us, a son given to us; authority rests upon his shoulders; and he is named Wonderful Counselor, Mighty God, Everlasting Father, Prince of Peace." (Isaiah 9:6)

213

Faith Fuel

A child has been born for us. This child was not born just for Joseph and Mary. A child has been born for us. This child was not born just for one race, nation, sex, or creed. A child has been born for us. This child is not a metamorphosis of God, as a butterfly is a metamorphosis of a caterpillar. God's promises–God's *Word*–have become flesh in order to pitch His tent among ours. This child, born for us, is the incarnation of God. A child has been born for us. In a world when the infant mortality rate approached fifty percent, this child was born to us. In a world when the average life expectancy of the population was under thirty years, a child was born to us.

A son has been given to us. The Creator chose to put up His only child for adoption. The risk was God's. Yes, He took a risk. There would have been no risk in sending a mighty and invincible warrior. There would have been no risk in bringing the world to an end right then, to bring immediate judgment. God has the power to bring on another flood, as in the story of Noah. God has choices. He can choose to withdraw from being involved in the world and leave us to our own devices. Deists claim that He has already done this. God can choose to wield destructive power. He continues to choose, however, the way of redemptive love.

Authority rests on Jesus' shoulders. That was and is God's choice. By giving authority to God-become-man, we are given someone we can deal with face to face. The birth of the Christ-child was the new beginning for humankind, and miraculously that birth continues to be the new beginning. The child developed in his mother's womb, just as we did. The child was nurtured, changed, bathed, taught, and disciplined. The child grew, worked, played, loved, and worshiped. The child struggled, experienced pain, knew sorrow, and found occasions for laughter. He breathed, ate, and slept. He knew what it was like to have acceptance and to have friends. He also knew what it was like to have enemies and to be rejected.

By sending a real, human son, God placed authority on real, human shoulders. Yet there is far more to say. Presidents, prime ministers, and monarchs have a tendency to become isolated from their subjects. They have a tendency to surround themselves with advisors who can be far more fallible than their bosses, because they do not carry an awareness of the burdens of responsibility. Jesus chose to have only the Creator as his advisor, and he could do so because of their unique relationship.

A child is born, a son is given, and authority is placed on shoulders fresh from their womb. It was an impossible task that was completed by the God who makes all things possible.

214

Faith Fuel

Born Into a World of Little Trust

"Though the fig tree does not blossom, and no fruit is on the vines; though the produce of the olive fails and the fields yield no food; though the flock is cut off from the fold and there is no herd in the stalls, yet I will rejoice in the Lord; I will exult in the God of my salvation." (Habakkuk 3:17,18)

Shortly before his death on the cross, Jesus condemned a fig tree that was in leaf but without fruit. During his ministry, he spoke of how he was the true vine, the Creator being the vinedresser. He told parables about fields and harvests, fish and fishermen, and sheep and shepherds. Jesus taught and healed with a confidence that comes from trust.

Jesus was born, however, into a world of little trust. In the years just before Jesus' birth the Jewish community nurtured hope for the coming of the Messiah. Then as now, hope was based upon trust in God. Over and over again, scriptures tell us that no matter what happens we should praise God anyway. More than that, we are to exult in God. It seems strange to many that we are to brag about what God is doing even when things are not going well, but that is our call.

Bragging about what God is doing, no matter what happens, is reflected in an old rabbinical tale. It seems that there used to be a rabbi who traveled from town to town on his donkey. His only possessions were his donkey for transportation, a hen for eggs, his scriptures, and a lamp to read by at night. One evening, when a town refused to provide lodging because he was a Jew, he went to the trees on a nearby hilltop for his night's shelter. He was not angry with the town, but simply said, "All that God does God does well." That night the wind blew so powerfully that it blew over and broke his lamp. As he curled up in his bedroll he said, "All that God does God does well." The next morning he found that his donkey had bolted and his hen had flown away. As he walked downhill to the town for provisions he said, "All that God does God does well." When he reached the town, he found the army there investigating the killing of all the townspeople during the night by a band of marauders. An army captain told the rabbi that if, during the night, the rabbi's lamp had been seen, his hen had clucked, or his donkey had brayed, the rabbi would also have been killed." The rabbi replied, "All that God does God does well."

When we read the above passage from Habakkuk, we are finding great inspiration from a passage written during some of the darkest days of Jewish history. At the time of the first Christmas,

215

Faith Fuel

Joseph probably experienced some dark days as well. He was responsible for a pregnant wife. He had very limited earthly resources to protect both the mother and a very important baby. According to the Gospel of Luke, they had to travel a great distance over difficult terrain to go to a census ordered by a repressive government. Joseph had to deal with large crowds and difficult living and traveling conditions. In the midst of all this, scriptures record no complaints from the one who society made accountable. Evidently, he praised God anyway.

Registration

"He went to be registered with Mary, to whom he was engaged and who was expecting a child." (Luke 2:5 NRSV)

Registrations can be frustrating. There is registering for the draft, registering mail, registering at a hotel or motel, registering for college, and many other opportunities to register. Then there are the opportunities to try to confirm your registration! Sometimes the very process of registration can be a nightmare!

Anyone who has ever registered for college knows what a tedious process it can be. When registering for college the process is made somewhat easier by the fact that registering is something we want to do in order to accomplish something. Such is not the case for registering for the draft, where often the person has serious concerns about what that registration means.

We do not know what registration for the census entailed for Joseph. According to the Gospel of Luke, a census had been ordered by the emperor of the Roman Empire. We do not know what Joseph and Mary went through in terms of a census process.

Since almost the entire population is highly visible during the Christmas season each year, it leads one to wonder what life at holiday time would be like if our country held a census each Christmas. Joseph had to go to a particular town to be with the rest of his family for the census. If we were compelled to gather as families for Christmas according to a particular formula, there would be both confusion and hardship. In a society of equality of the sexes, there would be difficult choices to be made with regard to whose families, the wives' or the husbands', would be the focus of gathering. An autocratic government might work out a formula for odd and even-numbered years. Then there would be the problems of divorces, remarriages, and children to be divided among multiple spouses. A bureaucratic machine would have to be built just to answer the questions and to coordinate the efforts each year.

On the other hand, each Christmas we remember indirectly the census in the Gospel of Luke in other ways. We update our memories of friends and relatives that we have not talked to since the previous year. We count the Christmas cards, seeing from whom we have not heard. We count up the gifts we have bought, making sure we have "taken care of" all the ones that should receive gifts. We add new friends to our lists and remove those we have lost to death or unaccountable separation.

Then there is the census of our blessings, which most count at Thanksgiving and many continue to count through Christmas. Later we count our bills. Mary and Joseph, in the census or not, had their own counting to do. One child, two earthly parents, three wise men, and countless angels, shepherds, and other well-wishers. That first Christmas involved a census of blessings, if nothing else.

A Familiar Story

"While they were there, the time came for her to deliver her child." (Luke 2:6 NRSV)

When it comes to the public speaking of scriptures, nearly everyone is familiar with the Christmas texts, even if they are heard in a translation that is not otherwise familiar to the listener. As we recite the Christmas story, it is fun to listen to where we place the emphasis on our words.

"**While** they were there, the time came . . . ." "While **they** were there, the time came . . . ." "While they were **there**, the time came . . . ." "While they were there, the **time** came . . . ."

"**While** they were there, the time came for **her** to deliver her child. . . ." "While they were **there**, the time came for her to deliver her **child**. . . ." "While they were **there**, the **time** came for her to deliver her **child**. . . ."

It is a most interesting experience to hear your own voice tell the Christmas story. If you record it and then play it back, you usually want to do it over again, often several times. If while you are driving along in your car, you listen to yourself tell the Christmas story, and then you hear it again, repeatedly, you soon begin to memorize it, like a favorite song.

Faith Fuel

Something even more remarkable happens! You begin to think of ways to share your experiences of Christmas with others, simply based upon the scriptures. People who have never preached a sermon before in their lives begin to think of sermons that they could preach on the Christmas story. Hearing the Christmas story almost compels us to share the good news in Jesus Christ.

For many of us Christmas is the beginning of the gospel. Never mind the fact that we would not celebrate Christ's birth if it were not for Easter. That is a theological technicality that most of us seldom think about. For so many in our world, the joy of knowing Jesus begins with knowing the child in the manger. We sense the joy of the shepherds, the reverence of the wise men, and the compulsion to sing like the angels.

For many of us it is easier to see the focus of God's love in the manger than on the cross. It is easier to share the joy of the shepherds and the angels than to share the joy of the disciples at Easter. It is easier to comprehend the reverence of the wise men than to comprehend the astonishment of those who saw the risen Christ. It does not need to be this way, but there is no harm in these preferences.

We cannot expect the un-churched to "come and see" like the shepherds, and we cannot expect the un-churched to have the wisdom of the wise men, bringing gold, frankincense, and myrrh. Christians have to share the joy and share the good news.

A Feast

"And she gave birth to her first-born son and wrapped him in bands of cloth, and laid him in a manger, because there was no place for them in the inn." (Luke 2:7 NRSV)

The sights of Christmas Day are a feast for the eyes. Even if we are inside, sick and confined to our bed, in our mind's eye on Christmas Day the sights are glorious. We see Christmas trees, both those of today and those of the past. We see faces around family dinner tables, perhaps the biggest and most formal of the year. We see presents under the tree, first unopened, and then opened. We see Christmas cards, some with notes and letters, from relatives, current friends, and friends of long ago. We see manger scenes, plain and fancy. We see the warmth of each other's hearts, warmed by the glow of the manger.

218

Faith Fuel

The sounds of Christmas are uninterrupted music. Even if time has deafened our ability to hear as much as we used to hear, there is still truth to the old song, "The Sweetest Sounds I'll Ever Hear Are Still Inside My Head" (Learner & Lowe). We hear Christmas carols, traditional and new, Handel's *Messiah*, shrieks of delight, and the giggles of children of all ages.

Many of the aromas of Christmas can be recalled from memory. We can remember the aromas of Christmas dinners being prepared and eaten, crackling fires, perfume counters in the department stores, and fresh cut trees at Christmas lots.

The tastes of Christmas go far beyond that of Christmas dinners, goodies, and desserts. Tastes also include the sweet kisses of loved ones.

Christmas touches us in many ways. There are the handshakes and hugs from those that we love and even from those that we hardly know. Sometimes there is trembling in our fingers as we wrap gifts for those that we love or unwrap gifts from the same. Gifts are often nice to touch as well as to see or hear.

Only through God's gift of imagination can we know what were the sights, sounds, aromas, tastes, and touches of the first Christmas. There were the sights of the Babe in the manger and the Christmas Star. There were the sounds of angels singling and a baby's low cry. There were the aromas of frankincense, myrrh, straw, and cattle. For the Special One, there was the taste of mother's milk, and for others there were more ordinary tastes. There was the embrace of parents for their child and the grasp of a tiny hand.

Each Christmas day we are confronted with many traditional and familiar things to do. We also have opportunities for new things to try and try on. We begin the day greeted with gifts wrapped in the tissues of expectancy. We fill the day with love, hope, peace, faith, and joy. It is truly the day that Our God has made, because God so loved the world.

Parents as Witnesses

"But Mary treasured all these words and pondered them in her heart." (Luke 2:19 NRSV)

Parents sometimes have strange and curious roles to play. At the time of a child's birth, parents usually receive all kinds of compliments and praise. Friends and relatives of the parents can usually find some nice things to say about a newborn, even if the child is not much to look at or has actual physical problems.

Joseph and Mary, however had things said to them that had not been ever spoken before, nor have those things been spoken since. Some no-collar workers, shepherds, told Mary and Joseph of seeing and hearing angels. They were not dreaming or hallucinating. Their experience was verified by group support, and without prompting by the parents, the shepherds confirmed what Mary and Joseph had already heard from their own angelic visitations.

Then there were some white-collar workers, Magi, who came a great distance to bring gifts of gold, frankincense, and myrrh. These visitors were a still stranger experience for Joseph and Mary. These men were not Jewish, and their religion was abhorrent to an orthodox Jew. God, through the Torah, had forbidden the involvement of the stars in authentic religion. Yet God used the foolish musings of wise men to bring them to witness the incarnation.

Both Mary and Joseph had been visited by angels before Jesus was born. Mary's pregnancy and Jesus' birth came wrapped in more than the usual mysteries. Parents usually wonder what their child will be like when he or she comes to maturity. Mary and Joseph knew what their child would become, but they had to wonder instead what it would all mean. Some parents wonder if their child will make a difference to their world, but Mary and Joseph had to wonder how that difference would be manifest.

As history began our new era, the first few days and weeks were very confining for both mother and child. Mary had to remain secluded until her ceremonial time of being unclean was over. All Mary could do was nurse her child and ponder. Was Mary to speculate about God's will and purpose? Was Mary to deliberate over what she and Joseph were going to have to do in order to be the parents of the Son of God? Perhaps Mary needed to muse over God's sense of humor, God's choosing two people such as these as tools of redemption.

Joseph and Mary had much to ponder, each from a unique perspective. Their perspectives were not different merely as male and female in a sexist society. If tradition is correct, Joseph was older and contemplated from the wisdom of life's other experiences. Mary considered what had happened from the innocence of adolescence. How they must have deliberated with a sense of wonder!

Faith Fuel

After Birth

"And having been warned in a dream not to return to Herod, they left for their own country by another road." (Matthew 2:12 NRSV)

There was the joy of anticipation throughout Mary's pregnancy. There was the joy that came with Jesus' birth. There was the joy of receiving the shepherds and wise men. For each of the parents there had been a dream at the beginning of the pregnancy. Now, once again, there was yet another dream. This dream for the wise men preceded a warning for Joseph and Mary to flee for their lives from the wrath of Herod.

"By another road" is an understatement, if we are to believe the gospel accounts, telling us that they went all the way to Egypt. In most cases today, the mother of a newborn is anxious to be at home in the midst of familiar surroundings. In their home, the parents can concentrate upon the basic challenges of rearing a child. Most parents would shudder at the prospect of having to flee to a distant and strange place instead of going home to care for a newborn.

A number of scholars have trouble believing that Jesus was born in Bethlehem, but rather they believe that he was born in Nazareth. In believing this, there is danger of missing an important point. The gospel accounts are not written to recite history but to proclaim faith. The gospel writers made choices as to what to tell and how to tell it, but they were not being selective of history. Rather, they made their choices in order to communicate their message to a particular audience. The story of Mary and Joseph going by another road, going to Egypt before returning to Nazareth, was a component of the writer's message.

The writer of this gospel was addressing a Jewish audience. It was and is important to understand that at the time of Jesus' birth there were those other than Mary and Joseph who knew of the importance of this birth. Of those who knew the significance of Christ's birth, there was at least one who greeted the good news with hostility. Far more than Luke's gospel, Matthew establishes the idea that from the very beginning some greeted Jesus with joy and some with much more negative emotions.

Such would be the story of Jesus' entire life on earth and the story of Jesus' presence in our world today. Non-Christians as well as Christians realize that Christmas is a celebration of the birth of Jesus. To those outside of Christ's church it is merely an opportunity to engage in a huge celebration and to possibly exchange gifts. Even

221

within the church, for some Christmas is merely an opportunity to feel good about themselves and about their world.

For the lost ones Jesus is in their vocabulary but not in their daily lives. They allow Jesus to touch their minds but not dwell in their hearts. As shepherds, we have to watch out for these lost sheep for whom Christ died.

The Blessing

"Then Simeon blessed them and said to his mother Mary, 'This child is destined for the falling and the rising of many in Israel, and to be a sign that will be opposed so that the inner thoughts of many will be revealed—and a sword will pierce your own soul too.'" (Luke 2:34-35 NRSV)

Evidently, Simeon was a very old man. We are told that within the Jewish community he was known as a man who was righteous and devout, and that the Holy Spirit rested upon him. We are also told that he was waiting for the consolation of Israel. This meant he was waiting for the vindication of Israel upon her enemies by God's messiah or savior. It had been revealed to him by the Holy Spirit that rested upon him that he would not see death until that happened. The scripture we are looking at today contains what Simeon said to Mary after he had praised and thanked God for what he was privileged to see.

Many years ago, a science fiction movie was made in which visitors from another civilization visited earth, and they left behind some strange little devices. As they were given into the hands of a wide variety of people, the people were told that the devices represented life and death. When the first device was activated, several thousand people died within the radius of hundreds of miles. As scientists clamored over the devices in order to study them, a great controversy arose as word of the devices spread. Power hungry people and self-proclaimed saviors wanted control of the devices because they represented life or death. Soon the whole world knew of the devices, and panic began to spread as people feared power that might get out of control when unleashed. Finally, one quiet individual understood what the aliens had really said. The visitors had spoken of the power of life and death and not life or death. Without asking anyone for permission that quiet person unleashed the power over the entire earth. Those who had compassion, caring, and love for others lived, and the rest did not.

Faith Fuel

That story is science fiction, but Simeon saw God's reality. Simeon saw not merely the consolation of Israel but the consolation of all humankind. Perhaps Simeon even realized that God's messiah was a redemptive and loving savior of life and death rather than a might warrior of life or death. Jesus, Simeon said, "...is destined for the falling and the rising of many...." What did Simeon see as he said that? We will never know. What did Simeon see when he said that Jesus was destined "...to be a sign that will be opposed...."? Again, we will never know.

There are things that we do know. We know of the falling of the Roman Empire and of the rising of Christ's church. We know about the opposition to Jesus' ministry, and how that opposition climaxed in an open tomb instead of a cross. The church is a Christmas people because it is also an Easter people. We are fascinated with the manger because of the empty tomb.

Remember the Real Story

"The child grew and became strong, filled with wisdom; and the favor of God was upon him." (Luke 2:40)

If you wish to do some research into the history of the Bible, you might find it fun to look at a group of writings known as the pseudopygrapha. Breaking down the meaning of that word, pseudo refers to "false" or "artificial." "Pyg" refers to a signature, and "grapha" refers to writings. In other words, these are writings that are written under the name of someone else. In Biblical times, it was considered a compliment to tell a beautiful story and give someone you admire credit for it. Thus, there are a number of pseudopygrapha supposedly written by the Apostle Paul, Peter, and others, written after the supposed author's death.

In keeping with those times, there are a number of things written about Jesus' boyhood and early manhood that we know are fictitious. There is the story of an angry little Jesus who had a bolt of lightning strike a playmate because the playmate would not play the way Jesus wanted. There is the story of Jesus making mud pies with his playmates, but showing off by breathing life into mud figures of birds and having them fly away.

These early writers wanted to make sure that history would record our Lord as being fully human as well as fully divine. A modern parallel to this is the conjecture by a Mormon scholar that Jesus may have looked down upon his wives and sons as he hung on the cross.

223

Faith Fuel

There is always the temptation to bring Jesus down to our level instead of trying to grow to his level. The scripture tells us that Jesus grew and became strong, and that is enough. We do not need to be told that he became strong as Superman. The scripture tells us that he became filled with wisdom. Scripture also tells us later that there were some things known only to the Creator. We are never told that Jesus knew everything.

The scripture tells us that the favor of God was upon him. This gives us a glimpse of what we mean by saying that Jesus is the incarnation of God. There is a difference between incarnation and metamorphosis. When a tadpole becomes a frog, or when a caterpillar becomes a butterfly, those are examples of metamorphosis. When Our Heavenly Father placed Jesus upon the earth, He watched over Jesus with such closeness that whatever Jesus experienced, The Father experienced with Jesus. The Creator did not leave heaven and transform himself into a baby. That would have been metamorphosis, but it would not have been incarnation. Whom did Jesus pray to throughout his ministry and in the Garden of Gethsemane? To whom was Jesus talking to on the temple steps on Maundy Thursday?

The celebration of Christmas helps us more fully understand who Jesus was and is–the Son of God. The birth of the Christ Child was the beginning of God's final redemption of humankind.

Remember the Reason

Sometimes during the so-called "Holiday Season," we see cards and signs that say, "Jesus is the reason for the season!" It seems curious that we do not hear that statement at other times of the year. For a Christian, Jesus can be seen as an integral part of every season. Ecclesiastes 3:1 says, "For everything there is a season, and a time for every matter under heaven . . . ." The wisdom of Ecclesiastes reminds us of the wisdom of Our Creator, and it helps put some things into perspective.

Most people think of pain as something negative or bad, but in reality, pain is good because it is a signal that there is something wrong. A headache may tell us that we are under too much stress or that we have a fever. In other cases, pain reminds us that we have damaged tissue that needs protection. Pain is a danger signal that protects us.

The spiritual equivalent of pain is guilt. When we feel guilty, we are being signaled by our spirit that there is something wrong with us

224

Faith Fuel

spiritually. Guilt is spiritual pain. There are some who refuse to feel guilty about anything. They have a philosophy of life that lets them ignore guilt and pretend it does not exist. The danger of this is the same danger we have if we take painkillers all the time without consulting a doctor. Serious damage–maybe death–can be the result!

In the thinking of Ecclesiastes, there is a time and a season for pain and guilt, just as there is a time and season for death of an individual or the dispersal of a group. Picture Jesus on the cross: On that day, Jesus showed us that there is a time and a season for divine forgiveness, and a time and a season for divine redemption. Shift the focus to our own lives. Are there not times and seasons for everything? Christmas is not simply an excuse for giving and receiving. It is a season with a reason. Just as surely as it is the season we celebrate Christ's birth, it can also be the season for lost people to be reborn.

Christmas in Perspective

I used to serve a church that had a sign out on the corner of a main street. Four days each week the sign had a short saying, and the other three days we posted the sermon title. The secretary had been in her position there for many years. When I arrived, she told me that she was going to have to start repeating herself, and she hated doing that after so many years. I happened to be a collector of epigrams, so I gave her a supply that would last her several more years.

In that little suburb of Los Angeles, many people would drive out of their way at least once each week on their way to or from work in order to see what the church sign had to say that week. As the pastor, I sometimes got feedback from people in town, and sometimes I got feedback by telephone.

The week before Christmas in 1982, I put on the sign, "Santa Claus never died for anybody." That got us a lot of memorable feedback. My favorite was an anonymous telephone call. The woman on the phone started by complimenting the church for its gifts of wisdom through the sign over the years. "Sometimes it is pretty good," she said. Then she began to get agitated as she began to talk about the celebration of Christmas. Just before slamming the phone down she closed her remarks about the epigram that week by saying, "I think it is inexcusable for a church to mix religion with a legitimate holiday!"

That remark made in all seriousness leads me to ask a question. Do the un-churched people you know see you as celebrating

225

Faith Fuel

the birth of the Christ Child, or just a warm and fuzzy time of "happy holidays?

Christmas Traditions

Christmas is a gigantic exchange of gifts, with gracious giving happening in varying parts of our lives. Most of Christmas each year involves two-way gift giving transactions between ourselves and our friends and family. Sometimes we step out and give a gift to someone who we know is not going to do the same for us. Sometimes this is done out of a sense of altruism and sometimes out of obligation. Sometimes we receive a gift from someone when we know we somehow either cannot or should not return the favor.

All of our giving seems to be earth-bound. Many of us respond to the call of the church to render a special offering. Having responded, many consider this to be all there is to do in a spiritual way for Christmas.

What about worship on Christmas Day and on Christmas Eve? Do we really fulfill our Christian obligations by being there at those times? If we go to worship in order to receive the Christmas message, to hear the Christmas music, and to see the sights of Christmas worship, we will be with plenty of people who are there for the same reasons.

In addition to all that, we can look up into the Lord's face, tell Jesus we have received His gift, thank Him for it, and offer ourselves in return. Each of us is the only thing that is really ours to give. If we give ourselves, then indeed Christmas is ours forever, and not just for the day!

Marriage Tradition

The Gospels tell us very little about Joseph, but it was customary for girls Mary to be wedded to their husband just as soon as they were physically able to have children. Mary was probably in her early teens when the Christmas story begins. How this couple got together is all conjecture. Romance and courtship were not major factors in ancient times. Most marriages were arranged between the parents of the couple, sometimes before the children were born. The marriages were sealed by a Rabbi, sometimes without the children

226

Faith Fuel

present. The bride and groom were not simply thrown together in a haphazard way, however. Directly or indirectly, comments and conduct of the children often alerted parents as to which family to contact, so love was indeed a factor in many of the relationships.

Joseph probably approached his parents one day and asked if he could marry a distant relative of his named Mary. The parents would consider parentage and ancestry, but they would probably not consider resources since both families were quite poor. Joseph's father would then call on Mary's parents, and the two fathers would do most of the negotiating. A marriage in those times was not just a covenant between the bridal pair but also between the two families.

After the fathers had agreed to a marriage contract, Joseph was brought before Mary, and parents uttered a formal benediction over them as they shared a cup of wine together. This legal betrothal was far more binding than today's engagement, because only divorce could break it. It was in essence the marriage. Unfaithfulness during the betrothal period was considered adultery and punishable by death. If Joseph died, Mary would have been his legal widow.

During the months between her engagement and her marriage, Mary's wedding preparations were interrupted by a visit by the angel Gabriel. Mary responded with simple trust. How many of us trust God so totally and completely?

Evolving Christmas Celebrations

Western culture has been observing an increasing role of the Christian origins of Christmas in our "Happy Holidays" observances. It has some people outside the church worried. It began when an obscure gospel singer began getting gold records and Grammys. Then, a rock and roll group was hurling Bibles into their audiences instead of dead chickens. Gospel records began to outsell classical records. Major newsmakers began to be "born again. A few years ago, a life insurance company took out full-page full color advertisements in magazines simply entitled "A Christmas Prayer." That year there seemed to be a new surge in civil religion, but it did not last. Pastors have not been asked to pray at a freeway openings or building dedication ceremonies for several years now. When the United States Supreme Court said that organized prayer in the public schools was unconstitutional, that decision sparked a new interest in prayer. Worse, there was an almost alarming significance to the combination of revived

227

interest in prayer and personal piety, along with the arrival of the Christmas season. The mix could have been potentially powerful.

When Peter Marshall was Chaplain of the United States Senate, he preached a sermon in his Washington church entitled, "Praying Is Dangerous Business," and he was right! We have to be careful about our prayers, because our prayers are likely to be answered! It is fun looking at our world upside down this way! Yes, prayer is powerful and potentially dangerous, but that is great news! People, churches, and even whole nations have come back from the grave's edge through prayer. If "too many" people accept the Christ Child as their Savior on Christmas Day, if "too many" people respond to church efforts, if churches get more than a 1% response to their direct mail advertising, if they do not have enough communion trays, offering plates, or enough food at the dinner??? It is scary to think about it! Yes, I would like to see every Christ-centered church have those problems!

The Calendar

A couple of years ago, actor Dean Jones wrote a book telling of his experience of being born again. He related his playboy lifestyle before his conversion. He also talked about how he had to grow once he decided to trust God with every aspect of his life. One of the points he made was regarding decision-making. Before his conversion, he made his decisions based on what seemed best for him or the right thing to do. After his conversion experience, he began praying about his decisions. He discovered that doing what is God's will involved his getting a sense of peace about that particular direction.

Following through on what God has given us to do is sometimes painful. The Apostle Paul discovered this when he was repeatedly imprisoned. At the close of one of his letters, he told how he bore on his body the marks of Christ. Shortly after Jesus said in the Garden of Gethsemane, "Not my will, but yours be done," he was arrested and went to the cross.

Most of us suffer on a smaller scale than He did, but many of our righteously intended decisions have painful consequences. Our faith rests in Christ's victory over the cross on Easter. That faith has been confirmed countless times by the saints and martyrs of these last twenty centuries. Knowledge of that history does not ease the pain much, but it helps keep our faith pointed in the right direction.

But when we begin Advent, the period of preparation for the celebration of the birth of Jesus the Christ, we approach the manger over four weeks. Let us remember that the cross always stands close to the manger, and it is Easter that makes Christmas important. Sometime after Christmas, we spend about six weeks getting ready for Easter. Then there's eight to nine months after Easter before Christmas. Is Christmas a prelude to Easter, or is Easter a prelude to Christmas?

Celebrations

The celebration of birthdays is a silly sport. Very few people on this planet care who was born on a Wednesday afternoon, the day after Halloween, just before the end of World War II. A hundred years from now, the day of my birth will be merely another of the countless days of history.

People's birthdays are only remembered because of what they did or said after they were born. Even the most important person's birthday is remembered only as long as people remember what that person did or said. When what was said or done is truly important to us, or if that person has personal importance to us, the silliness of remembering a day of birth is redeemed. At that point, the birthday becomes a handle by which we can grasp and remember what is really important to us.

Three of the greatest composers who ever lived were born in the year 1685–Johann Sebastian Bach, George Frederick Handel, and Domenico Scarlatti. 1685 would otherwise be an insignificant year in the march of time, but the music of those composers lives on, 1685 has become a reference point in time for truly great music.

A baby was born in a tiny town in a small province of the Roman Empire. The baby's birth would not even be a statistic in history if it were not for Easter. Thirty-three years later, in 29 AD, Jesus died on a cross, and He left His tomb empty before dawn three days later. Our celebration of Jesus' birth each year would be almost silly if Easter had not happened.

Is not it silly that so many people make a bigger celebration out of national holidays than out of Christmas? Is not it silly how most Christians make more of the celebration of Christmas than they do of Easter? In the midst of the tragedies of this world, we need to celebrate the blessings of God every chance we get! Let us keep up our silly celebrations of birthdays! Yes! But let us invite God to our parties!

Faith Fuel

Prince of Peace

"And he shall be called 'Prince of Peace'." In the Advent season, as we approach the birthday celebration of the Prince of Peace, we recognize that peace is possibly the major issue of our time. While our government talks about the necessity of a strong defense, we have distorted the meaning of the word "defense." Political paranoia was leading the United States in 2010 to spend more than a million dollars per minute on "defense." Scientific fact shows that 400 nuclear warheads could destroy all the industrial centers and one third of the population of the world, but our paranoia has led us to stockpile 30,000 of those warheads. During the Cold War, while the United States was building more, the Union of Soviet Socialist Republics was also increasing its "defense" spending in order to catch up with us. For years, there have been large numbers of people starving in Africa, but because of political paranoia about communist governments, those people went on suffering and dying until the problems went past the critical stage. Each of the superpowers has enough clout to wipe out in less than an hour the entire population of this planet, but we both are increasing our spending on "defense" in order to insure peace. Our departments of defense are actually departments of war.

In the midst of all this, there is hope: Jesus *is* the Prince of Peace, and our Heavenly Father is a God of justice and mercy. Our hope for the survival of the human race does not rest in stockpiles of weapons, nor does world peace depend upon the mechanism of the United Nations. The survival of the human race and our hopes for world peace depend upon the actions of individuals who will pursue peace with a passion. Few are willing to be peacemakers. Few are willing to make the effort to teach individuals in our world and their governments to have sufficient feelings of self-worth so that the process of peacemaking can succeed. Too few are willing to seek justice and do mercy, as well as walk humbly with our God. Instead of justice, there is competition. Our hopes for survival and peace are dependent upon our willingness to let God's power work through us. We need to let the Gospel permeate the consciousness of the world through our willingness to be witnesses. During the Christmas season, let us do more than just sing about "peace on earth, and good will toward men."

Faith Fuel

Holy Music

I remember hearing a recording of Kate Smith singing "Silent Night" one morning while I was at the office. The song, "Jingle Bells" brings visions of Santa Claus to little children. Bing Crosby singing "White Christmas" warms the cockles of most Americans' hearts. Christians around the world and some non-Christians as well associate "Silent Night" with the peace and joy that comes with celebrating the birth of Jesus Christ. Christians keep reminding the world that it is *not* the silence of that night that we are celebrating.

When I was completing my course work for a degree in music, one of my professors challenged the class to define "music" in one sentence. The result? "Music is an ordered sequence of sounds and silences." Sometimes we do not recognize sounds as beautiful until they are set against a backdrop of silence. Every piece of written music contains rests as well as notes. Yes, there was silence that first Christmas night, but a part of every night in every part of the world is silent. On the day our Savior was born, that silence was broken by a baby's low cry accompanied by choirs of angels singing of the mighty glory of our God.

Holy night? Yes! Silent night? Not entirely!

Gifts of Honor and Grace

Of what value were the gifts brought by the Magi to the baby Jesus? Did Mary and Joseph put the gold into a certificate of deposit or savings bonds for Jesus to have when he became a man? Did Mary and Joseph burn the frankincense for household odor control, or did they use it for a fragrant offering when they dedicated Jesus at the Temple? How did they use the myrrh? Was it used as baby oil? Did Mary use it as a beauty treatment? Was it used later to prepare Joseph's body for burial?

Were not the wise men actually bringing Jesus honor and glory in the best way they knew how? Is not honor of more value than gold, frankincense, or myrrh? With music, the angels brought Jesus glory, but was it not his already? Fame can be historic, and glory is but for a moment. Honor is harder to describe. Honor seems to be in scarce supply in the 21st century.

231

Faith Fuel

Gene Roddenberry's Lieutenant Worf, one of his more colorful characters in the Star Trek saga, is portrayed as valuing honor above everything else. A Klingon, Worf has few of the refined characteristics that we associate with the better part of modern human society. Seemingly, barbaric Klingons are almost always honorable people because they work at it. Klingons pursue the maintenance of honor just as passionately as they engage in fierce battles for their empire. They were remarkably like their counterparts in the Roman Empire into which Jesus was born. For Romans as well as Klingons, glory without honor was–and is–worthless.

In today's society, leaders of business, industry, and politics often pursue glory without giving any thought to being honorable. Worse, this lack of values has infected much of our society. If a person dishonors friends, family or even country, there is little concern so long as the result does not damage us personally. There is little or no thought given to the damage it does to our children's values. There is even less thought given to how a precedent will impact us in the future.

What about the gold, frankincense, and myrrh of today? As in the time of Jesus, money, fragrances, and cosmetics are still commodities, but can we still use them to give glory and honor? Absolutely! We can still give glory to God and honor the Savior sent by God to pitch His tent among us. We can honor Jesus, rather than simply honor his teachings. We can honor Jesus because of who He is in the world. We can honor Him by living according to His example. We can honor God's supreme effort for us, and thus we can fulfill the most important relationship we have. We can live lives of disciplined obedience to the God who loves us. We can still give of ourselves and give what we value to God. Yes, we can still follow the path of the wise men, who gave in order to honor God. How much of yourself can you surrender to God? Your gold? Your frankincense? Your myrrh?

Watching

Watching and waiting is essential to celebrating a new year. Before the first Christmas, Jews were watching for the coming of the Messiah for centuries. Sometimes being a spectator can be boring, and sometimes it can be exciting. How we experience being a spectator depends upon our perspective. I have a friend who does not want to hear the truth if it makes her feel uncomfortable. If you tell her something that she needs to hear but does not want to hear it, she tells me it is "inappropriate." I just had to watch when I knew her boyfriend was cheating on her.

I have friends who know the truth of what the Bible says, but if the Bible says something that conflicts with their perspective on life, they just do not want to hear it. I just have to watch as they suffer through the consequences. As we watch Christmas decorations going up, they are called "holiday" decorations in order to be politically correct. As a spectator, what we see depends upon our perspective.

Watching

Each one of us that walks this earth finds brilliant times we love.
We see our lives so clearly strong and blessed by God above.
At first, we stop with awe and thanks, but then proceed with zest.
Inspired, there is nothing small or great that keeps us from our best.

At other times, our way seems dark–we strive to keep awake.
Our zest's been tapped, our best's been tried–
no path seems ours to take.
Our ears are pricked, our eyes are focused out beyond our scope.
Our watching's ache is just bearable with faith that is fueled with hope.

Our watching's painful when we wait as loved ones fade and die.
Our watching's painful when the truth is scorned with someone's lie.
Our watching's mad when scheming foes
do not care what conflict costs.
Our watching's sad when dreams are dashed
or when our love's been lost.

Some watching's easy on the eyes, when beauty comes our way.
Some watching's fun when laughter fills another fertile day.
Some watching's entertainment as we root for favorite teams.
Some watching's preparation for a quest to fill our dreams.

We watch because we are human, and
we've learned that patience pays.
It is not enough to wait and hope–we watch for better days.
We watch because instinctively we know that God's above.
We watch because our world's a gift
that's wrapped with grace and love.

Faith Fuel

Maybe Next Year

Earliest records show the Advent season to be one of fasting, but few Christians today practice this aspect of Advent. The first record of such fasting is found in the Calendar of Perpetuus, bishop of Tours, in CE 491. It lasted from November 11 to December 25, and it was for three days a week. In 1581, The Council of Macon appointed for all a fast on Mondays, Wednesdays, and Fridays for the same period. Consequently, Advent became known as *St. Martin's Quadragesima*. In Rome, Advent has never been for more than five Sundays. Since the Middle Ages, the fast has died out in the West to become simply a solemn time for prayer.

Advent is not a time when Christians simply say, "Season's Greetings," and let it go at that. This is a time rich in history, from the time of the birth of Our Savior to the present. The history of the celebrations of Christmas is a breathtaking panorama. The rich traditions of Christmas have fascinating stories to tell, and we should pass them on to our children and theirs. There is much more to Advent than its history and traditions, however. The very best celebrations are those for which we carefully prepare. Most of us have gotten in the habit of making the physical preparations, but also there are spiritual preparations. We could spend one or more days a week fasting as an acute reminder of the approach of Christmas. This also might be good for some people's diets! Taking just liquids for a day also does wonders for most of our systems.

Since some people cannot fast due to health restrictions, however, the other possibility is daily time for serious prayer. I always pray we will bring many of our neighbors to know Jesus at Christmas. It is a time to be excited about the Christmas season! Christians plan to invite people to go to church with them. Christians also set aside time on Christmas Eve to be in church with their church family. Advent is more than a time for decorating homes and buying gifts. It is more than a time for exchanging Christmas cards. Perhaps people outside the church will see us preparing in ways that they do not prepare. Perhaps if they notice, they too will end up glorifying God instead of simply saying Merry Christmas. It is good to be able to say that we helped someone find Jesus at Christmas!

Faith Fuel

"As the angel choir withdrew into heaven, the sheepherders talked it over. 'Let us get over to Bethlehem as fast as we can and see for ourselves what God has revealed to us.'" [Luke 2:15 (MSG)]

As we consider this passage of scripture, one wonders if maybe our churches have Christmas celebrations planned backwards. The shepherds had a desire to "go and see." The motivation came from within the shepherds. Mary and Joseph did not send out birth announcements saying,

> By the grace of God
> Joseph and Mary
> Cordially Invite You
> To their temporary home
> at the
> Stable at the Inn
> to Celebrate
> The birth of Their Son
> Jesus Emmanuel

Such an invitation did not go out. The angels did not even invite the shepherds. They wanted to go! Each Christmas season, churches spend a lot of money on publicity, and Christians do a lot of inviting. We should be inviting our un-churched friends all year around. It is easier at Christmas. Some think all we have to do is spend the time and the money it takes to get some "exposure" of churches and their worship services.

It might be possible to turn things around, the way they were that first Christmas. On Pentecost, the preaching led the people to ask the question, "What must I do to be saved?" The circumstances led to the question! That first Christmas the circumstances led the shepherds to say, "Let us get over to Bethlehem...." Each Christmas season the Crystal Cathedral in Anaheim, California, does a lot of advertising for a spectacle of entertainment entitled The Glory of Christmas. Many people have said to one another "Let us go and see," but they go to be entertained. They are thrilled, perhaps, but few are converted. They are offering an answer to a question that people are not asking!

It is easy to provide answers people need to hear. It is harder, much harder, to set the tone that leads people to ask questions about the Christ Child. The answer does not lie with the clergy, though a unified effort helps. The answer cannot be found in church programming either, though good programming helps. The answer lies

235

Faith Fuel

in each individual Christian, setting the tone—each of us! The answer lies in un-churched people knowing Christ is at work in us. The choice is ours for each of us. Do we take the easy path, and advertise and invite? Do we accept the challenge of letting other people see Christ at work in us? Do we do both?

Between Christmas and New Year's

Each January, many of us find occasion to shout, "Happy New Year!" Our New Year may not be really happy. The peace and joy of the little Christ child may or may not still linger with us throughout the year. Most go back to business as usual after Christmas is over.

It is amazing how each year people go to such elaborate means to prepare for Christmas. The day after Christmas, they return from the mountaintop experience back to the valley of the shadows like a dive-bomber. So few people linger at or near the top! Few come down at a more leisurely pace! Some of us leave the decorations up until after New Year's Day, but talk of peace, joy, and good will all stop on December 26.

In the 17th chapter of the gospel according to Matthew, Jesus, Peter, James, and John go up on top of a mountain. There the disciples see Jesus transfigured before them. That particular vision was the greatest experience those men had in all their lives up until that time. Peter wanted to preserve the event, and he offered to build "booths" there, or a kind of monument. Immediately, Jesus led them back down the mountain! Jesus went back to work, business as usual, and healed an epileptic.

Peter, James, and John had to come down off the mountain and return to the valley of the shadows, but Jesus came down the mountain with them. It is true that at Christmas we have an intense awareness of the Christ-child in our midst, much like seeing a transfiguration. Jesus is just as much with us on the day after Christmas. When the decorations are down, we just have to have a keener awareness to notice Jesus' presence.

Therefore, it is back to "business as usual," back to the valley of the shadows, after Christmas. For those who have the eyes to see, the peace, joy, and good will can linger. We consign our bodies to the valley, but our hearts can linger on the mountaintop!

Faith Fuel

Christmas is a time when we can see our spiritual journey's progress more clearly. Along the way in our journey, we can see four "mileposts" that mark our progress. Those mileposts are spectator Christian, seeker Christian, disciple Christian, and kingdom-builder Christian. Seeing these "mileposts" help us understand our own spiritual development and maturity.

For spectator Christians, Christmas is centered on decorating for the holidays, exchanging presents, and experiencing the sights and sounds that are unique to the "holiday season." Being part of a religious celebration of Christmas is mostly an afterthought–one of the many options in a season full of celebration options. In complete seriousness, an un-churched woman once told me that she thought it "inexcusable for Christians to try to mix religion with a legitimate holiday." Spectators and spectator Christians want to experience the pleasures of the season in whatever ways necessary and deemed possible. They do not recognize what is missing in their celebrations.

Seeker Christians want all of the pleasures that spectator Christians enjoy, but they sense deep down that there is more to the holiday celebrations than just pleasure. They look beyond all the trappings of the holidays and wonder about the roots of the celebration. Seeker Christians want to experience the older traditions and learn from them. They recognize the value of the season's religious roots, and they want to integrate those values into their lives in some way that gives their lives more meaning. Seeker Christians have begun to recognize that there is a spiritual dimension to life, and they want to develop that part of themselves. Music that glorifies the King of Kings may awaken within them a part of themselves they did not know existed. Seeker Christians may even recognize their spiritual hunger and instinctive longing after God.

Disciple Christians enjoy all the pleasures of Christmas celebrations, and they are aware of their need to have Jesus in their lives in a personal and intimate way. Disciple Christians want to have a bond with Our Savior, and they want nothing to interfere with that bond. Disciple Christians see Christmas celebrations as opportunities to strengthen that bond and to nurture their relationship with God through Jesus Christ. They see that walking in the footsteps of the shepherds or of the wise men is a way to improve one's walk with Jesus. As Disciple Christians experience Christmas, their focus is less on the decorations, music and gifts–and more focused on the experience of celebrating the birthday of Jesus.

Kingdom-builder Christians are so confident or comfortable in their walk in the footsteps of Jesus that they want to share their Christmas experiences with others, wanting to share their joy with those less far along in their spiritual journey. For them, kingdom building may be a matter of helping others move from spectator to seeker, or from seeker to disciple. A few kingdom-builder Christians also want to share their faith experience of Christmas with non-Christians.

Christmas is a good time to ask ourselves the question: "Am I a spectator, a seeker, a disciple, or a kingdom-builder?" Wherever we are on our spiritual journey, Christmas is a great opportunity to move further along.

Publicity

A stranger approached the late Will Rogers in his hometown and asked, "Do you have a criminal lawyer in town?" "A lot of us think so," he drawled, "but no one has been able to prove it yet." Is there anyone following in the footsteps of Jesus in our community? A lot of us think so, but can anyone prove it?

We can admit that it would be really great if people outside the church would point to us and say, "They walk in the footsteps of Jesus." Yes, and it would feel good if someone were to say that about me. It would be good publicity if someone were quoted as saying this about a church in the newspaper, and it would be even better if someone were seen saying it on a newscast. On the other hand, it would not be Christ-like if we were to seek actively such publicity.

Is it important for Christians to want to live so as to give the term "Christian" a good name? Some would say so. Those who teach communications like to say, "Perception is reality." By that, they mean simply that if a person perceives us as Christ-like, then for that person we are indeed Christ-like. If we are being hypocritical and they do not see it, to them at least we are Christ-like. Many of us go to a lot of trouble to keep up appearances.

When I was growing up, I was taught the importance of being honorable. I was told countless times that the biggest advantage of always telling the truth is that you do not have to try as hard to remember what you said. As a variation on this, some like to say we have to be true to ourselves. From a Christian perspective, this is a good "plan B."

"Plan A" for Christians is to be true to Jesus Our Lord. What others say about us is not nearly as important as what Jesus thinks of us. Walking in the footsteps of Jesus is more important than what we hear others saying about us. Being obedient to Christ's call upon our lives is more important than responding to others' praise or criticism.

The Christmas season continues to be a good time to examine ourselves. If we decorate our houses, are we trying to glorify God or to impress the neighbors? When we give our gifts, do they reflect our love, our generosity, or both? When we go to worship, are we going out of commitment, dedication, community, compassion, or a hunger to praise God? Some people put a nativity scene on their front lawns during this season. It is extremely rare to see a cross as part of Christmas decorations. If we think about it, the cross is in fact rather uncomfortably close to the manger. The cross stands only 33 years from the manger, while we look back over 2000 years at both.

We cannot prove we are walking in the footsteps of Jesus, and we do not need to prove it to anyone. It is simply a matter of doing it.

Jellybeans

In 1976, I got a call to preach at First Christian Church in Wheatland, California, on the first Sunday in December. I did not have a congregation to serve at the time, and it was the second Sunday of Advent. I remember the title, "Christmas and Jelly Beans" because through the years several people have reminded me of the title and the smiles it brought.

I have observed over the years that people have various attitudes towards Christmas that have a remarkable parallel in people's attitudes towards jelly beans. Some just do not like jellybeans. Some eat only the colors and flavors they like. Still others enjoy all the colors and flavors. People on President Ronald Reagan's staff used to say they could judge his mood by the way he consumed the Jelly Belly candies that were invariably on the table near them.

The people who do not like jellybeans are like those who reject Christmas as part of the season. Some focus on the strictly secular symbols of the "holiday" season, and a few do not celebrate at all. The emotions of these people reflect the extremes of moodiness and everything in between. Some go through the motions for appearances or for the approval of family or friends. Some use the season as an excuse to do what they want to do anyway. 2 Timothy 4:3,4 says, "For the time is coming when people will not put up with sound doctrine, but having itching ears, they will accumulate for themselves teachers to suit their own desires, and will turn away from listening to the truth and wander away to myths." (NRSV) To say that these people do not know what they are missing is a gross understatement.

Some of us, who have Christmas as a vital part of the season, pick carefully what we do, the way some people pick out colors of jellybeans. Sometimes it is because we are wrapped up in traditions and other things we have always done. In other cases, it is because of either personal limitations or the limitations of those with whom we celebrate. In still other cases, it is a matter of personal preferences regarding music, decorations, and other things associated with the season.

Finally, there are some of us who embrace everything associated with Christmas, whether we have tried it before or not. We are like those who simply grab a handful of jellybeans out of a bowl and enjoy them all. When the Holy Spirit fills us with boundless joy over the Christ child, it gives us a hunger to celebrate. We bring that joy into all that we do. We want to find the energy and the resources to explore all the opportunities to celebrate Christmas that come our way. Such joy can be contagious.

Let us not ask people to limit their joy to Christmas however. Joy is one of the primary indicators of healthy faith. When someone in the community of faith has a lingering negative attitude that suppresses their joy, one can only wonder what The Devil is whispering in hat person's ear. I am so grateful that God forgives and redeems—how about you? Christmas can be the catalyst that brings healing and reconciliation to broken relationships. It can also bring comfort to those who are angry or grieving. May your celebration of Christmas be filled with contagious joy.

Christmas Images

What is the image that we want to see?
What's in the mirror that we want to be?
Yesterday's heroes are not what we want,
Our precious egos' what we want to flaunt.
'Me' generation and me on the line.
'Me' for self-help so more me we can chime.

Faith Fuel

Who are our heroes and who seeks the fame?
Heroes in everyone, that is our game.
Even in church we find much of the same,
Self-esteem's hype is a Christian's cocaine.
Charges so strong are not gentle to hear.
Being a sheep seems like self-esteem's smear.

Di'gnosis is painful and yet there is hope.
Hope springs eternal and more for God's "dopes."
Setting their hopes on that bright Christmas star,
Brought "home" some "wise" men who came from afar.
Manger's sweet wisdom made theirs into waste,
Hope born of woman so young and so chaste.

Hope also flowed from some shepherds who came,
Listening to God who had called all the same:
"Leave now your flocks and come now into town–
Meet now your shepherd and worship bowed down."
They wanted care being known who they were,
Found care in him knowing just whose they were.

See in the manger the image of God,
Then see your mirror and be truly awed.
Yes, we are made in that image and more.
"Image" but not the true God, just a door.
If, when you're opened there is love there to see,
Then you are who God's created to be.

'Me' Generation, O people take note,
Salvation's ours, but its not by our vote!
Self-help is out, only fools will defend–
Death brings a helplessness to this life's end.
There are no keys found in riches or lands–
All the control is in God's mighty hands.

Christ is the firstborn of all human race,
Rebirth begins seeing Christ's baby face,
Which is confirmed in the empty tomb's grace.
Image of God, we have found our home base,
Nurtured in swaddling cloths rather than lace.
Walk with Him, talk with Him, now, face to face.

Faith Fuel
INDEX

Faith Fuel

Faith Fuel

Faith Fuel

Faith Fuel

246

Faith Fuel

Faith Fuel

NOTES

www.ingramcontent.com/pod-product-compliance
Lightning Source LLC
LaVergne TN
LVHW051501080426
835509LV00017B/1862